A COMPREHENSIVE GUIDE TO
MEN'S FLAT SKETCHING

CROQUIS
SHIRTS
PANTS
JACKETS
COATS

NICK VERREOS
DAVID PAUL

"A Comprehensive Guide to Men's Flat Sketching"

This helpful guide is for anyone interested in learning the fundamentals of drawing Fashion Flat or Technical Sketches by hand. In addition, what makes this guide unique is that it is entirely about drawing MEN'S flat sketches. We identified the need to help students of fashion design, apparel manufacturing and product development learn the specific details of hand drawing flat sketches for men's garments.

In a comprehensive step-by-step format, this book will guide you through the basic steps of creating a Men's Croquis specifically made for drawing flat sketches. In addition, you will learn to draw the fundamental garments in Men's Fashion, including Basic T-Shirts, Dress Shirts, Jackets, Pants, Jeans and Shorts. "A Comprehensive Guide to Men's Flat Sketching" not only shows you how to sketch the garments, but also teaches the specific details within each garment, such as sleeves, collars, stitching, plackets, cuffs and other aspects of garment construction.

You will learn all the essential skills to help you master all the fundamentals of drawing Flat/Technical Sketches by hand. Once you have learned this, you will be more than prepared to learn the CAD/Computer Aided Design methods of drawing flat sketches via computer.

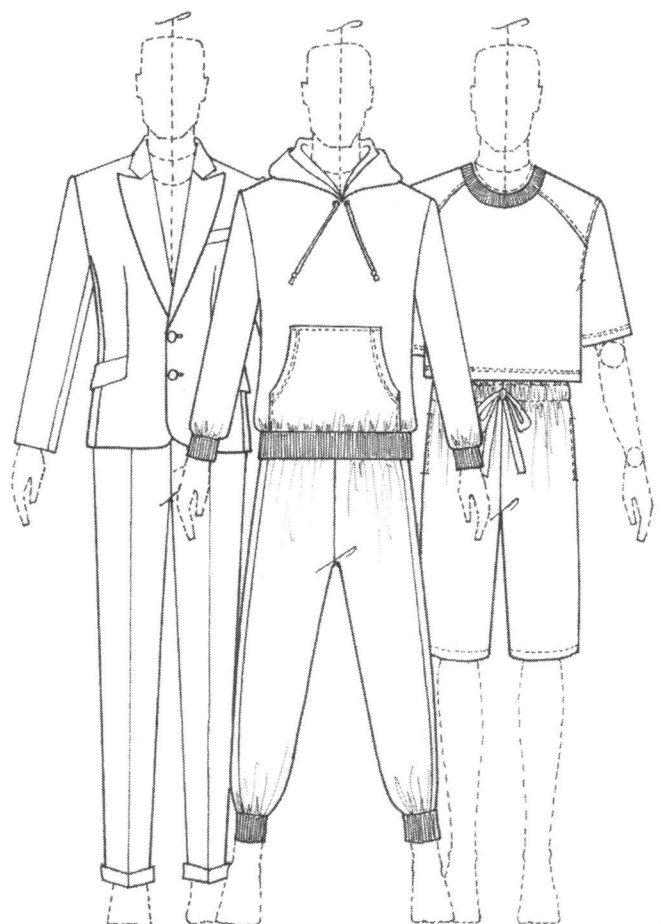

BIOGRAPHY

Nick and David co-founded NIKOLAKI, in 2001. Their collections of upscale red carpet gowns and cocktail dresses have been worn by celebrities such as Beyoncé, Katy Perry, Heidi Klum, Eva Longoria and Carrie Underwood. NIKOLAKI has been carried in over 100 stores across the US and abroad.

Additionally, they design and produce NV Nick Verreos a clothing line which is available on major Home Shopping Networks including Evine Live (USA), QVC UK, QVC Italy and The Shopping Channel (Canada).

Nick was the Winning Mentor of Project Runway: Under the Gunn and first received national and international attention after appearing on Project Runway. He is a red carpet fashion expert and correspondent for various networks including E! Entertainment and ABC's "On The Red Carpet" LIVE from the Oscars.

Nick Received his Bachelor of Arts in Political Science at the University of California, Los Angeles/UCLA. He then continued on to the Fashion Institute of Design & Merchandising/FIDM, where he graduated from the Advanced Fashion Design Program.

As an educator, Nick has been an instructor at FIDM where he taught Fashion Sketching, Draping, Patternmaking and Design.

A native of Southern California, David Paul Attended the University of California, Los Angeles/UCLA where he received his Bachelor of Arts in Theatre Arts and subsequently, his MFA in Costume Design.

David went on to build an extensive resume in the world of entertainment and fashion styling for over 20 years. As a member of IATSE Local 705, David designed costumes and worked on shows such as "Queer Eye for the Straight Girl", "Passions", "Undressed" and numerous other productions for MTV, ABC, FOX, NIKELODEON and the WB.

David has also worked alongside Andre Leon Talley and Lisa Love for Vogue Magazine and with such illustrious photographers as Arthur Elgort, Regan Cameron, Noe DeWitt and Amanda DeCadanet, styling for Kate Hudson, Heidi Klum, Vanessa Paradis, Twiggy and Heather Graham.

Nick and David are Co-Chairs of Fashion Design, Advanced Fashion Design, Advanced Theatre Costume, Film & TV Costume, Jewelry and Footwear at the Fashion Institute of Design & Merchandising/FIDM. They also co-authored the best-selling book, A Passion for Fashion, which was the #1 New Release on Amazon for Fashion and Textile Business.

Published by NIKOLAKI PUBLISHING
© 2019 NIKOLAKI, INC.
Nick Verreos and David Paul assert their rights to
be identified as the authors of this work.

All rights reserved. No part of this publication my be
reproduced or transmitted in any form or by
any means electronic or mechanical, including
photocopy, recording or any information storage
and retrieval system without permission in
writing from the publisher.

TABLE OF CONTENTS

INTRODUCTION

- FLAT SKETCH DEFINITION...1
- FLAT SKETCH W/ FASHION ILLUSTRATION................................2
- TECHNICAL SKETCH...3
- LINE SHEET..4

TOOLS & SUPPLIES

- PAPER, PENCILS & ERASERS..6
- PENS..7
- MARKERS..8
- STRAIGHT RULERS..9
- CURVED RULERS & CIRCULAR STENCILS......................................10

CROQUIS

- DRAWING A CROQUIS..12
- CROQUIS: FRONT..15
- CROQUIS: BACK...16
- CROQUIS: SPREAD LEG...17
- CROQUIS: PLUS SIZE...18

TABLE OF CONTENTS

- CROQUIS FRONT: ENLARGED ... 19
- CROQUIS BACK: ENLARGED ... 20

KNIT SHIRTS

- SLIM FIT T-SHIRT ... 22
- LOOSE FIT T-SHIRT ... 24
- TANK TOP ... 26
- SLEEVELESS MUSCLE TEE ... 27
- KNIT COLLARS & NECKLINES ... 28
- BINDING & COVERSTITCH ... 29
- TRACK JACKET ... 30
- DRAWING A HOOD ... 32
- HOODED TRACK JACKET ... 36
- KNIT SHIRT STYLES ... 38

WOVEN SHIRTS

- BASIC SHIRT COLLAR ... 42
- FITTED DRESS SHIRT ... 44

TABLE OF CONTENTS

- UNFITTED DRESS SHIRT...46
- LONGLINE SHIRT..48
- SLEEVES...50
- CUFFS..51
- COLLARS..52
- PLACKETS...53
- YOKES...54
- TOP STITCHING..55
- DARTS...56
- POCKETS...57
- TUXEDO SHIRTS...58
- BUTTONS...59
- WOVEN SHIRT STYLES..60

PANTS

- STRAIGHT LEG PANTS..64
- JOGGERS..66

TABLE OF CONTENTS

- DROP CROTCH..68
- JEANS...70
- JEANS TOPSTITCHING...72
- WAISTBANDS...74
- PANT LENGTHS...75
- FRONT POCKETS..76
- BACK POCKETS...77
- HEMS...78
- DRAWSTRINGS...79
- PANT STYLES..80

JACKETS

- NOTCHED COLLAR..84
- NOTCHED COLLAR JACKET..86
- NOTCHED COLLAR JACKET: UNFITTED..................88
- SHAWL COLLAR..90
- SHAWL COLLAR JACKET..92

TABLE OF CONTENTS

- DOUBLE BREASTED COLLAR...94
- DOUBLE BREASTED JACKET...96
- SINGLE BREASTED COAT..98
- DOUBLE BREASTED COAT..99
- JACKET SLEEVE..100
- JACKET VENTS... 101
- SINGLE BREASTED VEST.. 102
- DOUBLE BREASTED VEST.. 103
- PUFFER VEST... 104
- SINGLE BREASTED JACKET STYLES.. 105
- DOUBLE BREASTED JACKET STYLES.. 106
- JACKET STYLES... 107
- COAT STYLES... 108

Flat Sketch

A Flat Sketch (also known as a Technical Sketch or more casually, as "Flats"), are drawings of garments done without the 3-dimensionality of a body inside.

- They are drawings of garments done to show a one-dimensional 'flat' view of the garments.
- Think of it as if the garments (shirts, pants, suits, jackets, etc.) are on a table, lying neatly flat, or as if the garment is on a hanger, hanging perfectly still.

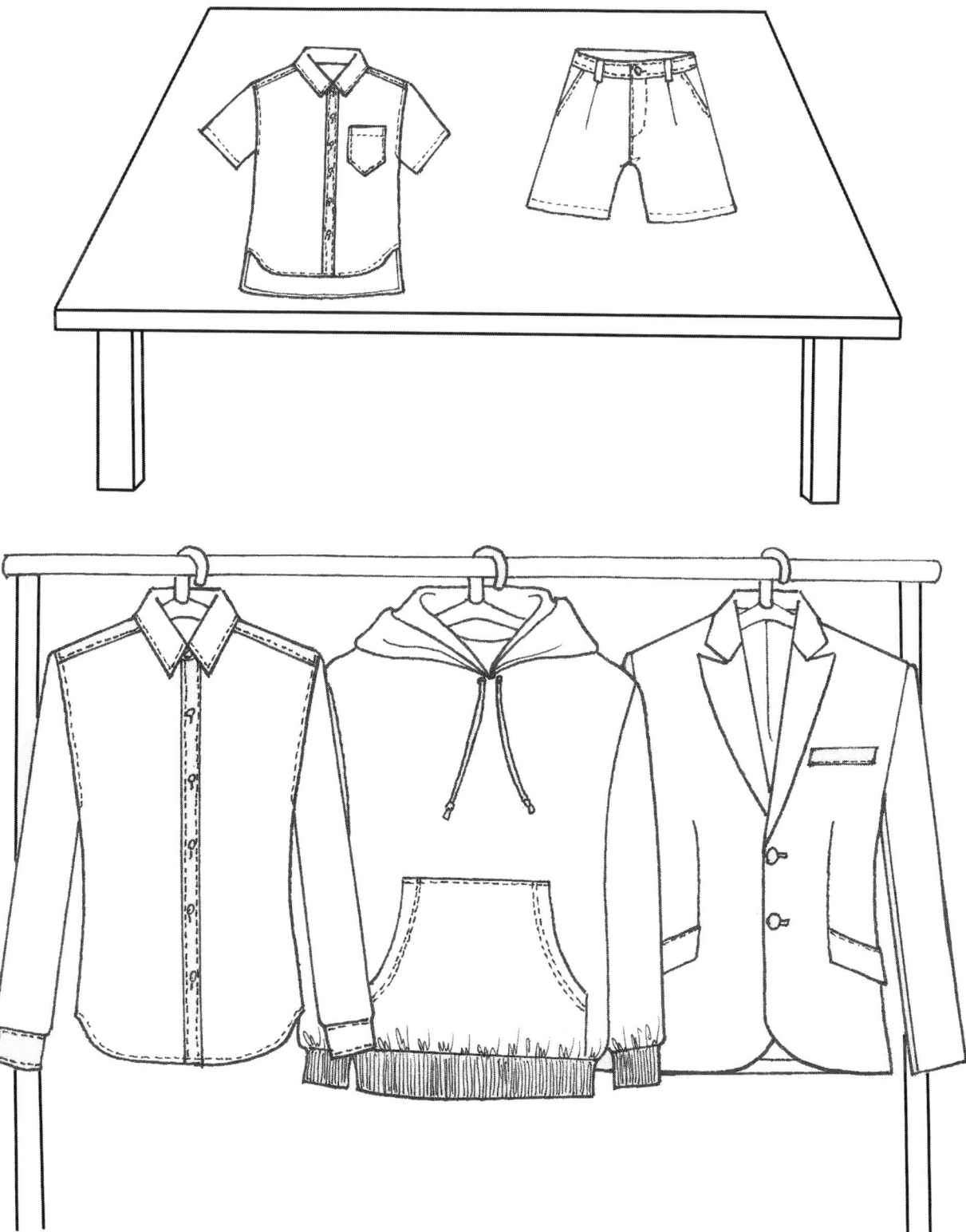

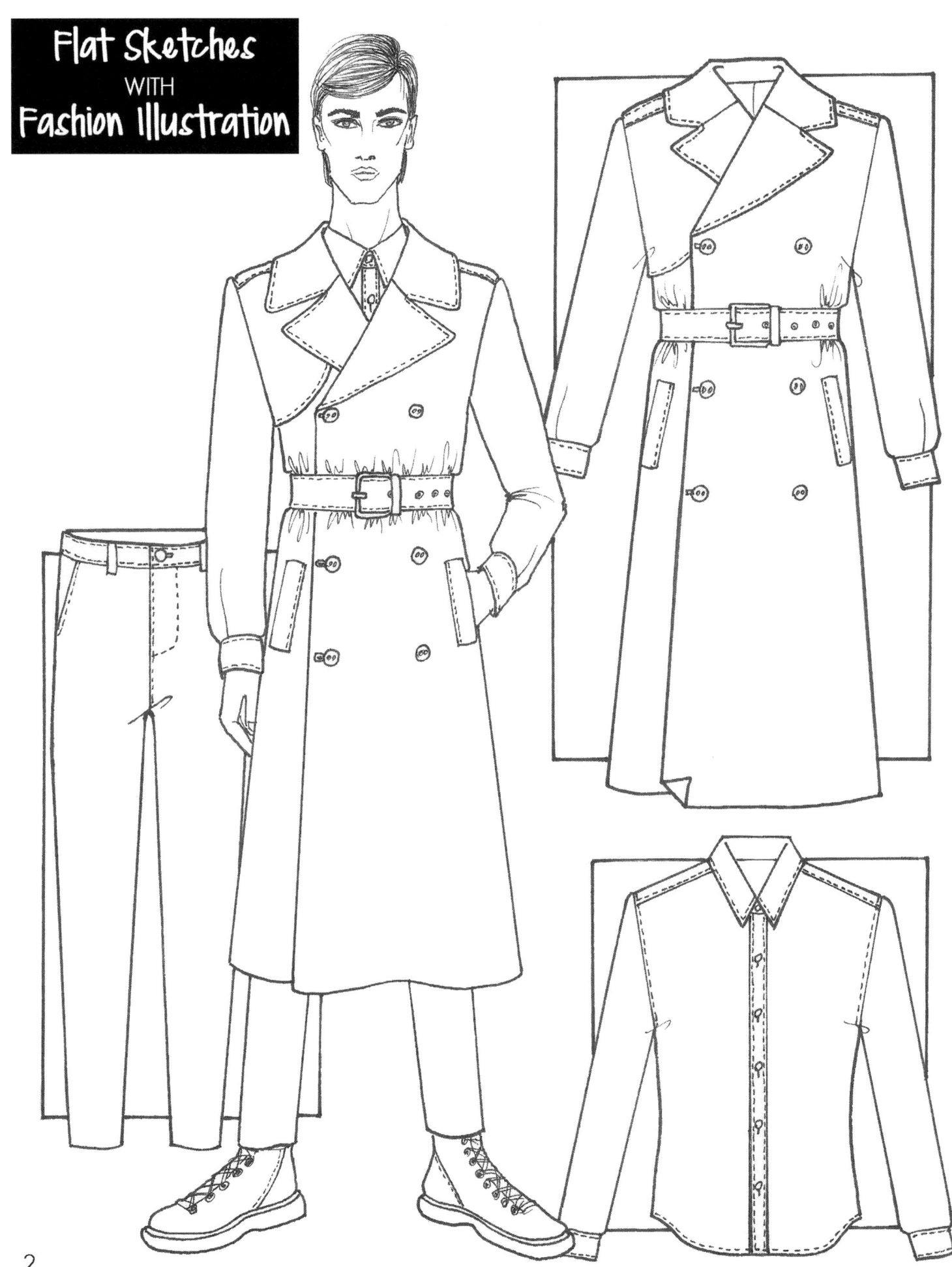

Technical Flat Sketch
USED IN A SPEC SHEET

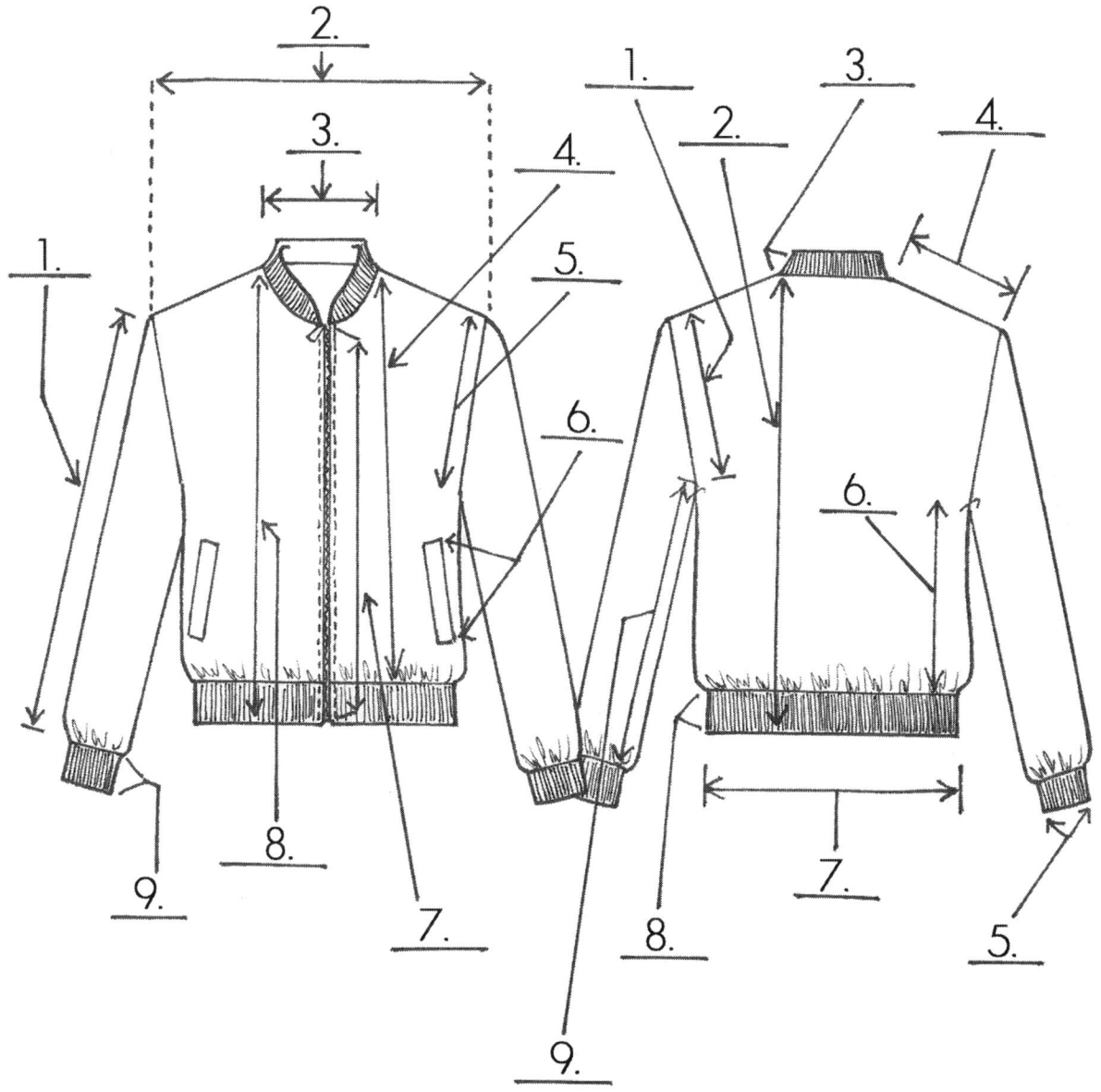

FRONT		BACK	
1. Sleeve length	24"	1. Back armhole-straight	9.5"
2. Shoulder to shoulder	17.5"	2. Back HPS neck to bottom of jacket	26"
3. Neck width	6"	3. Neckband ribbing width	1.75"
4. Front HPS to beginning of hem ribbing	24.5"	4. Shoulder width	7"
5. Front armhole-straight	9.5"	5. Sleeve band/cuff width (half)	4"
6. Welt pocket length	7"	6. Side seam bottom of armhole to top of ribbing	13"
7. CF/zipper length	22"	7. Width of jacket, at hem (half)	18.5"
8. Front HPS to bottom of jacket	26.25"	8. Hem ribbing band width	2.5"
9. Sleeve band/cuff length	2.5"	9. Undersleeve length	17"

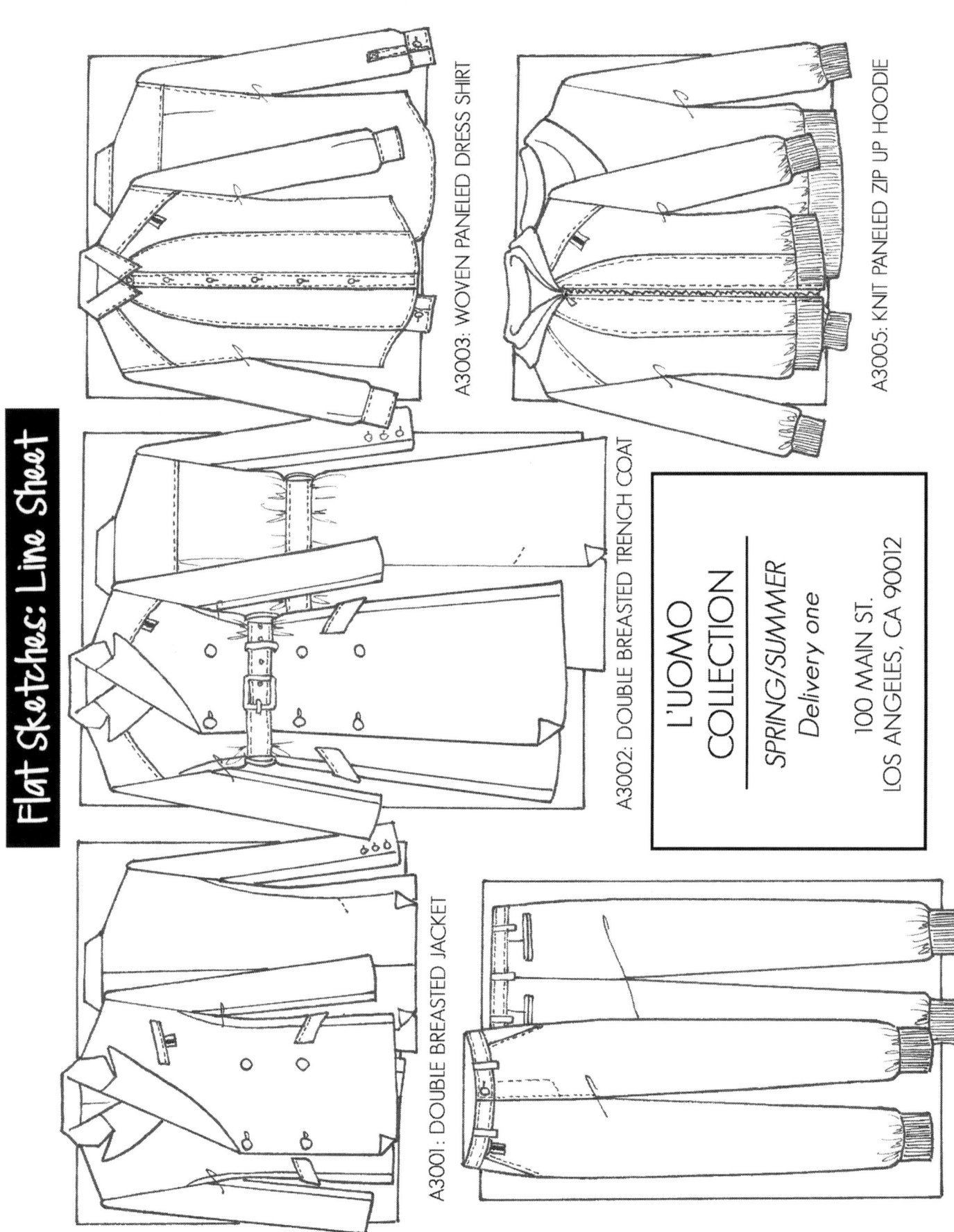

Tools & Supplies

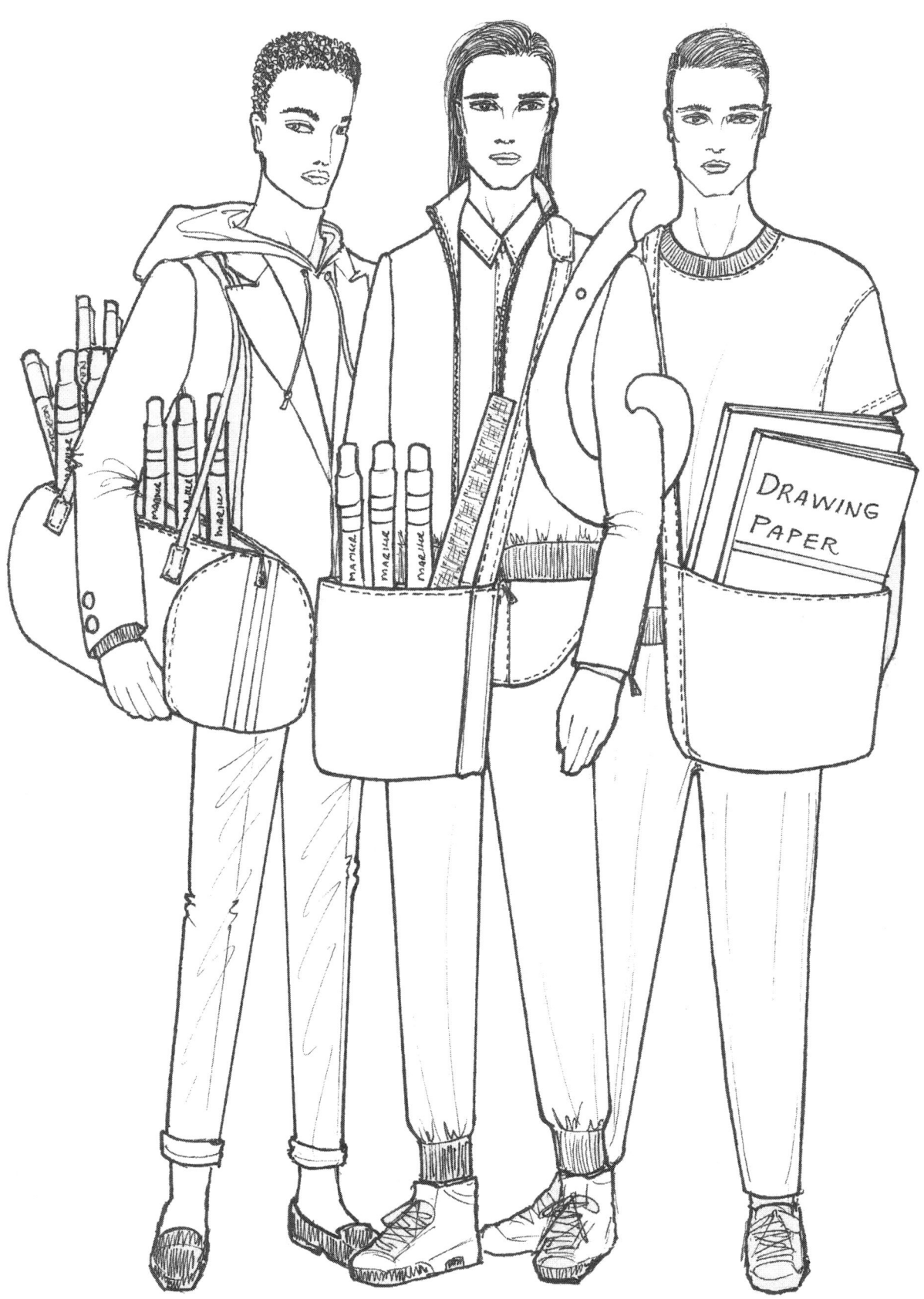

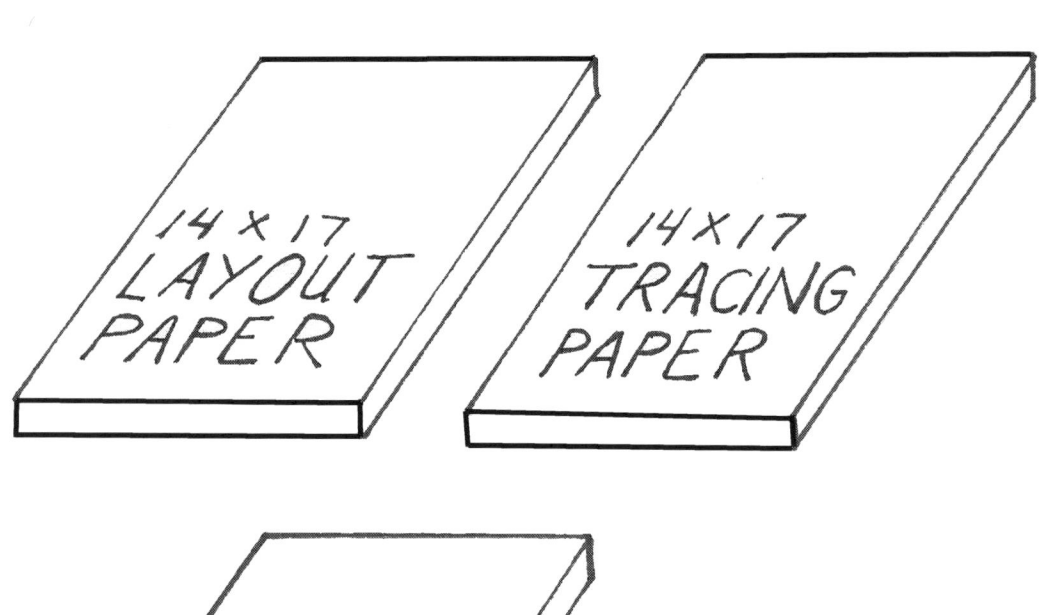

Paper

- Various types of drawing paper can be used when creating Flat Sketches by hand.

- These are the mostly used types:
  14" x 17" Layout Paper
  14" x 17" Tracing Paper
  14" x 17" Marker Paper
  8 ½" x 11" Copy Paper

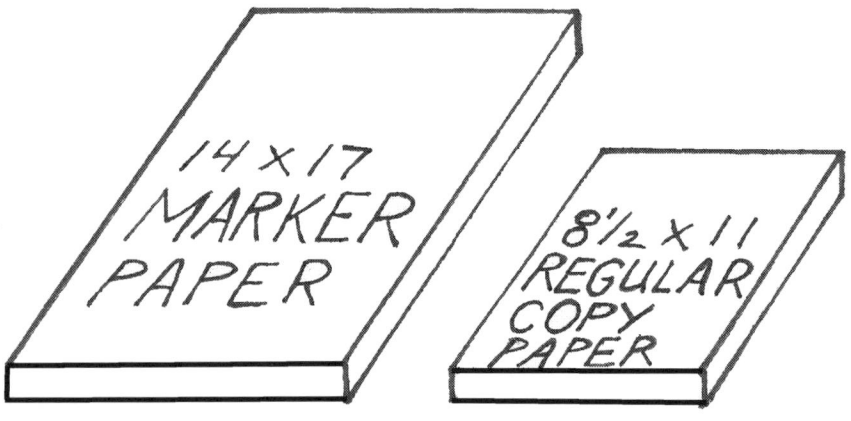

Pencils & Erasers

The following pencils can be used for drawing the first flat sketch prior to inking:
- Regular #2 Pencil
- Mechanical Pencil
- Lead for Mechanical Pencils: 0.7mm is a nice sturdy choice but you could use a smaller lead size.

Erasers:
- Hi-polymer Eraser is ideal for erasing drawings.
- Retractable erasers; eraser sticks.

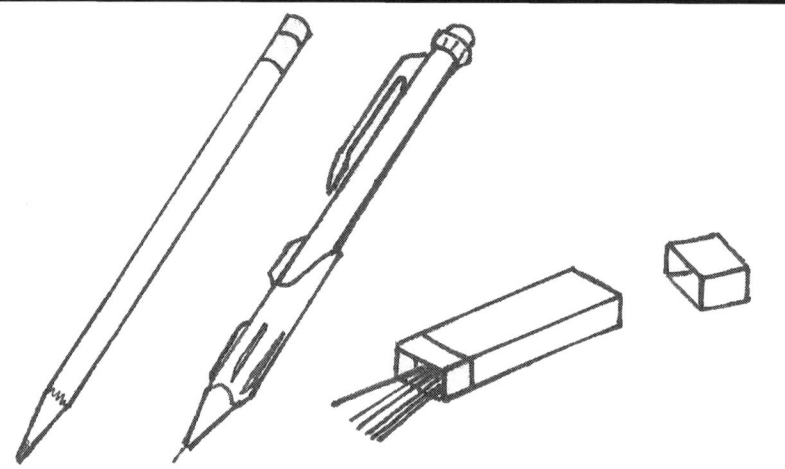

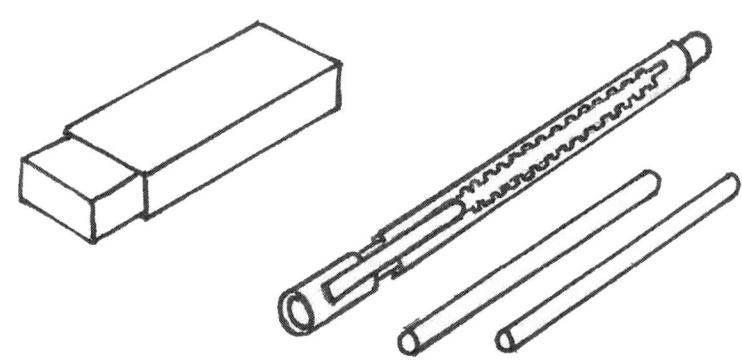

Pens

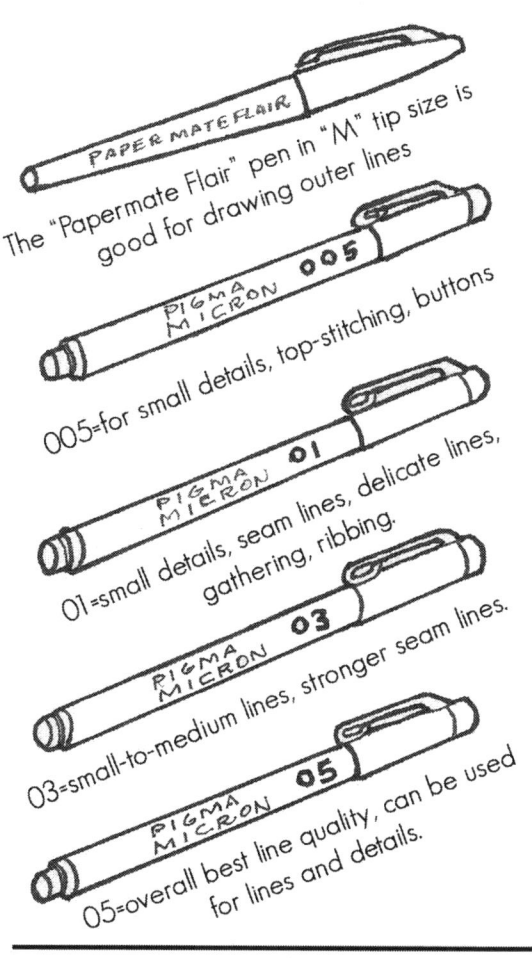

- The "Papermate Flair" pen in "M" tip size is good for drawing outer lines
- 005 = for small details, top-stitching, buttons
- 01 = small details, seam lines, delicate lines, gathering, ribbing
- 03 = small-to-medium lines, stronger seam lines.
- 05 = overall best line quality, can be used for lines and details.

- Ink pens are used in the process of hand drawing Flat Sketches. After you have drawn the Flat Sketch in pencil, making sure it is correct with all the proper details, the next step is to go back and retrace over the same lines, in pen.

- The most widely used styles of ink pens include the "Papermate Flair" and the "Pigma Micron" ink pen brands.

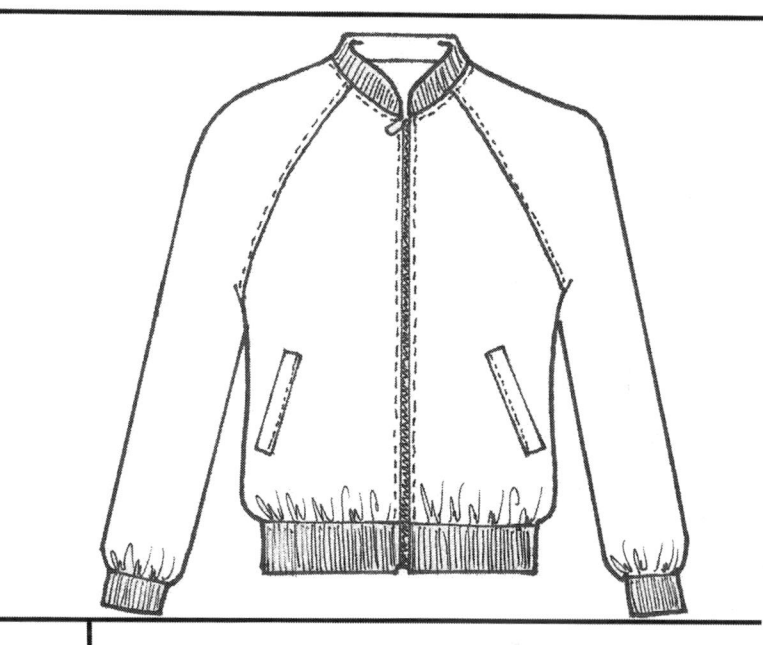

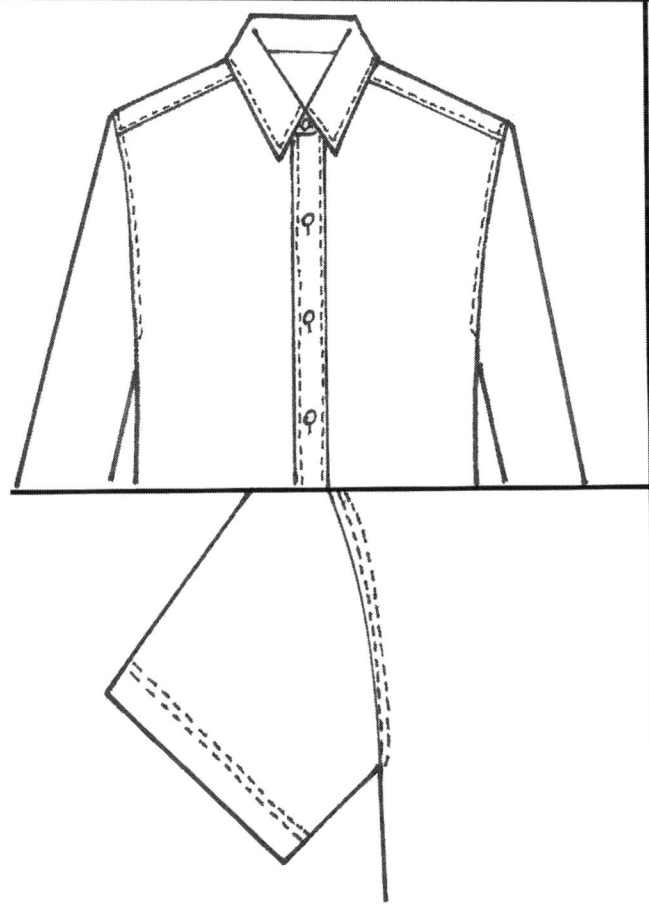

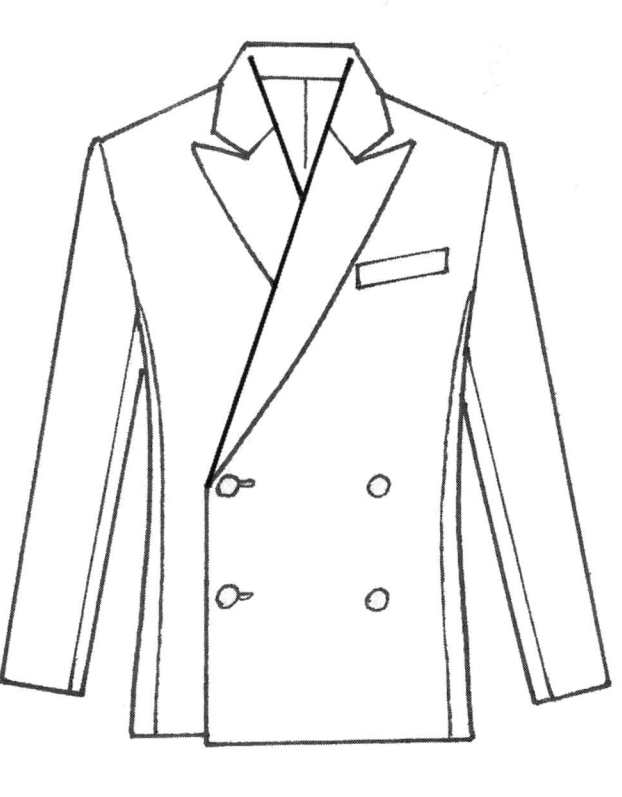

Markers

Drawing Markers, such as *Prismacolor* or *Copic*, are great to use as supplemental tools in enhancing the look of a Technical/Flat Sketch. They are used to highlight certain areas of the garment, emphasize gathering, pleating and shading in areas that show the inside of the garment.

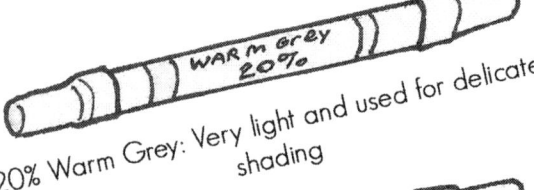
20% Warm Grey: Very light and used for delicate shading

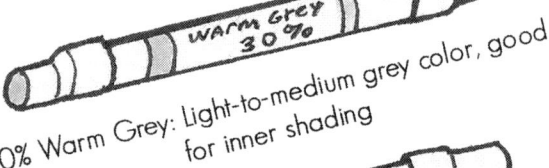
30% Warm Grey: Light-to-medium grey color, good for inner shading

40% Warm Grey: Medium gray color, good for darker inner shading, highlighting edges and seams.

60% Warm Grey: Darker grey color. Good for emphasizing outer edges of the flat sketch.

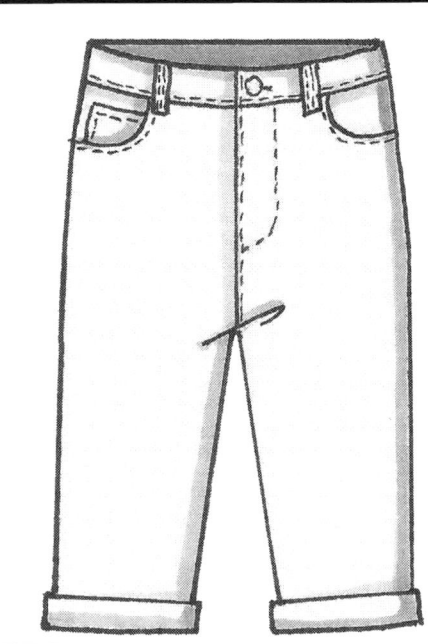

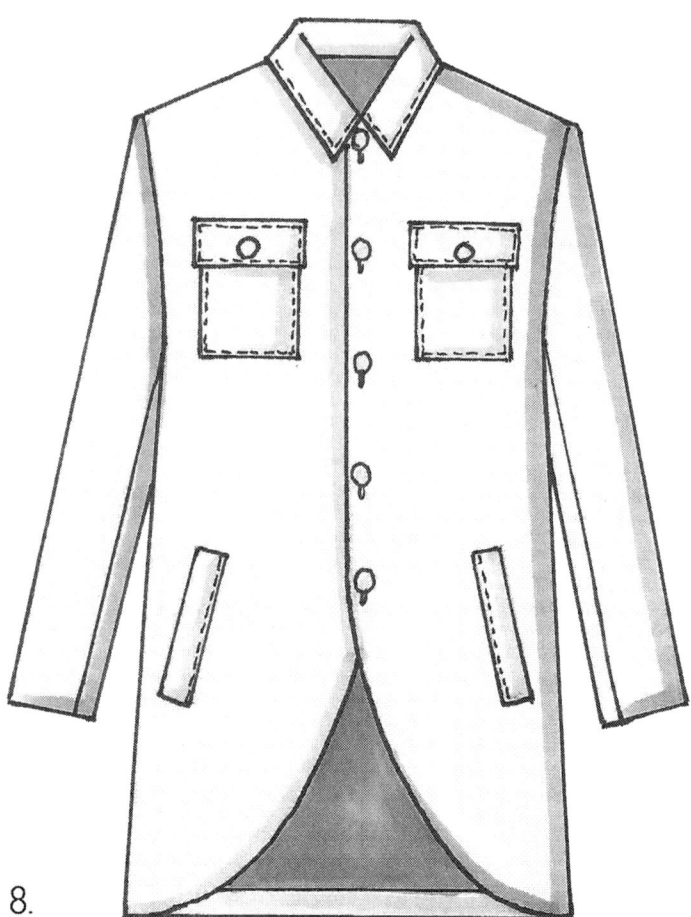

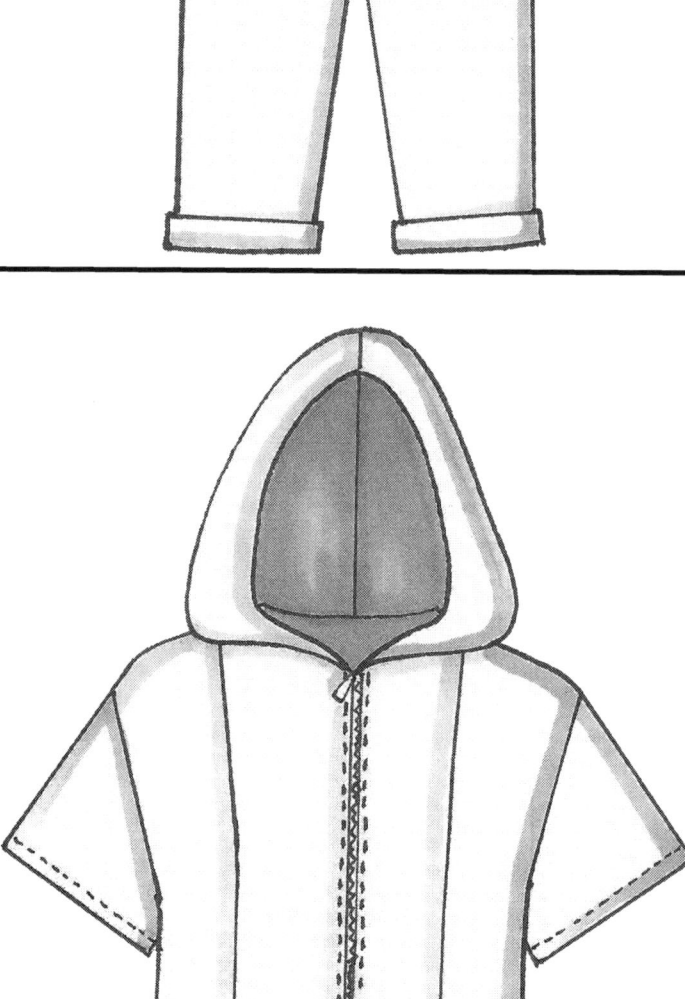

Rulers

- Clear beveled plastic rulers are the best types of rulers to use when drawing Flat Sketches by hand.
- They allow you to see the measurements and be more precise with the quality of your lines.
- Rulers are great for helping draw straight lines such as collar edges, shoulders, sleeves, hems, waists and seam lines.
- Clear rulers come in a variety of sizes including:
1" x 6"
2" x 12"
2" x 18"

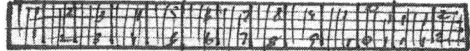
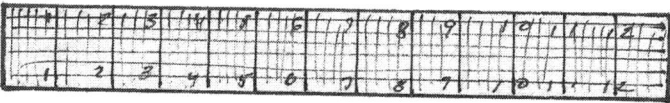
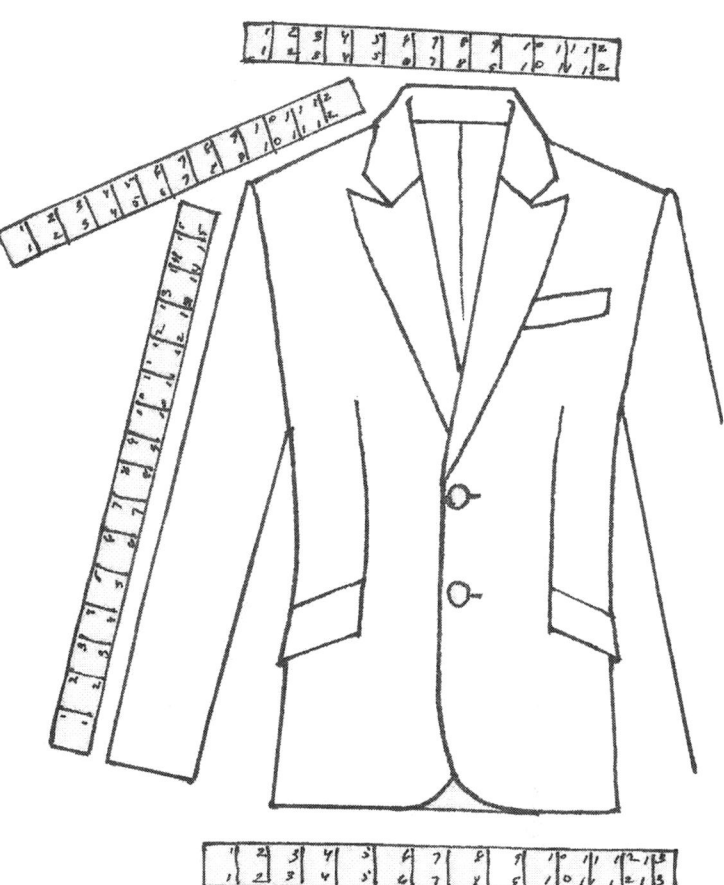
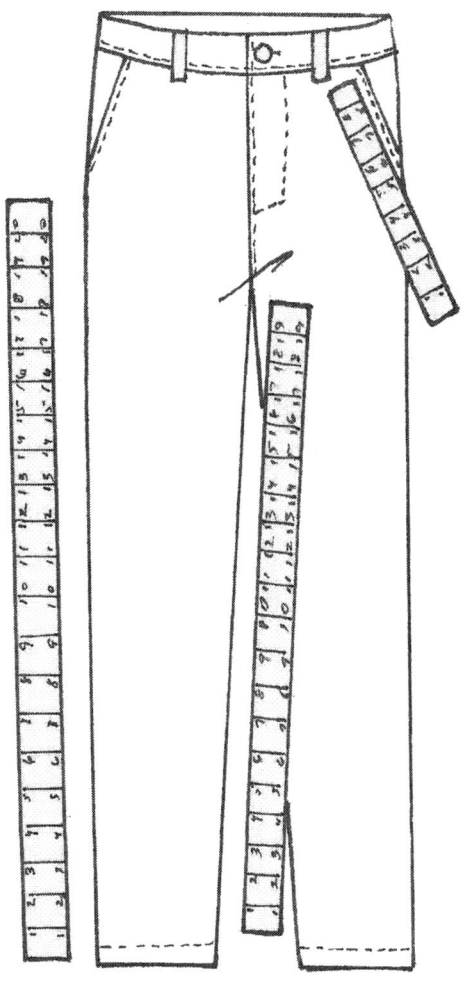
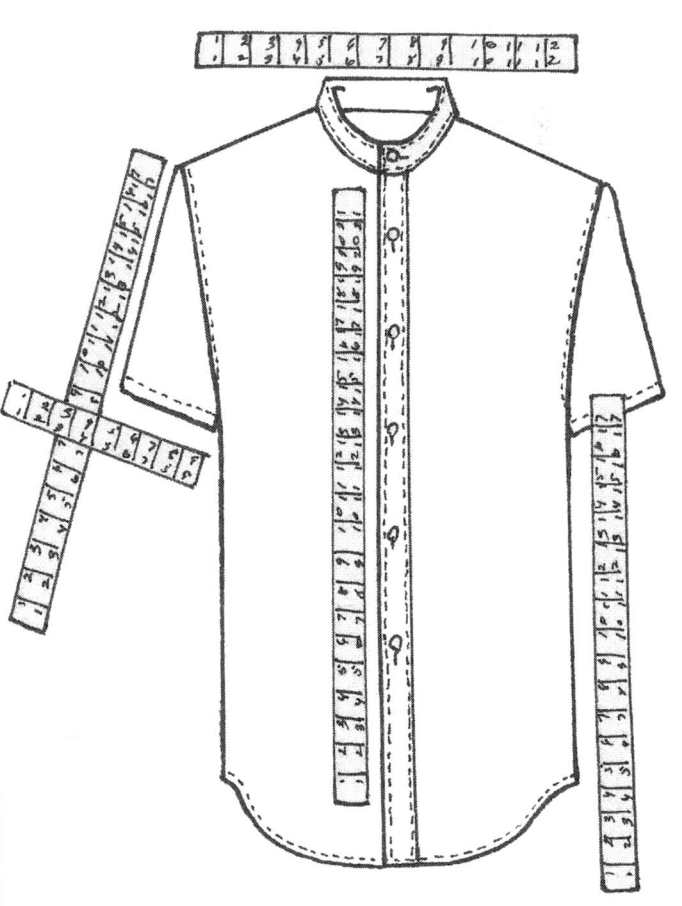

French Curve Circular Stencils

- Clear French Curves are great when drawing curve details of fashion flat sketches. They can aid in drawing necklines, armholes, or any curved seaming or garment silhouettes.
- Circle Stencil Templates are the perfect tool when drawing buttons, snaps or other small circular shapes needed for garment details.

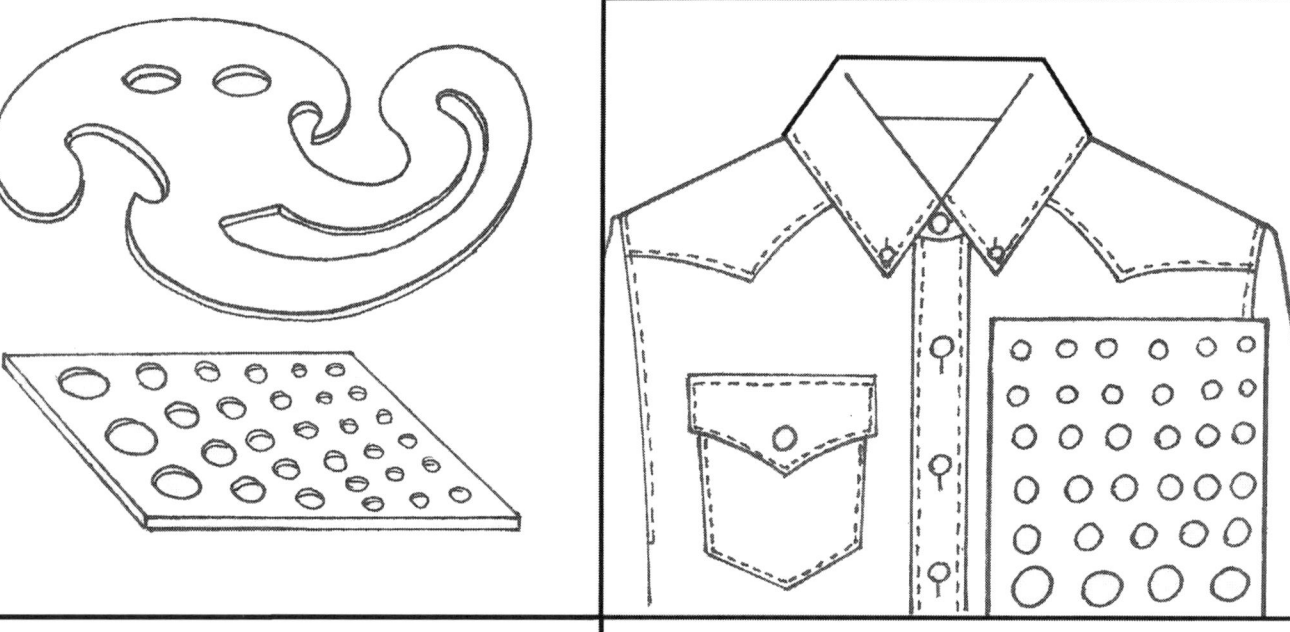

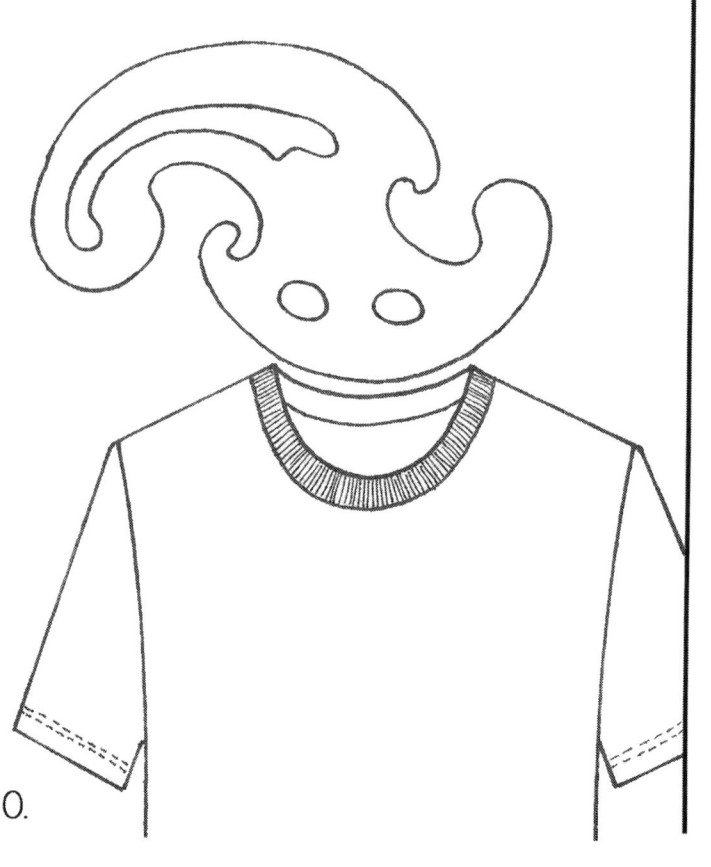

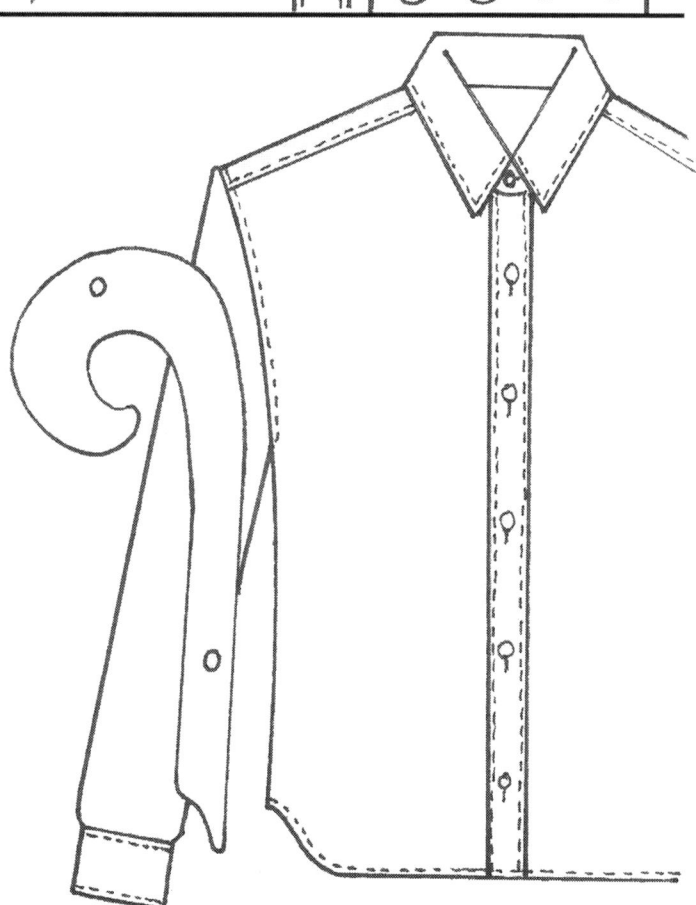

Croquis

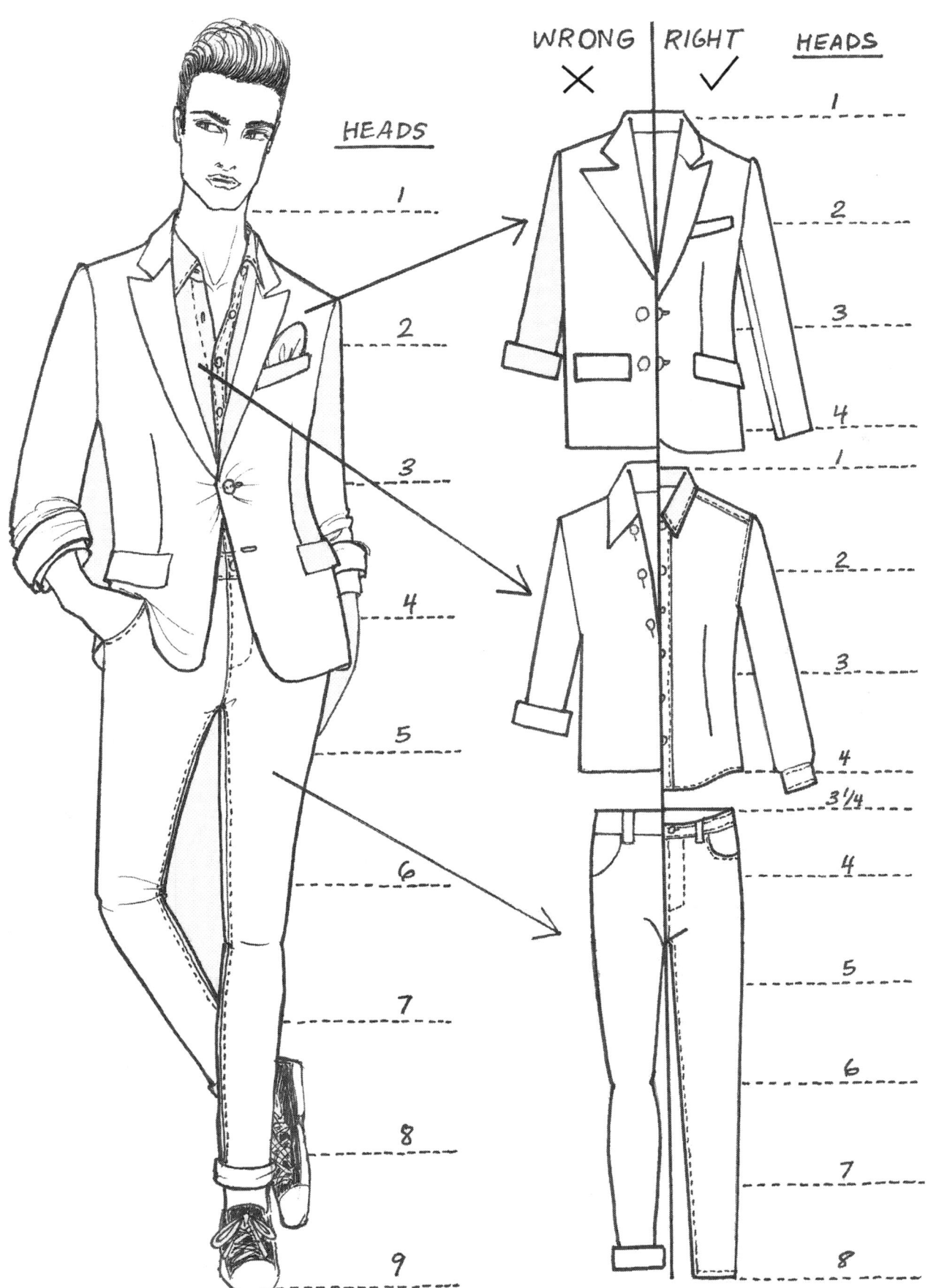

Men's Croquis

1.
- Draw a straight line on the paper.
- Divide the line into NINE even spaces. Mark #1-9 as shown. These spaces represent the "9 Heads".
- Each #/Head will represent a specific part of the Croquis' body.

2. Head, Neck and Shoulders
- From the top, draw the head of the Croquis, ending with the chin at the #1 spot.
- Between #1 and #2, draw a broken line, marking #1 1/2 Heads. This mark is where the Shoulders end.
- Draw the Neck from the Head, then the Shoulders.
- Draw light broken lines to show the back and front Necklines.
- The width from one shoulder point to the other is the same amount as 1 1/2 Heads.

3. Upper Torso, Upper Arms
- #2 represent the Chest position.
- #2 1/4 is right BELOW the Chest position.
- #3 is the Natural Waist (or High Waist), as well as Elbow position.
- This Natural Waist Width is slightly wider than the 1 Head length.
- Draw the Upper Torso and top half of Arms starting at the Shoulder points as shown, ending at the #3 position on the Croquis.
- Draw a small circle at the Elbow.

4. Waist-to-crotch, Lower Arms
- #3 1/4 is the Modern Waist position.
- #3 1/2 is the Low Waist position.
- #4 is the position for the Hips and Wrist.
- #4 1/2 is the Crotch position.
- Draw the lower half of the arms and Waist-to-Crotch section of the body.
- Make the Hips Width slightly WIDER than the Waist.
- Draw smaller-than-the-elbow circles at the Wrist positions.

5. Hands, Upper Legs
- #5 is the "Finger Tips" (end of hand) position.
- #6 is the Knee position.
- Draw the Hands and the Upper half of the Legs.
- First, draw the Hands from the Wrist/#4 position to the #5 position.
- Next, draw two straight lines per Leg; one from Crotch to Knee position (inner leg) and the other from the Low Hip to Knee position (outer leg).
- Draw a circle at the knees.

6. Lower Legs, Feet
- #7 is Mid-Calf/Middle of Lower Leg.
- #8 is the Ankle
- #9 is the bottom of the Feet.
- Draw the Lower Legs from #6/Knee position to #8/Ankle position. Notice the shape is wider at the Knee and smaller at the Ankle.
- From #8, draw the Feet, down to #9.

1.

—	1
—	2
—	3
—	4
—	5
—	6
—	7
—	8
—	9

2.

1
1½

3.

1
1½
2
2¼
3

13.

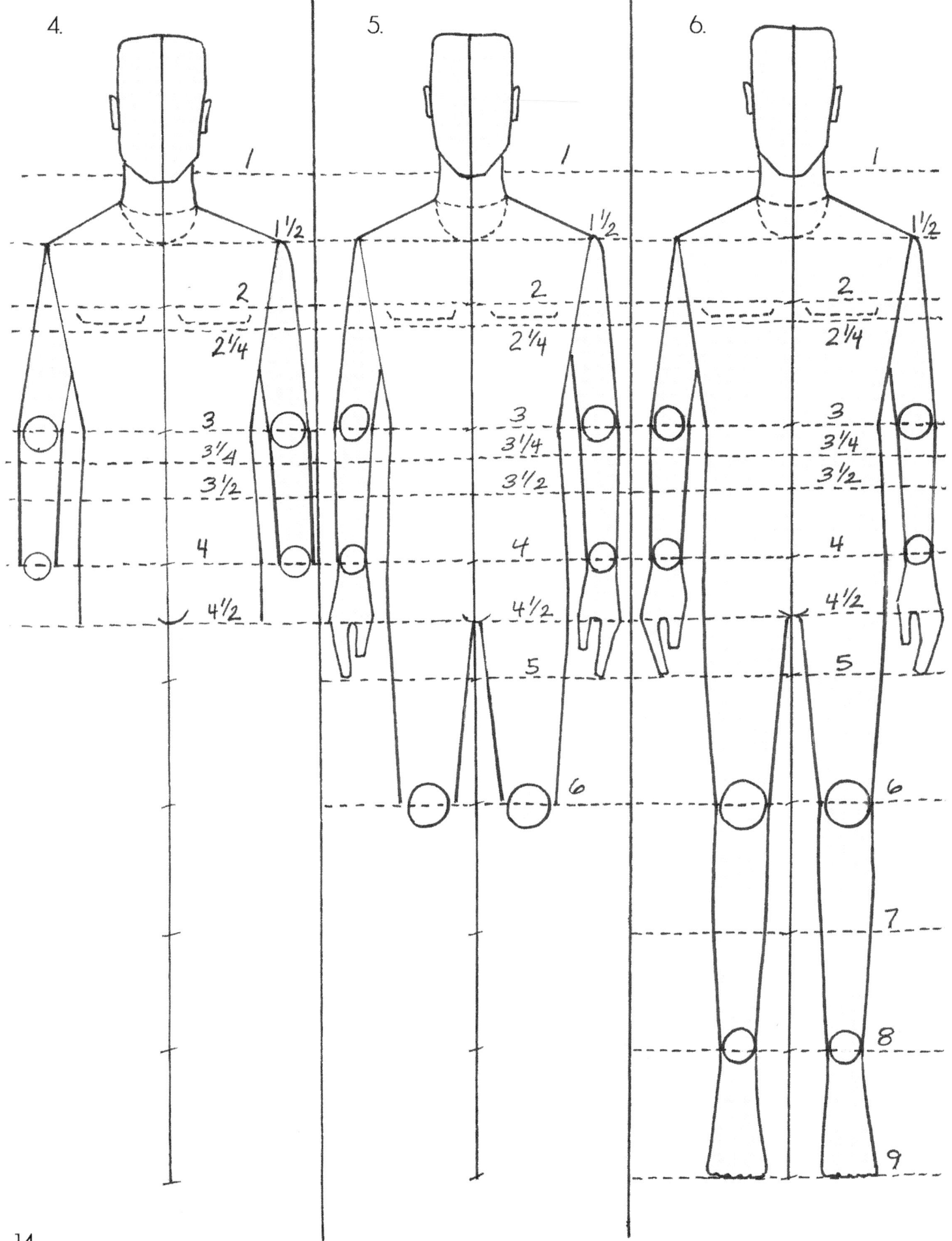

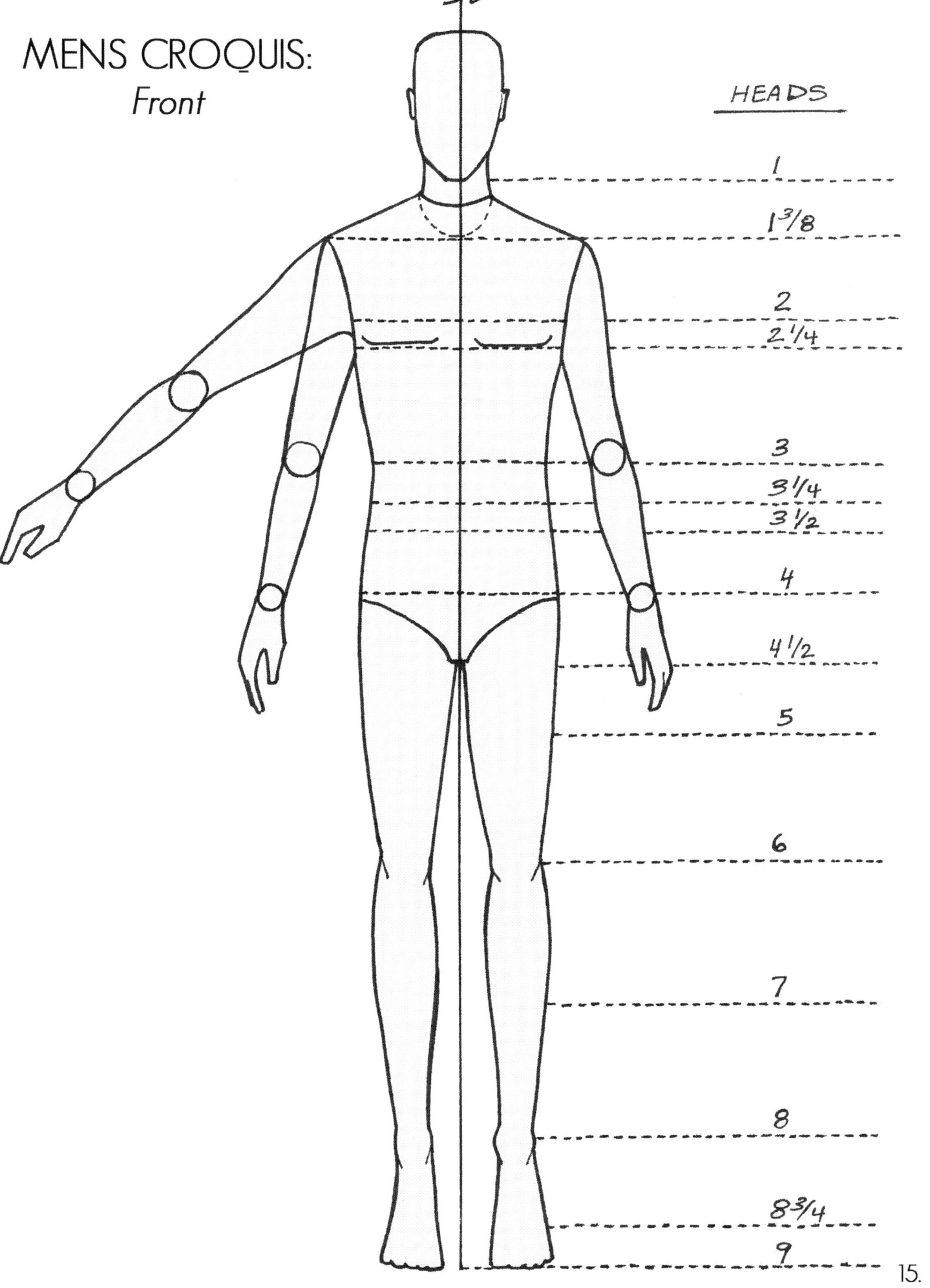

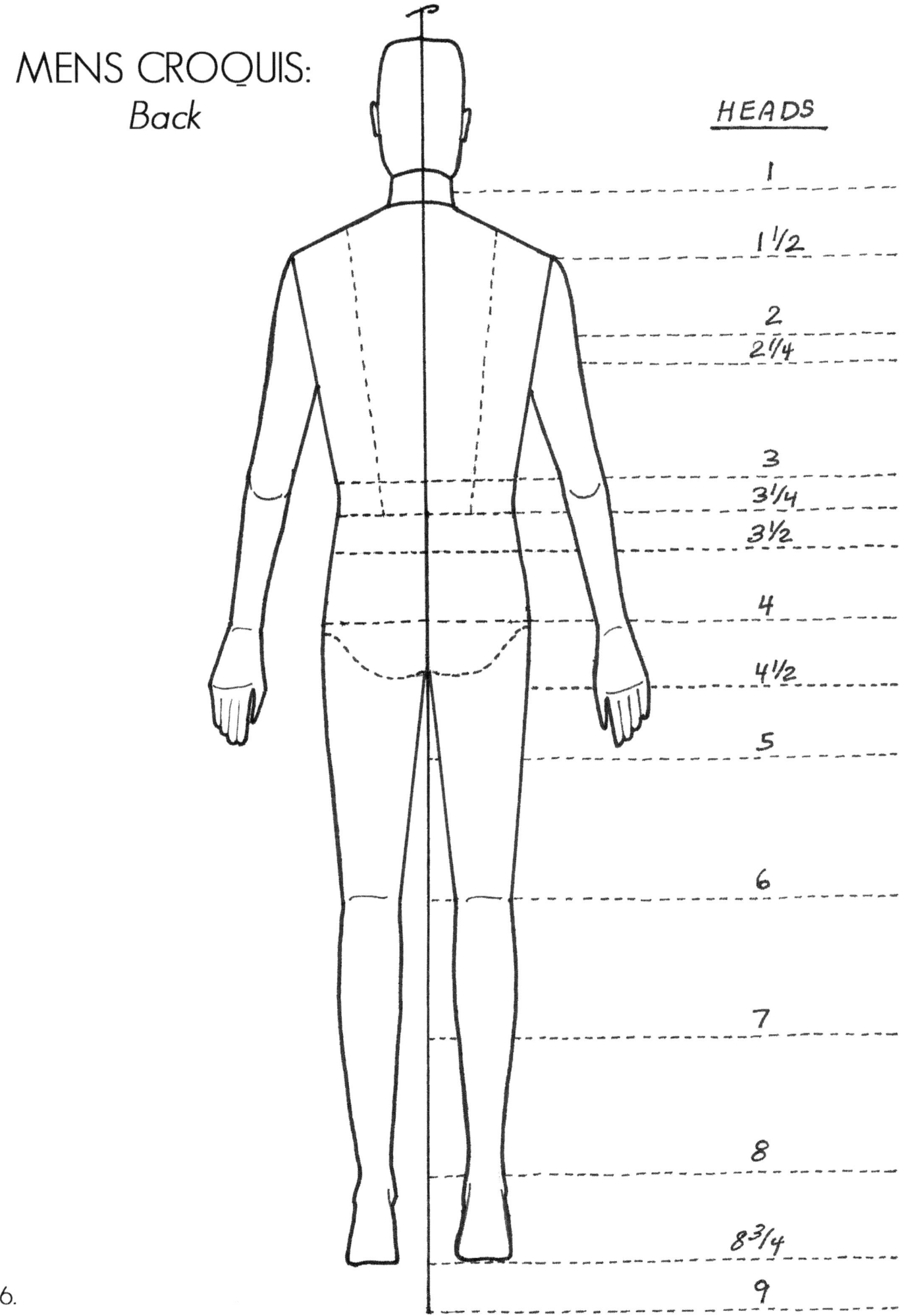

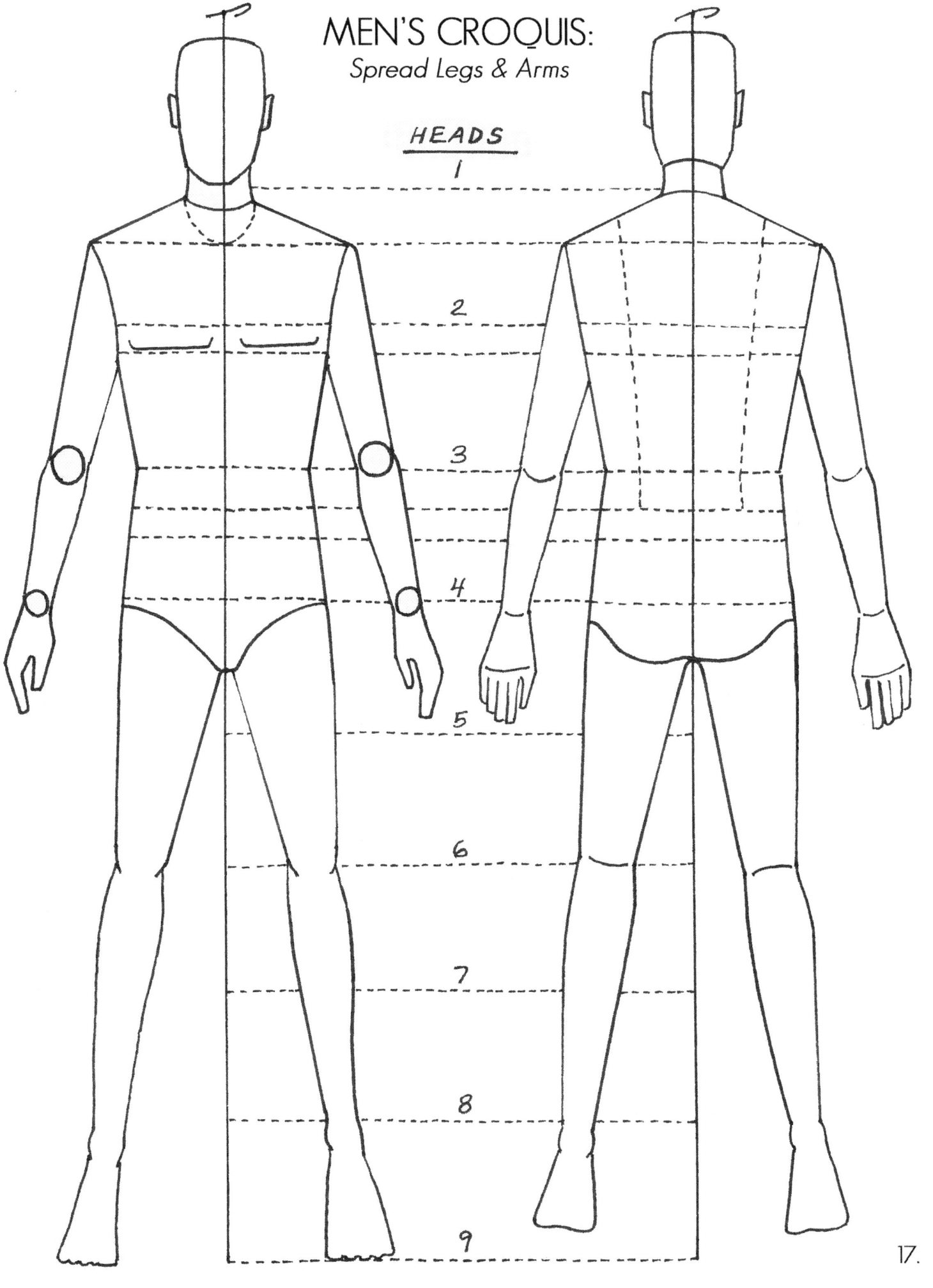

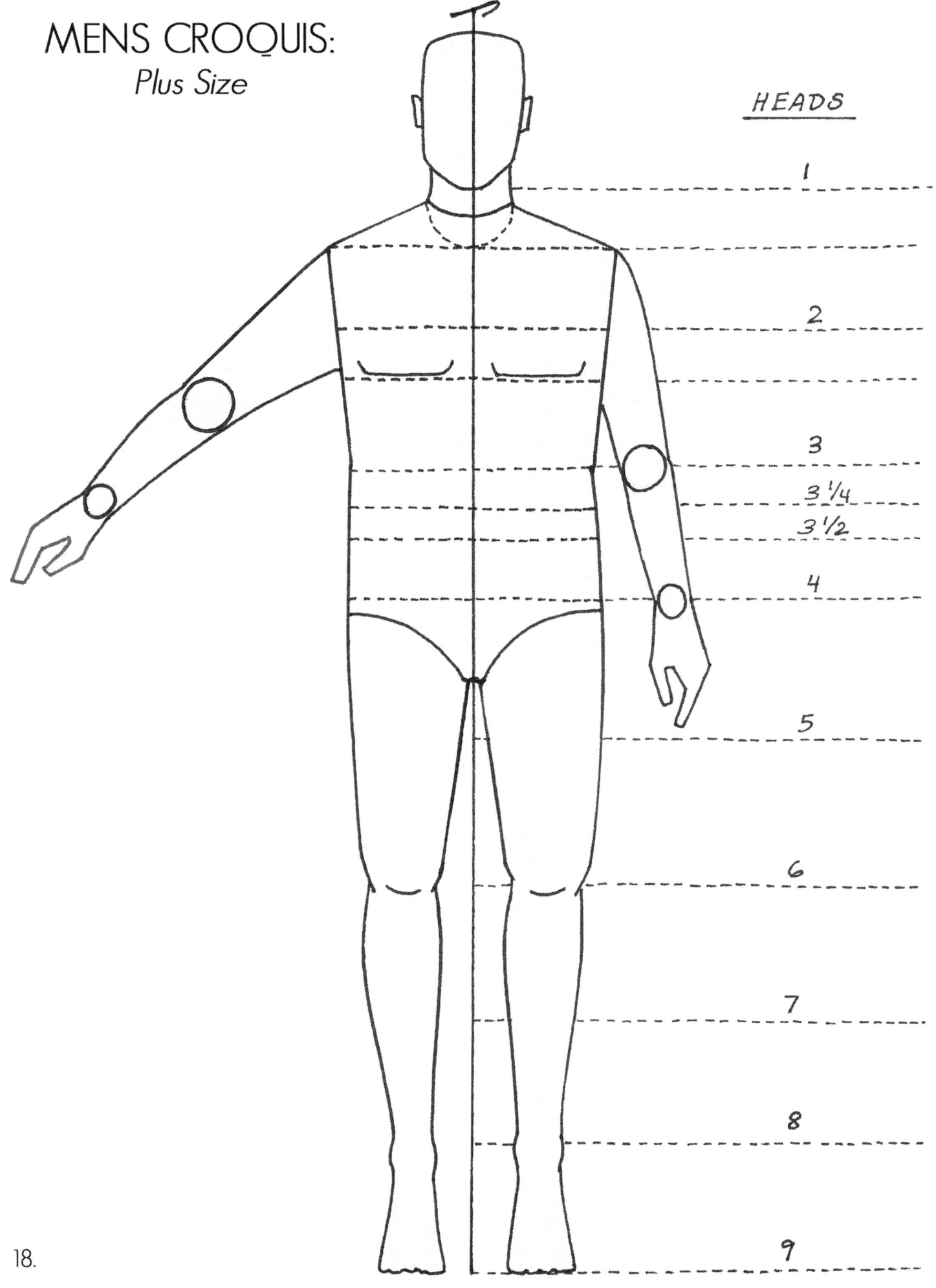

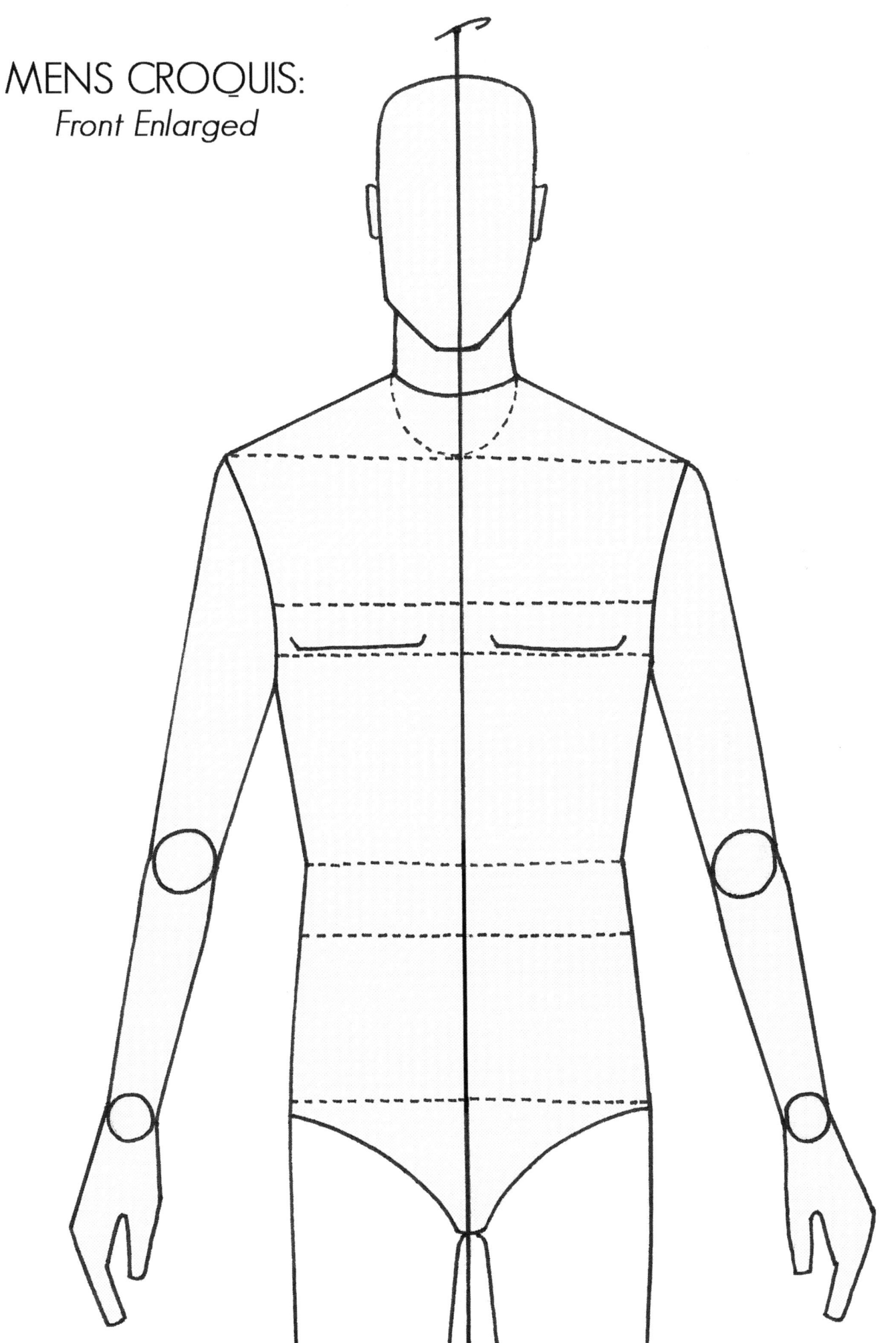

MENS CROQUIS:
Front Enlarged

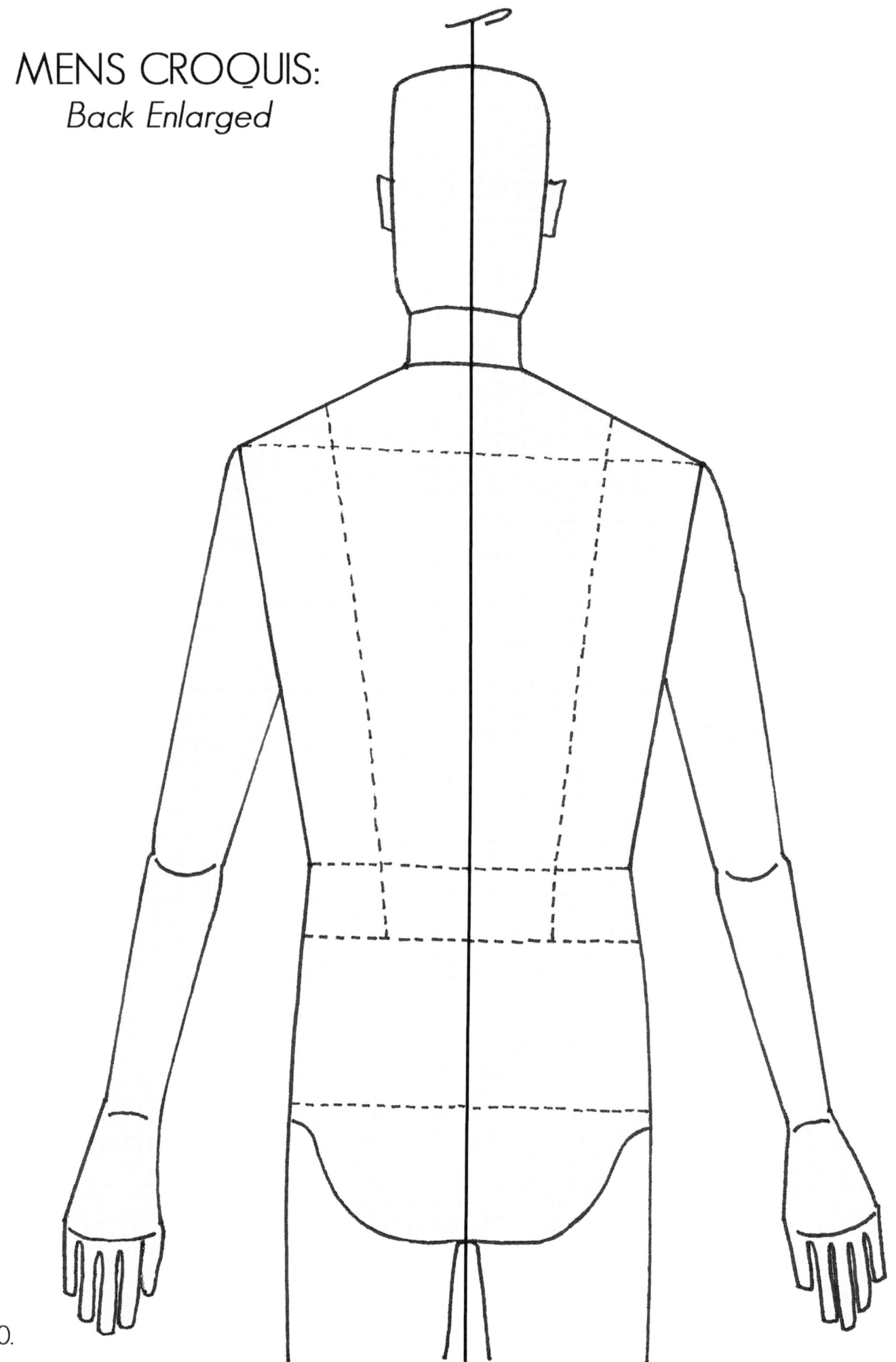
MENS CROQUIS:
Back Enlarged

Knit Shirts

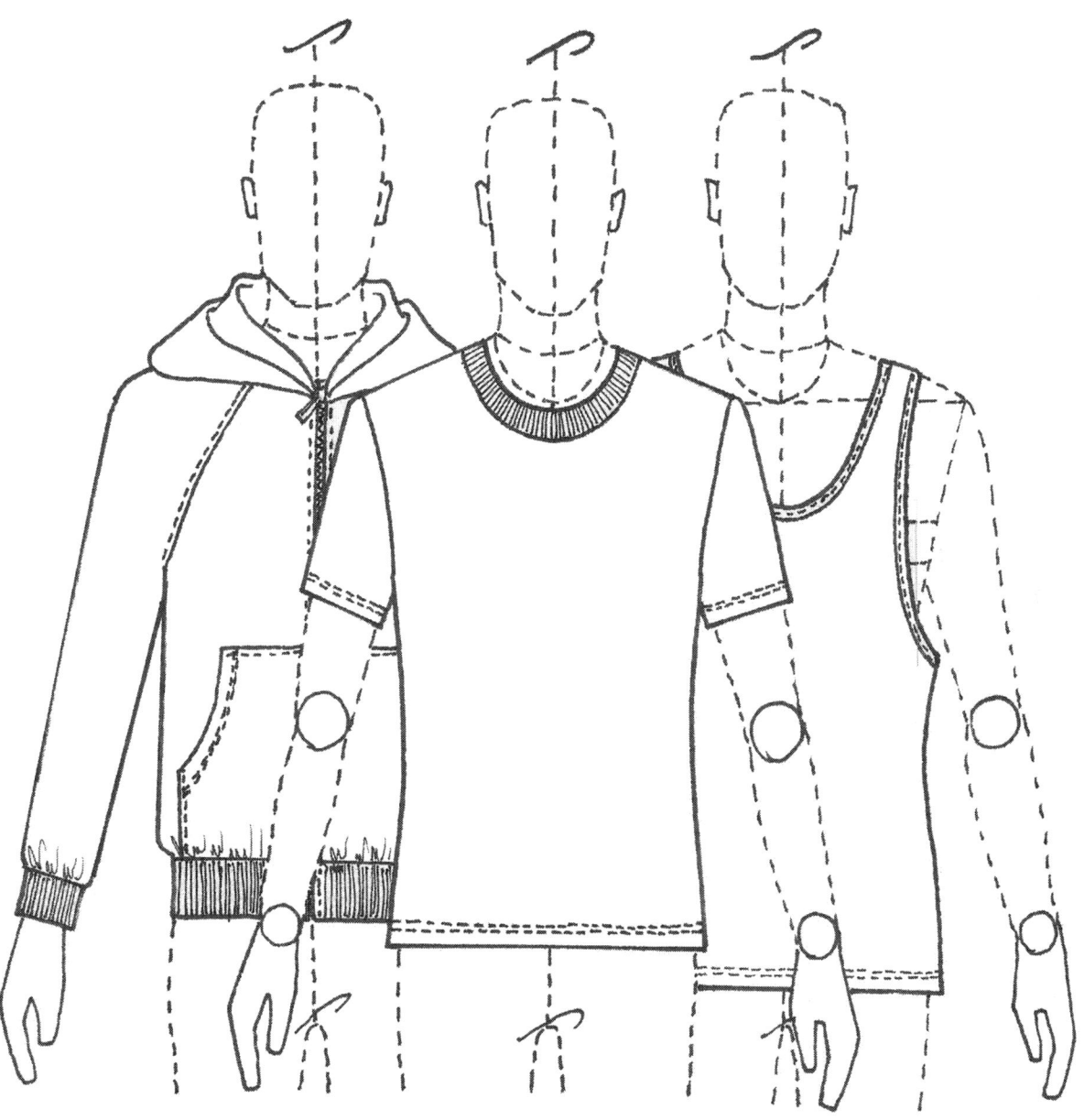

Knit Shirts

Slim Fit T-Shirt

1.
- Draw half of the neckline, both front and back.
- Continue by drawing the shoulder line.

2.
- Draw the armhole and side of T-Shirt of your croquis.
- Since this is a "Slim-Fit" T-Shirt, make sure to curve ever so slightly near the waist as shown, but do not make it too shapely.
- End this line right below the hip level, above the crotch. Draw the hem line.

3.
- Draw the sleeve. Since this is a sleeve for a Slim Fit T-Shirt, the sleeve will follow the arm of your croquis very closely.

4.
- Draw the other side of the T-Shirt including the sleeve, following the same instructions above.
- Draw the front neckline banding. Draw a curve about 1/8" below the first original neckline.

5.
- Finish by drawing small lines on the neckline band; this will represent the knit ribbing.
- Draw inner back neckline.
- Draw the coverstitch at the hems of the sleeves and T-Shirt. Coverstitching is the most common hem finish seen in knit shirts; they are drawn by sketching TWO rows of broken lines.

6.
- Draw half of the back neckline right below the croquis' neckline.
- Draw the shoulder line.
- Draw the armhole line and the side of the T-Shirt line.
- Draw half of the hem line.
- Draw the sleeve. Follow the same instructions as the front sleeve.

7.
- Draw the other side of the T-Shirt including the sleeve.
- Draw a curved line right below the first neckline. This will be the back neck band.

8.
- Finish the back by adding short lines inside the back neckband. These lines will represent the knit ribbing.
- Draw the coverstitch (2 rows of broken lines) at the hems of the T-Shirt and sleeves.

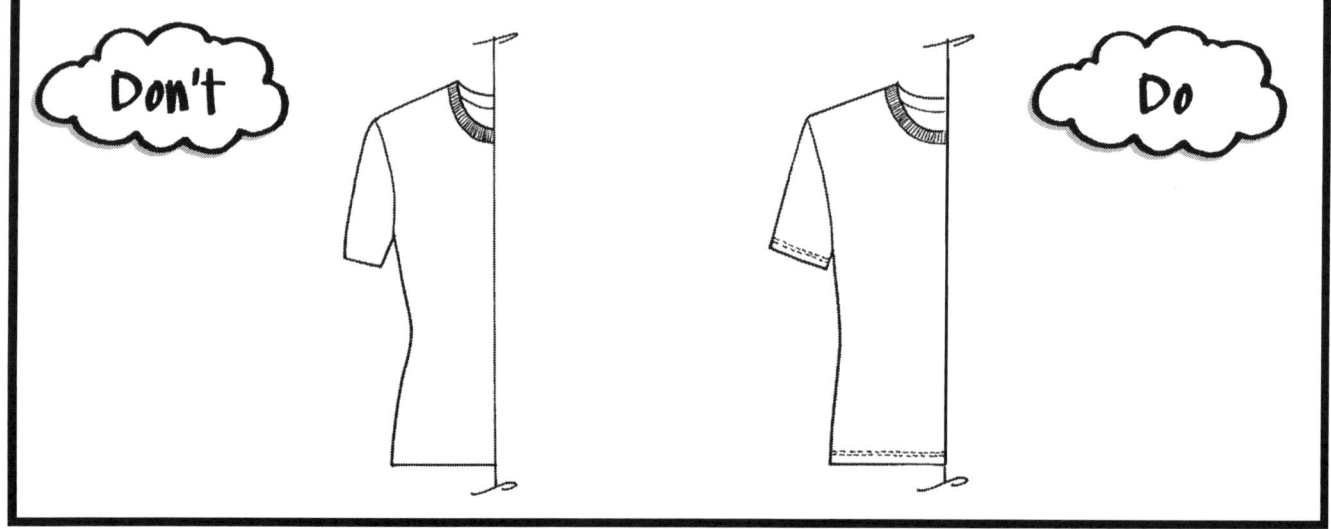

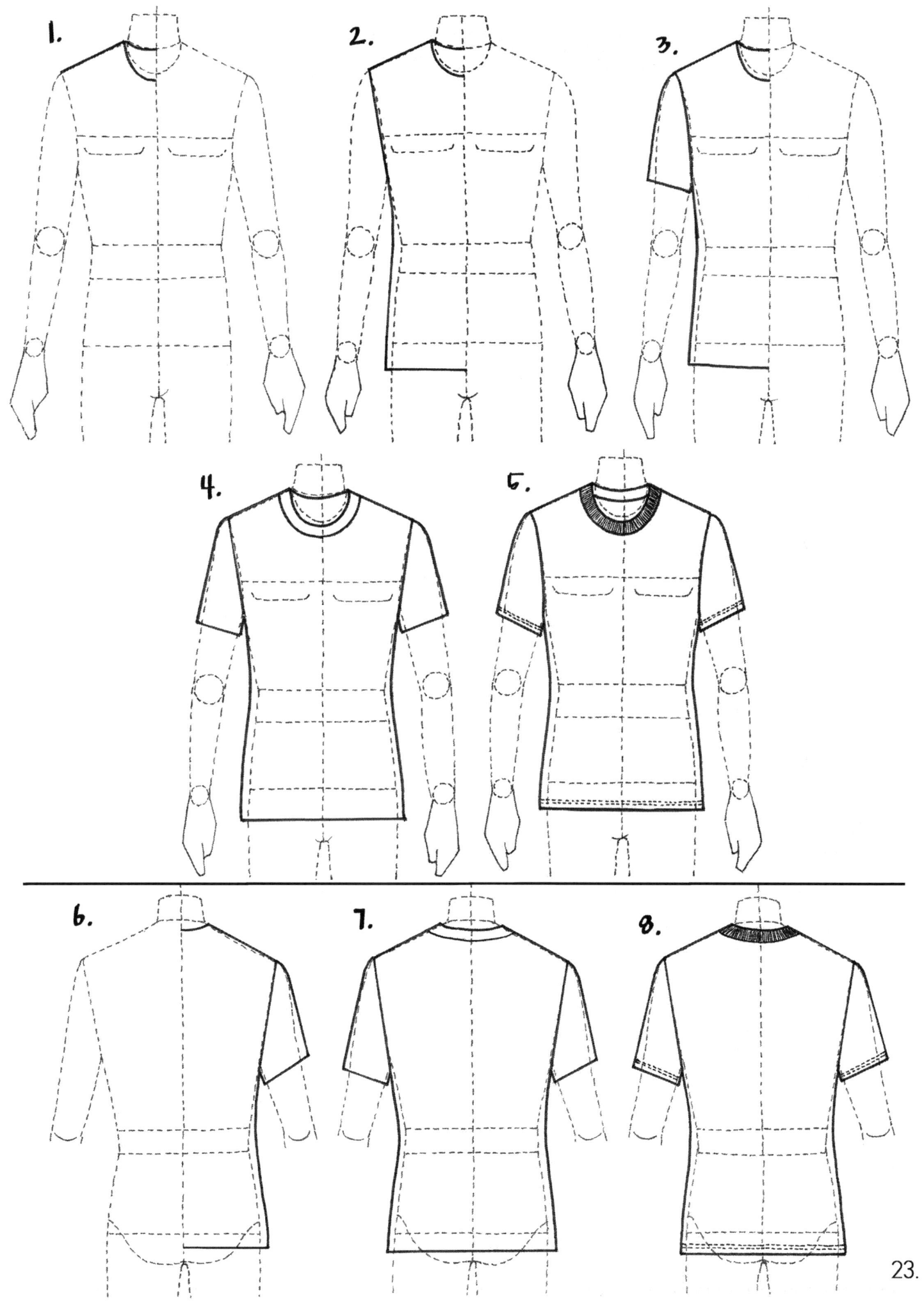

Knit Shirts

Loose Fit T-Shirt

1.
- Draw half of the neckline, both front and back.
- Continue by drawing the shoulder line.

2.
- Draw the armhole and side of T-Shirt. Continue the line, as a straight line, from the armpit to bottom of T-Shirt, ending below the hip and above the crotch.
- Make sure this line is STRAIGHT and away from the torso of your croquis, this is what makes it a Loose Fit T-Shirt.
- Draw the hem line.

3.
- Draw the sleeve. Since it is for a Loose Fit T-Shirt, the sleeve will be wider and more of a square shape.

4.
- Draw the other side of the T-Shirt including the sleeve, following the same instructions above.
- Draw the front neckline banding. Draw a curve about 1/8" below the first original neckline.

5.
- Finish by drawing small lines on the neckline band; this will represent the knit ribbing.
- Draw the inner back neckline.
- Draw coverstitch at the hems of the sleeves and T-Shirt. Coverstitching is the most common hem finish seen in knit shirts; they are drawn by sketching TWO rows of broken lines.

6.
- Draw half of the back neckline right below the croquis' neckline.
- Draw the shoulder line.
- Draw the armhole line and side of T-Shirt line.
- Draw half of the hem line.
- Draw the sleeve. Follow the same instructions as the front sleeve.

7.
- Draw the other side of the T-Shirt including the sleeve.
- Draw a curved line right below the first neckline. This will be the back neck band.

8.
- Finish the back by adding short lines inside the back neckband. These lines will represent the knit ribbing.
- Draw the coverstitch (2 rows of broken lines) at the hems of the T-Shirt and sleeves.

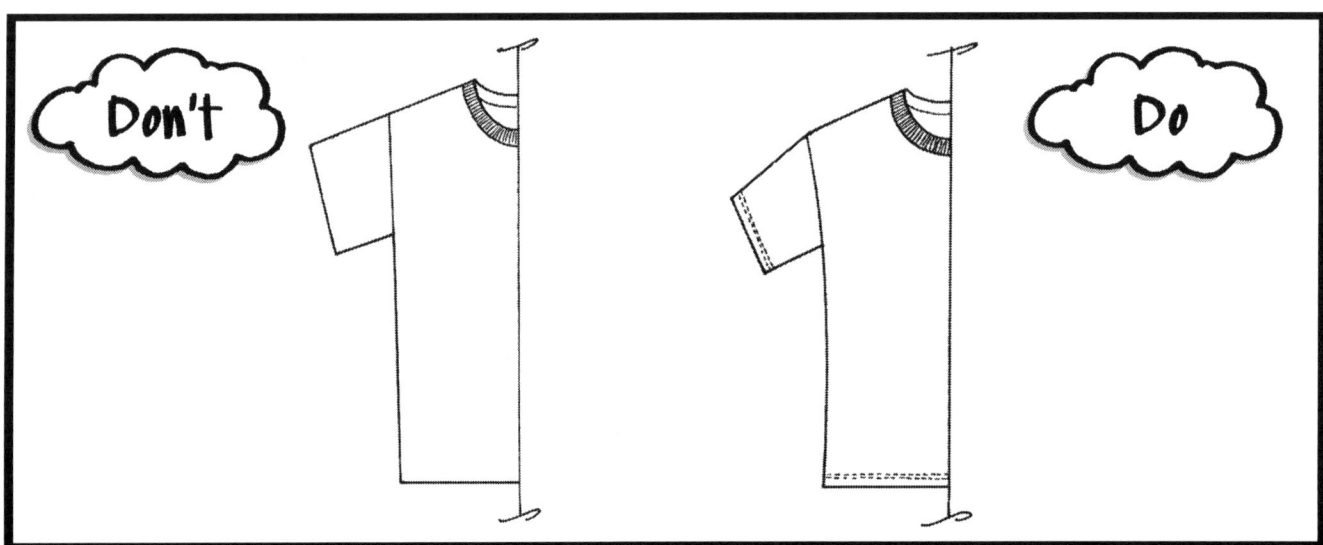

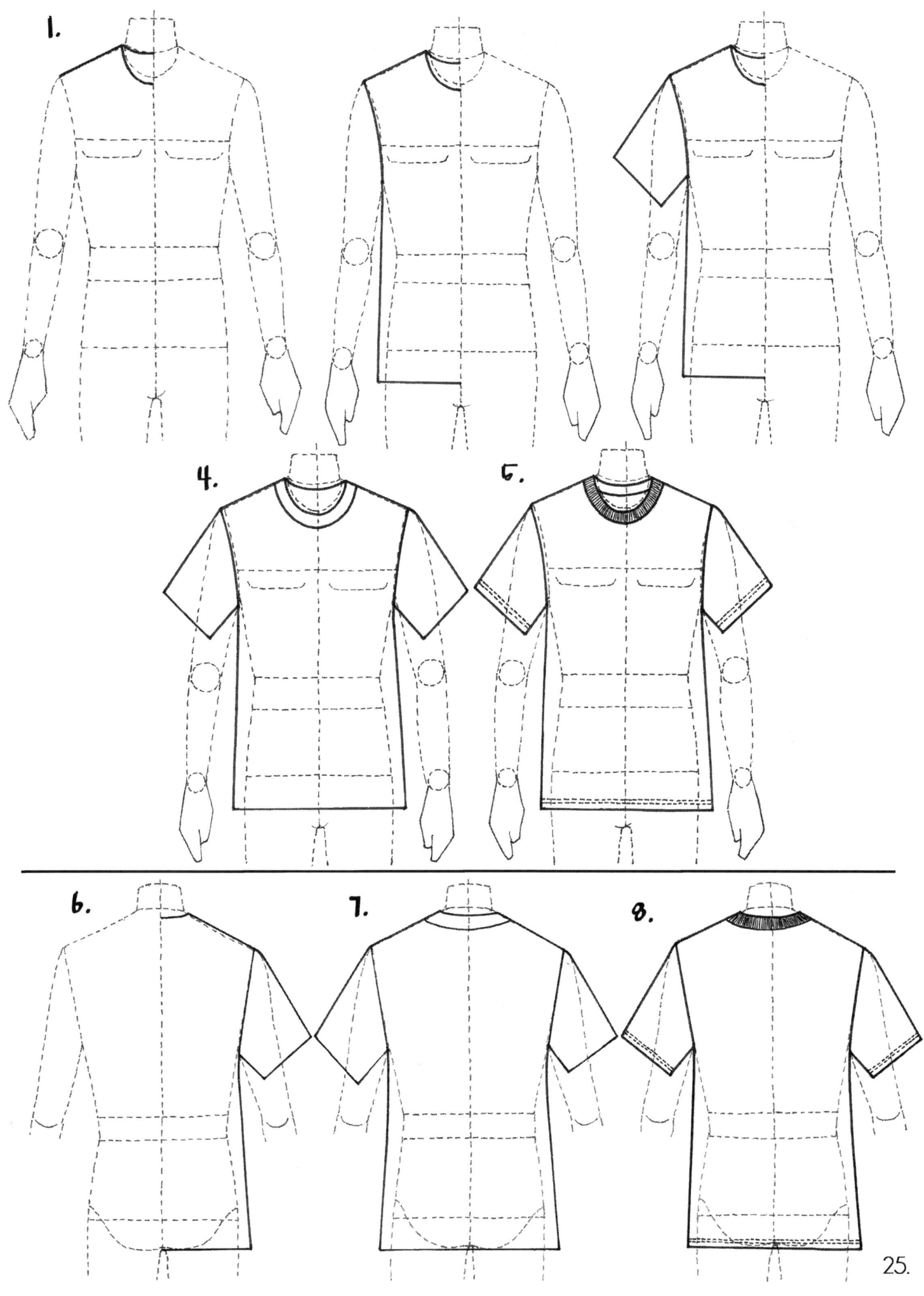

Tank Top

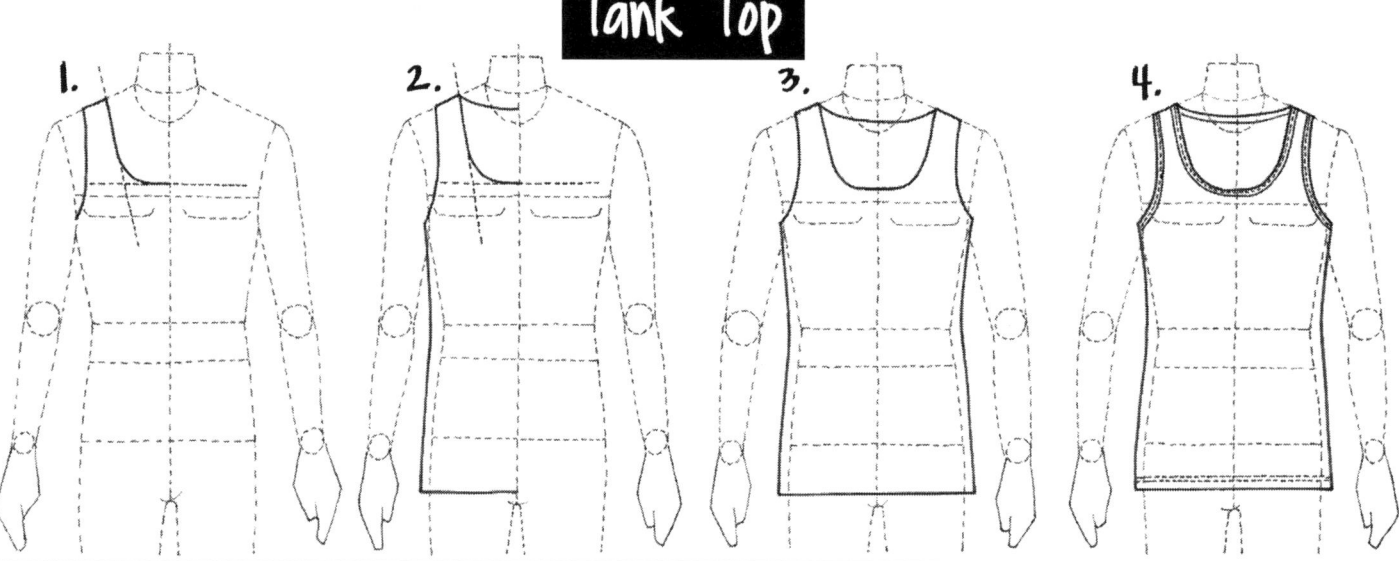

1.
- Start by drawing a short line in the middle of the shoulder.
- Draw a broken line as shown (that will be erased later) to help you in creating the shape.
- From the shoulder, draw half a "U" shape, stopping at mid-chest.
- For the armhole, beginning at the other side of the small shoulder line, draw a slightly curved line in a "J" shape ending at armpit/underarm level.

2.
- Draw the back neckline, side and hem.

3.
- Draw other side of Tank Top following the same instructions as above.

4.
- Finish the Tank Top by drawing binding at the armhole and neckline edges, as well as the coverstitch at the hem.

5.
- Draw the back neckline beginning at the center back as a straight line that then curves to the shoulder.
- Draw the shoulder as a short straight line in the middle of the shoulder.
- Draw the armhole as a curved line, from shoulder to underarm/armpit.

6.
- Draw the side of the Tank Top and hem.

7.
- Draw the other side of the Tank Top following the same instructions as above.

8.
- Finish the Tank Top by drawing binding at the armhole and neckline edges, as well as the coverstitch at the hem.

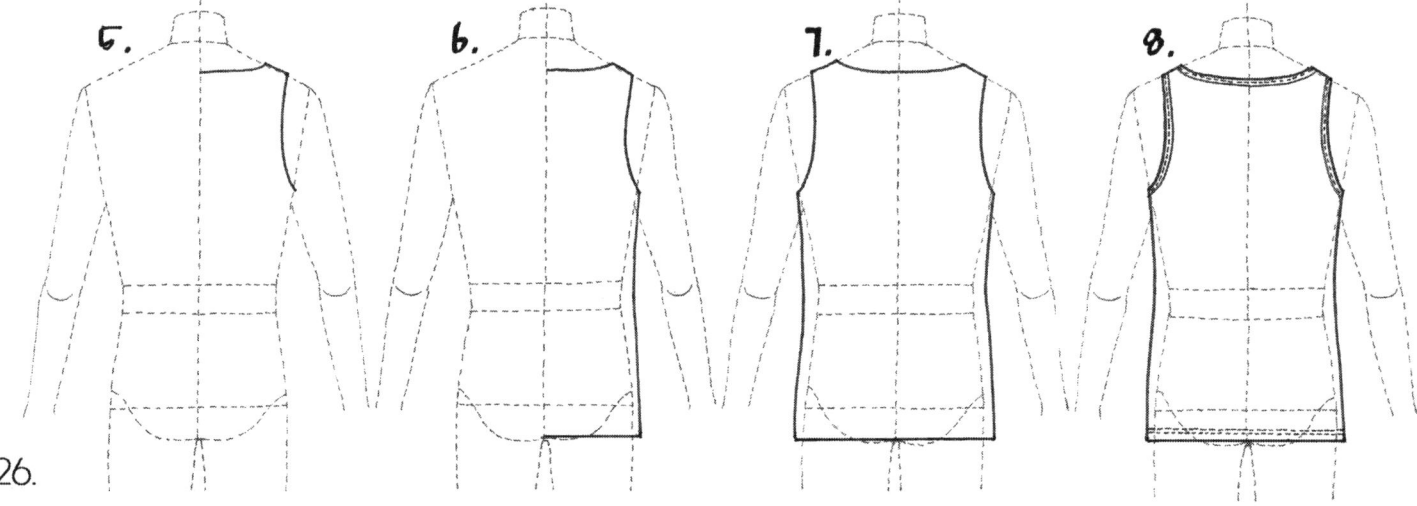

Sleeveless Muscle Tee

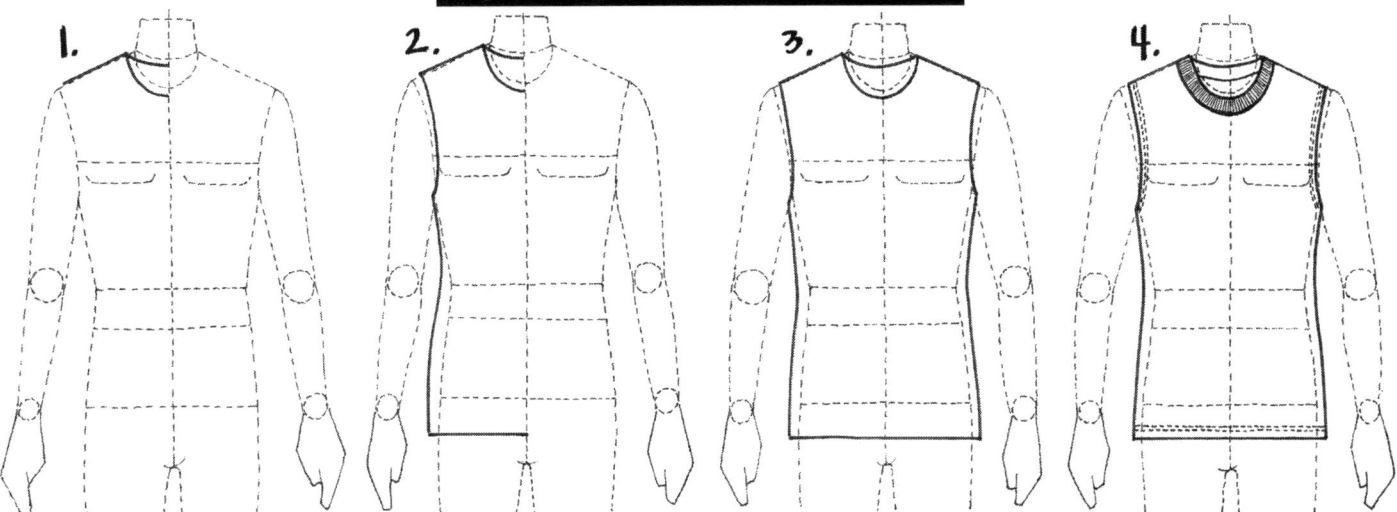

1.
- Draw half of the neckline—front and back by following the broken line curves on your croquis.
- Draw the shoulder line. Stop right before the shoulder tip.

2.
- Draw the armhole line. Beginning at the shoulder, draw a slightly curved line down to the armpit level.
- Draw a slightly curved line following the torso of your croquis that ends below the hips and above the crotch.

3.
- Draw the other side following the same instructions as above.

4.
- Finish by drawing the neckline bands (front and back), adding small lines inside the neckband to represent ribbing. Sketch the coverstitch lines at the hem and edges of the armholes.

5.
- Draw half of the back neckline and shoulder line stopping right before the shoulder tip.

6.
- Draw the armhole line, side of T-Shirt line and hem.

7.
- Draw the other side of the Slim Fit Muscle T-Shirt following the same instructions as above.

8.
- Finish by drawing the back neckline band, adding small lines inside the neckband to represent ribbing. Sketch the coverstitch lines at the hem and edges of the armholes.

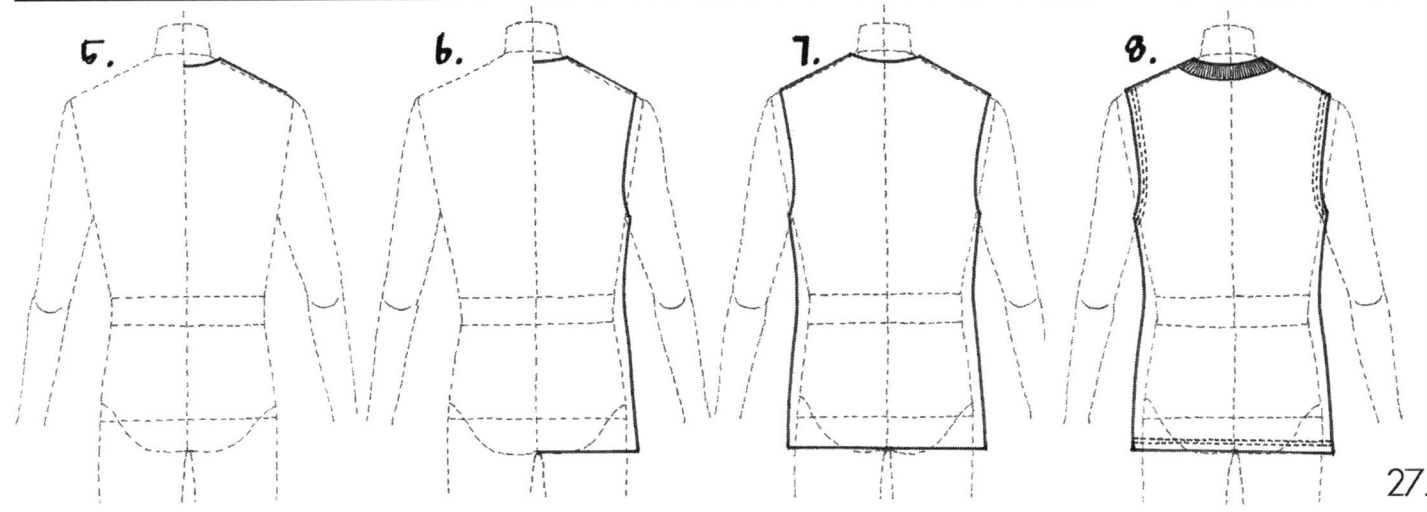

Knit Collars and Necklines

CF — Crew neck	CF — V-neck
CF — Turtleneck	CF — Mock Turtleneck
CF — Ribbed Knit Collar	CF — Henley Collar

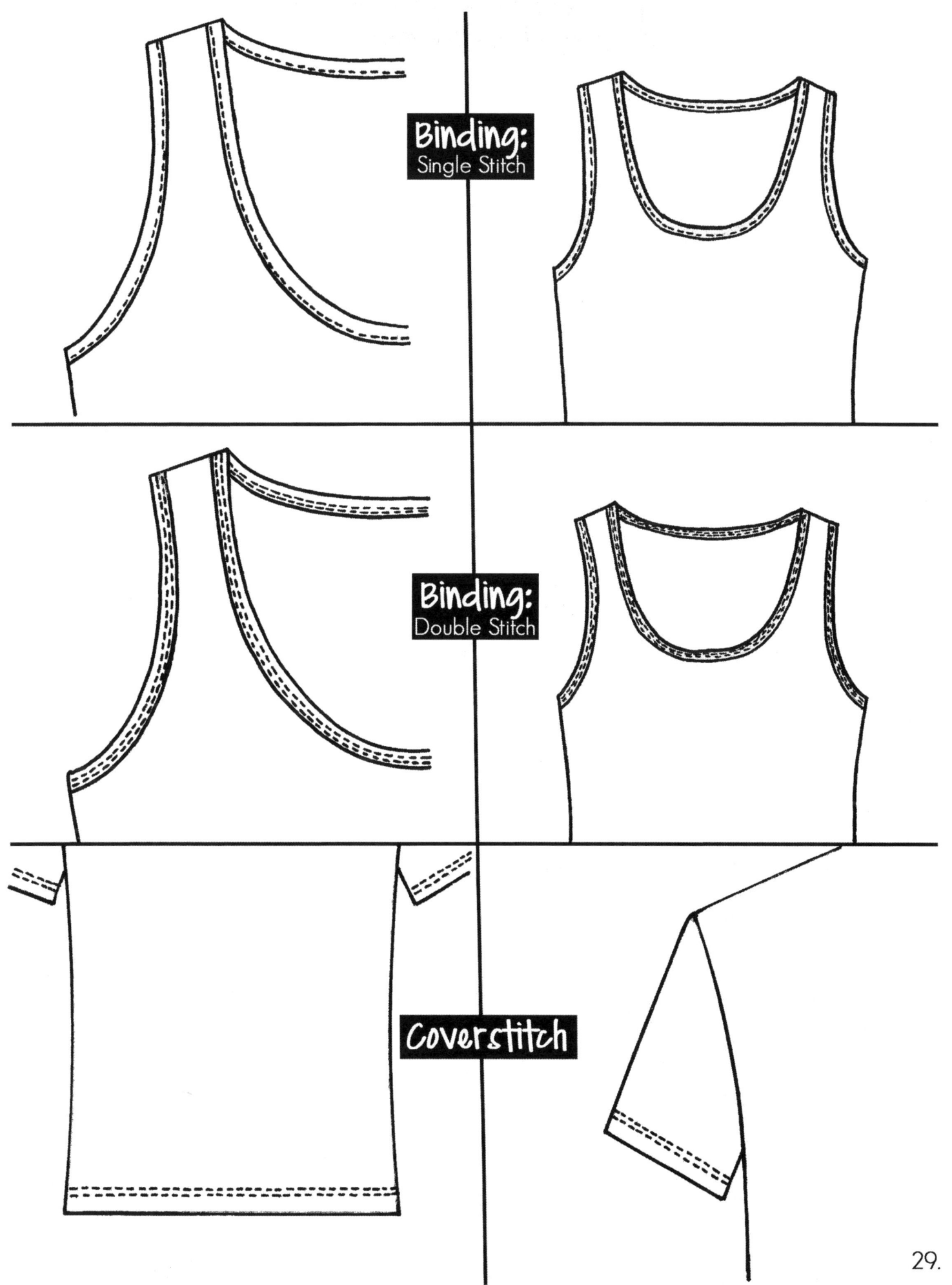

Track Jacket

1.
- Begin by sketching the band collar first. This will be slightly higher than a regular band collar. Leave a small open space in the center front.

2.
- Draw the shoulder line from the neck to shoulder tip area.
- For the sleeve, continue shoulder line curving slightly at shoulder area and continuing into a straight line down to the wrist.
- Draw a slight curve near the wrist and then a short vertical straight line representing the outside of the sleeve cuff.
- Draw the inner sleeve line as a straight line from the armpit to the wrist area. Draw the slight curve and short vertical straight line in the same manner as the outer sleeve.
- Finish the sleeve with a short horizontal line at the wrist to show the hem.

3.
- Draw the side of the jacket with a line beginning slightly above the armpit, down the side of the torso, ending around hip level with a slight curve. From there, draw a short vertical line down the side of the croquis' leg.
- Draw the hem of the jacket as a straight line from the hips to the center front.
- Draw the front of the jacket with a straight line slightly away from the center front and NOT at the center front.

4.
- Draw the other side of the jacket following the same instructions as above.

5.
- Finish drawing the Track Jacket by adding all the necessary details:
- Draw the raglan seams as slightly curved lines, from armpit to mid-neck.
- Draw front zipper and zipper pull in the center front of the jacket.
- Add short straight lines on the cuffs and jacket band to show ribbing material.
- Draw welt pockets as thin, slightly angled rectangles. The pockets should begin around waist level.
- Finish by adding any necessary topstitching around raglan seams, welt pockets and zipper.

6.
- Draw the back of the band collar.
- Draw the shoulder line beginning at the neck to shoulder tip.
- For the back sleeve, follow the same directions as the front sleeve.
- Draw the hem of the jacket as a straight line from hips to center back.

7.
- Draw the other side of the jacket following the same instructions as above.

8.
- Finish drawing the Track Jacket by adding all the necessary details:
- Start with drawing the raglan seams as slightly curved lines, from armpit to mid-neck.
- Add short straight lines on the cuffs and jacket band to show ribbing material.
- Finish by adding any necessary topstitching around raglan seams.

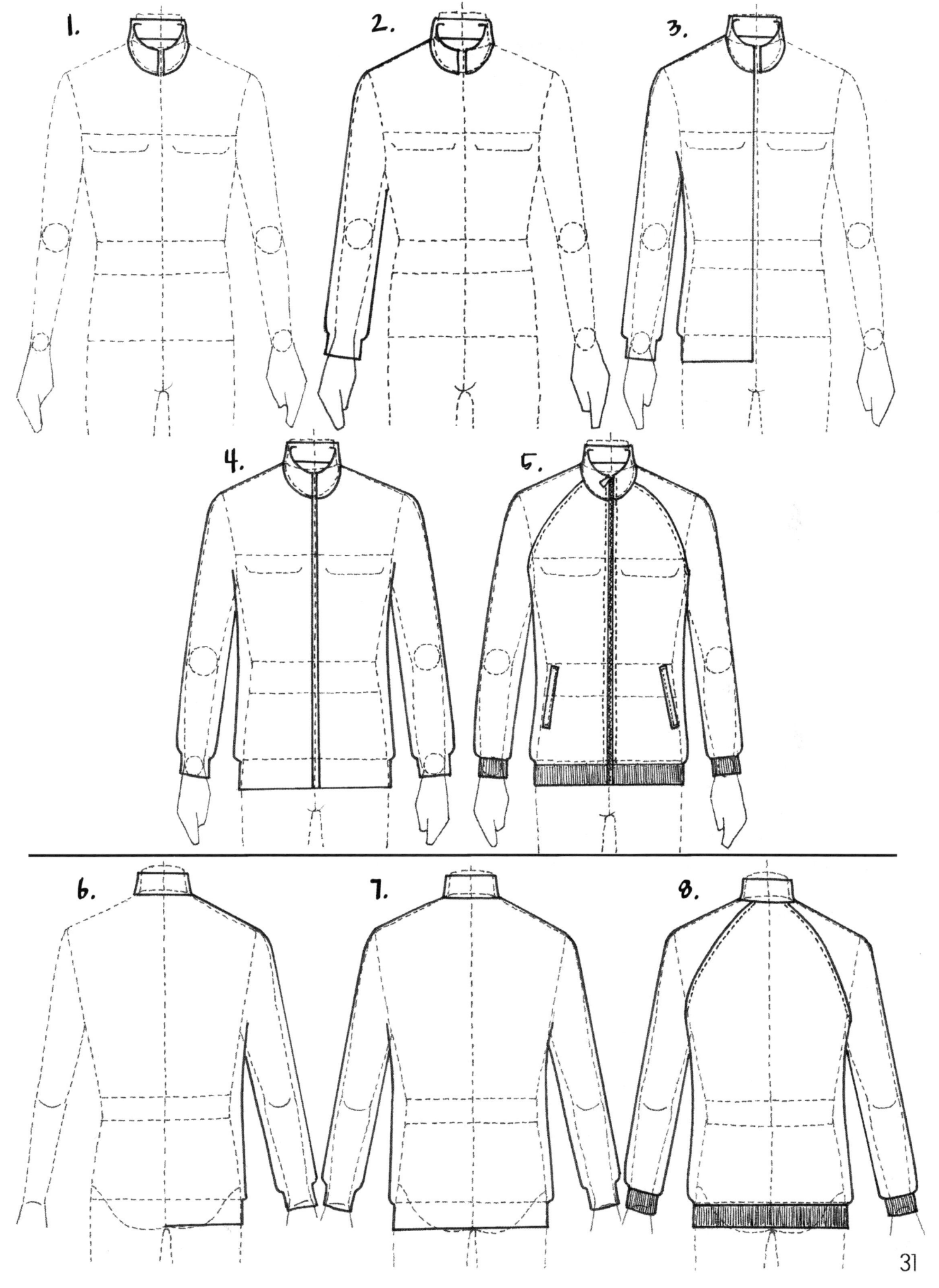

Hoods: Front

Flat Hood

1.
- Draw the outline of the "flat" hood: Sketch a line beginning at the shoulders then rising up toward the neck, as shown.

2.
- Draw curved inner necklines as well as additional outer curved lines showing the flattened hood, from center front neck toward the shoulder area.

3.
- Finish by drawing the draped hood lines, curving from the CF neck area toward the shoulder and curving around the back.
- Next, draw inner neckline as a small curved line.
- Add the hood ties, center front zipper and topstitching.

Fitted Hood

4.
- Draw the outer line of the Fitted Hood: Starting at the shoulder, draw a straight line following the shoulder, then beginning at the neck area, continue drawing the outer line of the hood around the head of the Croquis in the shape of a rounded cone, as shown.

5.
- Draw the neckline as a curved line from shoulders to center front, following the broken lines of the Croquis' neckline.
- Draw the inner opening of the hood like the shape of a balloon.
- Draw a short straight line from the top of the hood to the inner hood opening; this represents the center seam of the hood.
- Next, draw the inner neckline as a small curved line.

6.
- Finish drawing by adding details including ties, center front zipper and topstitching.

Traditional Large Hood

7.
- Draw the hood outline shape starting near the center front, slightly below the center front neckline. Continue onto mid-shoulder, curving to the top of the Croquis' head and ending back to CF neck area. The shape should resemble a wide cone shape, as shown.
- From the mid-shoulder, draw shoulder lines to the shoulder tips.

8.
- Draw the inner opening of the hood, following the same shape as the outer hood line.
- Draw a short straight line from top of hood to the inner hood opening; this represents the center seam of the hood.
- Next, draw inner neckline as a curved line.

9.
- Finish drawing of the Traditional Large Hood by adding the necessary details including ties, center front zipper, inner seam line (inside the hood) and topstitching.

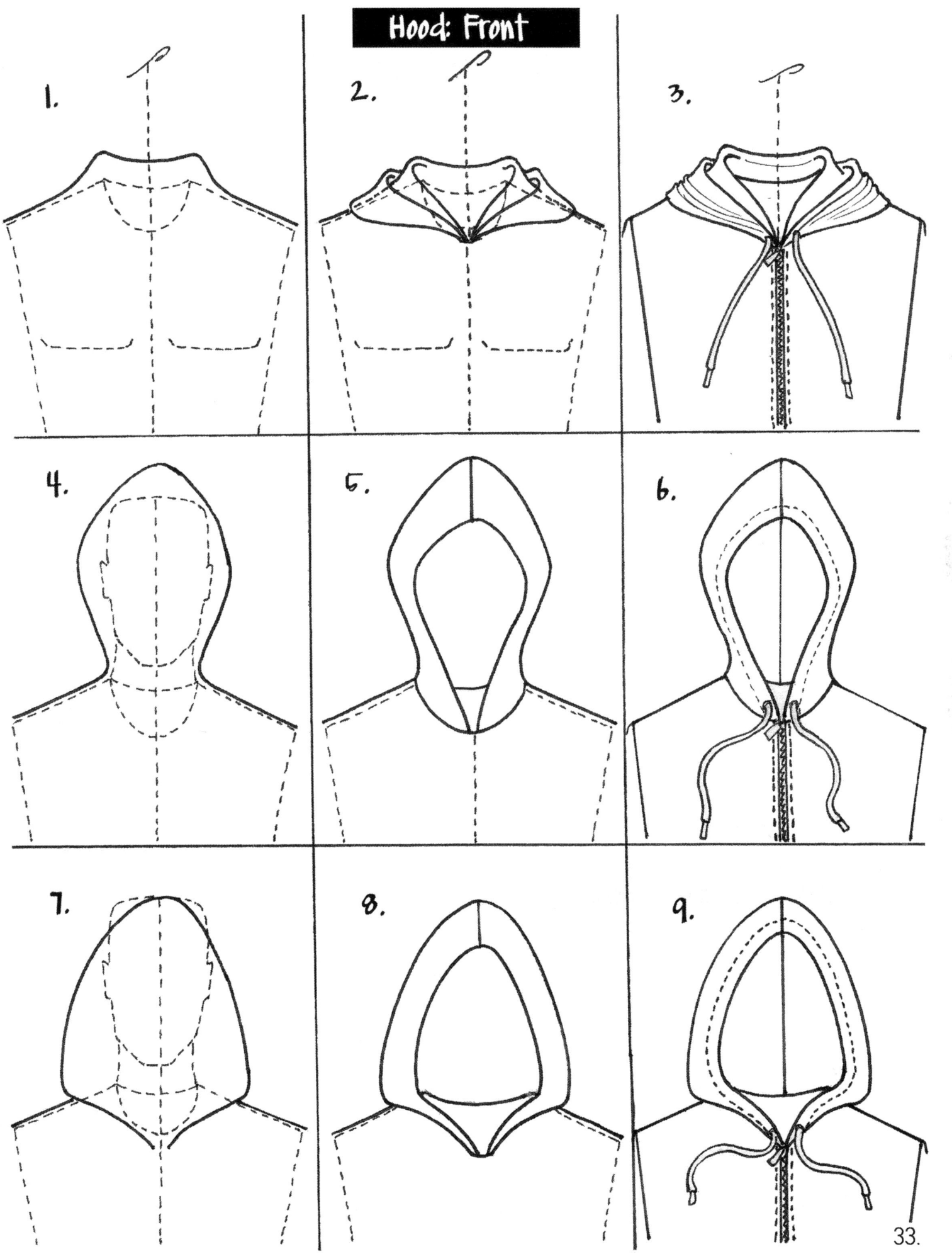

Hoods: Back

Flat Hood

1.
- Draw the outlines of the "flat" hood: Sketch a line beginning at the shoulders then rising up toward the neck, as shown.

2.
- Draw the outline of the back hood, draped over the back. Start at the raised neckline, following the shoulder line and curving in a cone-like shape finishing back at the opposite side of the raised neckline.
- Add an additional curved line around the neck.

3.
- Finish by drawing the back hood lines, showing the draped effect.
- Add a line in the center back of the back hood, to show the seam in the hood.

Fitted Hood

4.
- Draw the outer line of the Fitted Hood: Starting at the shoulder, draw a straight line following the shoulder, then beginning at the neck area, continue drawing the outer line of the hood around the head of the Croquis in the shape of a rounded cone, as shown.

5.
- Draw the back neckline as a curved line slightly below the Croquis' back neckline.
- Draw a line at the center back of the hood, to show the seam in the hood.

6.
- Finish by adding topstitching right below the back neckline.

Traditional Large Hood

7.
- Draw the back hood outline shape starting from the left shoulder tip, then onto mid-shoulder, curving to the top of the Croquis' head and ending back to the right shoulder tip. The shape should resemble a wide cone shape, as shown.

8.
- Draw the back "neckline" of the hood as a slightly curved line right below the Croquis' neckline.
- Add a line at the CB of the back hood, showing the back hood seam.

9.
- Finish drawing the back by adding topstitching right below the back neckline.

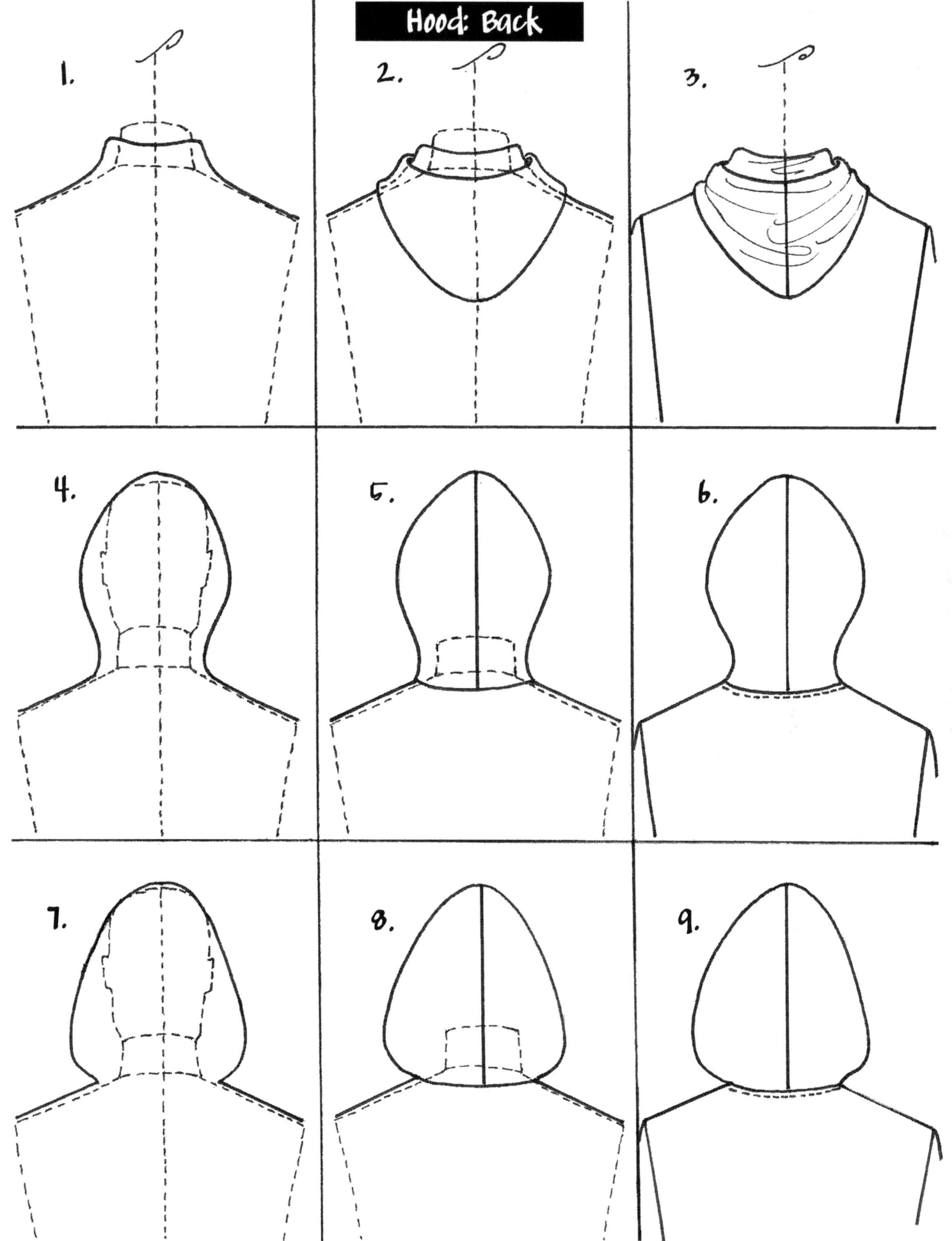

Hooded Track Jacket

Front:
1.
- Draw the hood as shown (refer to "Hoods: Front" for detailed instructions).

2.
- Begin by drawing the shoulder line from the edge of the hood to shoulder tip.
- Draw the armhole line as a straight line from shoulder tip to underarm.
- From the underarm, draw the side seam as a straight line to the hip area.
- At the hip area, curve in as shown and then draw a short straight line showing the side of the hem.
- Draw the hem as a horizontal line from the side of the leg to the center front.

3.
- Draw the outer sleeve from shoulder tip to wrist area as a straight line, curving in at the wrist.
- Draw the inner sleeve from underarm to wrist area as a straight line, curving in at the wrist.
- Draw sleeve cuff outlines on the side and hem.

4.
- Draw the other side of the hooded track jacket and sleeve following the same instructions as above.

5.
- Draw the center front zipper.
- Add the front "kangaroo"-style pockets.
- Draw the hood ties.
- Draw short straight lines at sleeve cuffs and hem band to show the knit ribbing.
- Lastly, add topstitching wherever needed including around the zipper and pocket.

Back:
6.
- Draw the back of the hood as shown (refer to "Hoods: Back" for detailed instructions).

7.
- Begin by drawing the shoulder line from the edge of the hood to shoulder tip.
- Draw armhole line as a straight line from shoulder tip to underarm.
- From the underarm, draw the side seam as a straight line to the hip area.
- At the hip area, curve in as shown and then draw a short straight line showing the side of the hem.
- Draw the hem as a horizontal line from the side of the leg to the center back.
- Draw the outer sleeve from shoulder tip to wrist area as a straight line, curving in at the wrist.
- Draw the inner sleeve from underarm to wrist area as a straight line, curving in at the wrist.
- Draw sleeve cuff outlines on the side and hem.

8.
- Draw the other side of the hooded track jacket and sleeve following the same instructions as above.
- Draw the back hood lines, showing the draped effect.
- Draw top cuff line and top waistband line.
- Draw short straight lines at sleeve cuffs and hem band to show the knit ribbing.
- Add small gathering lines at edges of the sleeve cuffs and hem band.

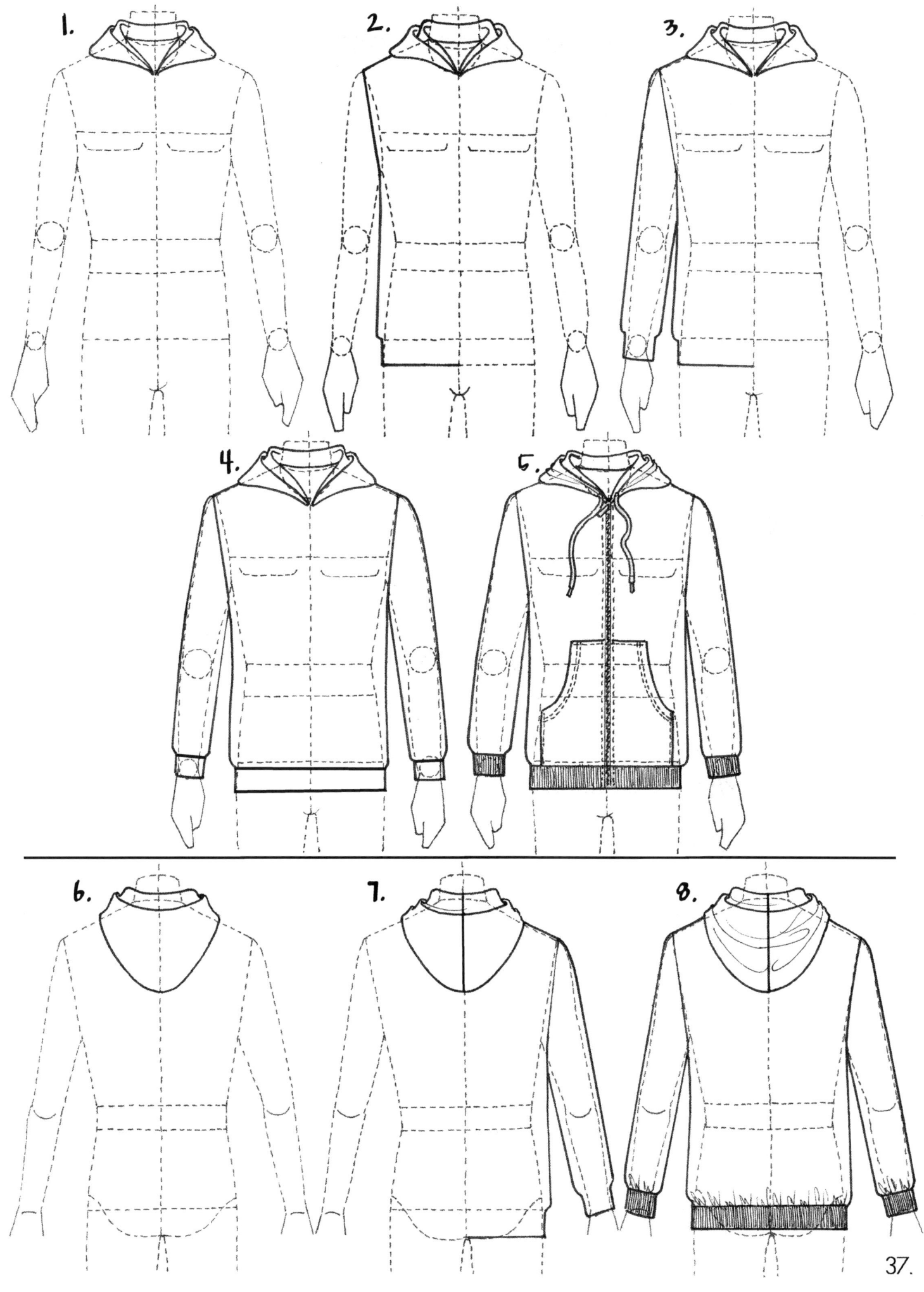

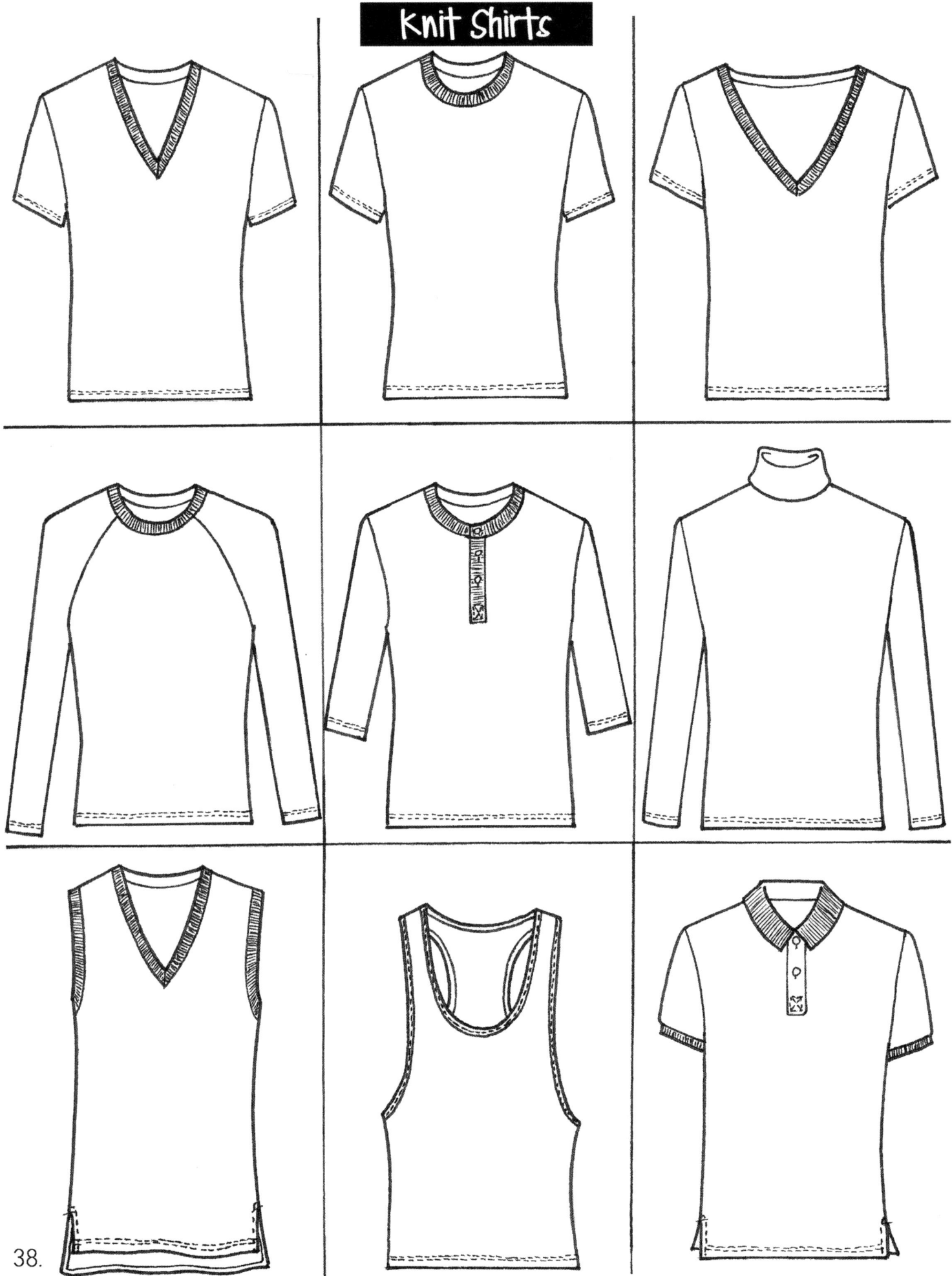

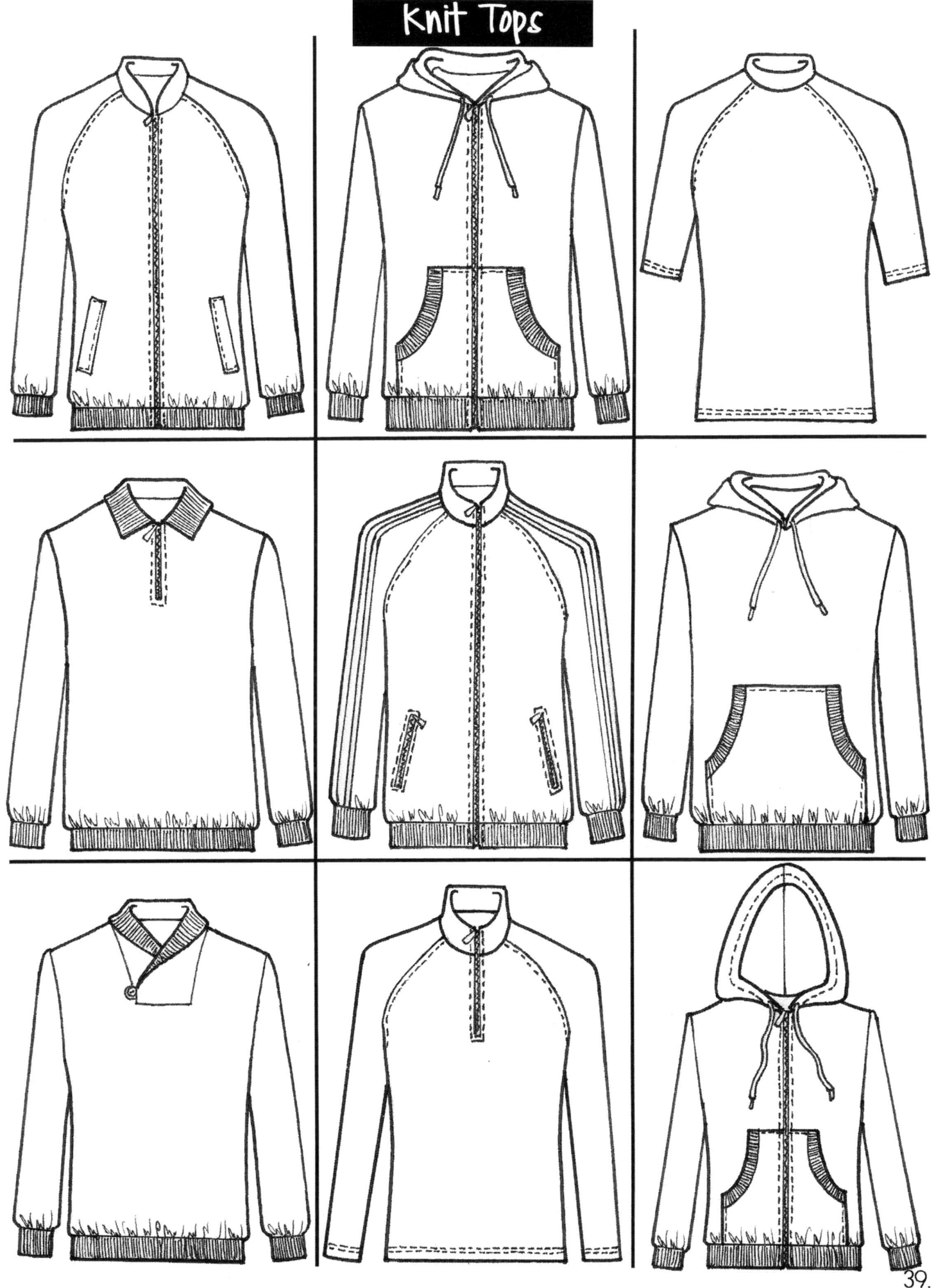

Woven Shirts

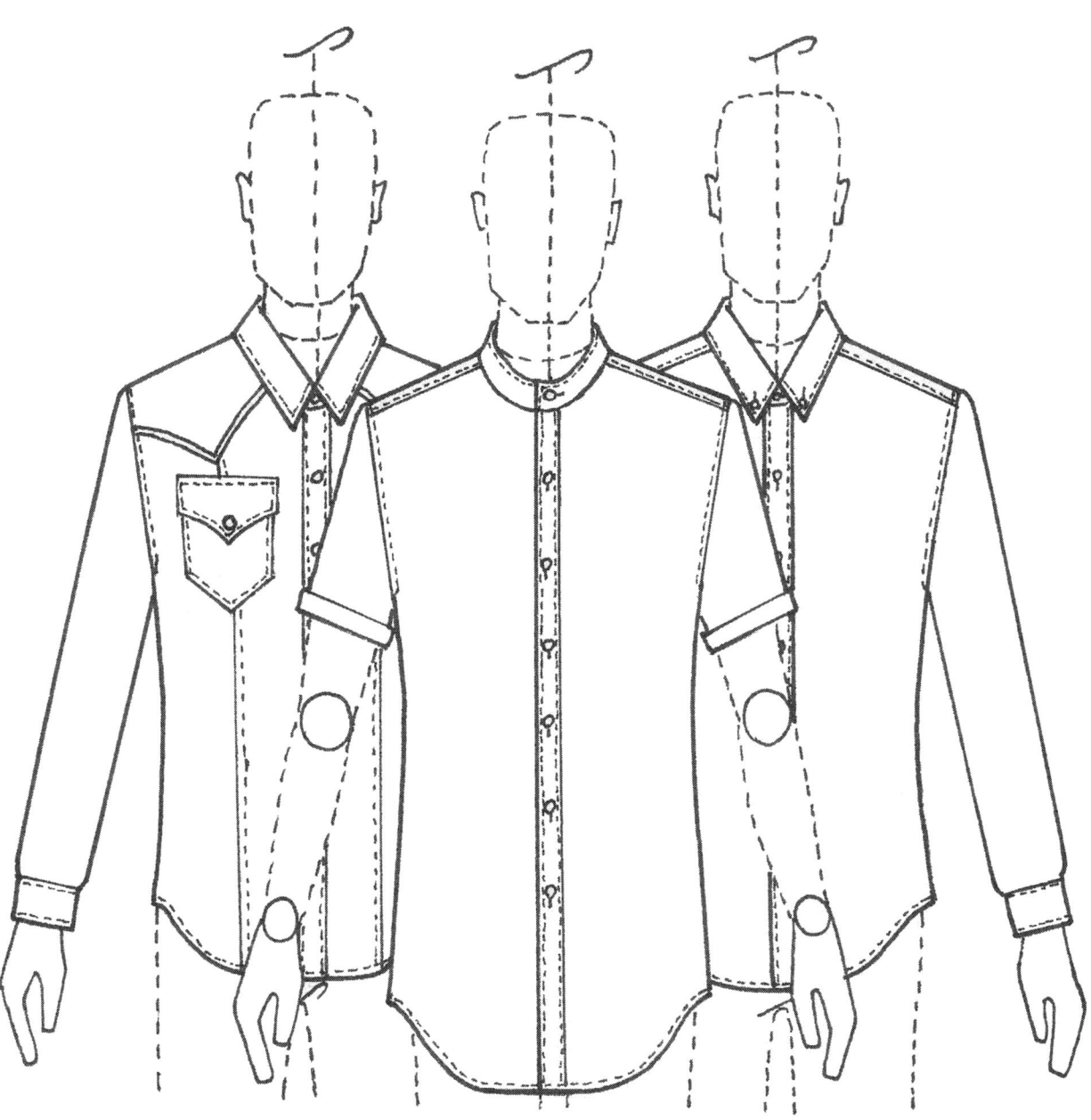

Basic Shirt Collar

Front:

1.
- Draw a "halo" line above the neckline of the croquis.

2.
- Draw a "V" shape with the point touching the center front of the neckline. Make sure the open edges of the "V" DO NOT touch the "halo" line.

3.
- Draw a smaller upside-down "V" shape from the point of the larger "V". The end result will resemble an uneven "X".

4.
- From the "halo" line, draw short angled lines that end at the shoulder. These lines should be the same length as the small upside-down "V" lines at the center front.

5.
- Draw a straight line connecting the above-the-shoulder lines to the upside-down "V" lines in the front.

6.
- Draw the front opening of the shirt slighty to the LEFT of the center front of your sketch (for women's shirts, this line would be drawn slightly to the RIGHT).

Back:

7.
- Draw a "halo" line above the back neckline of your croquis.

8.
- Draw two slightly angled lines starting from the "halo" line, stopping at the shoulders.

9.
- Draw a straight line below the back neckline of the croquis, connecting the two short angled above-the-shoulder lines.

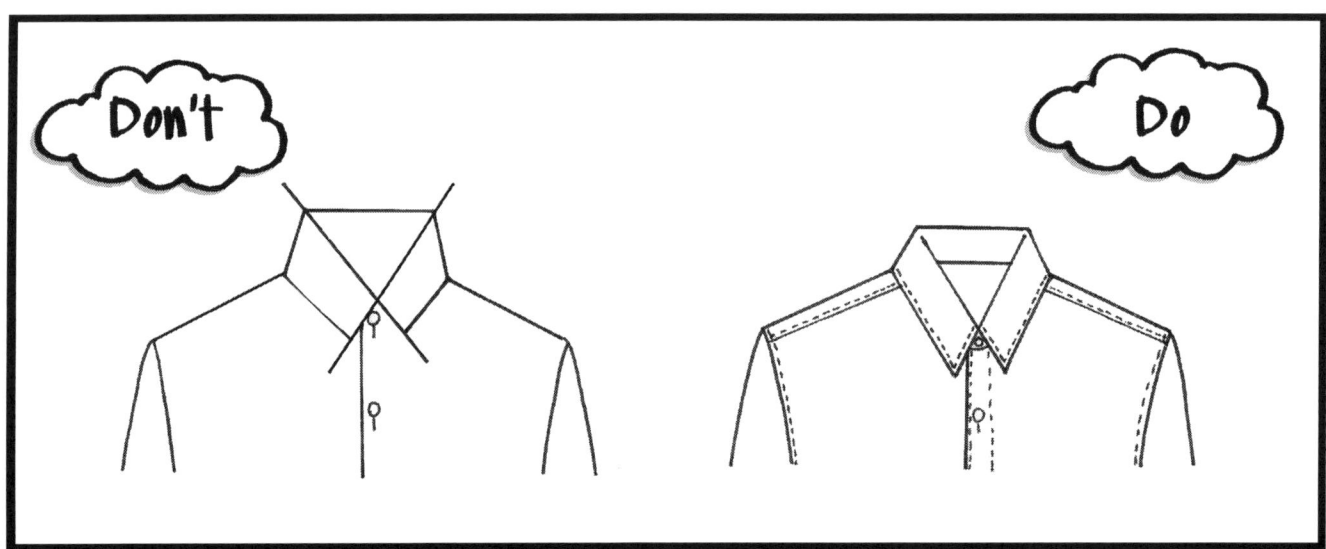

42.

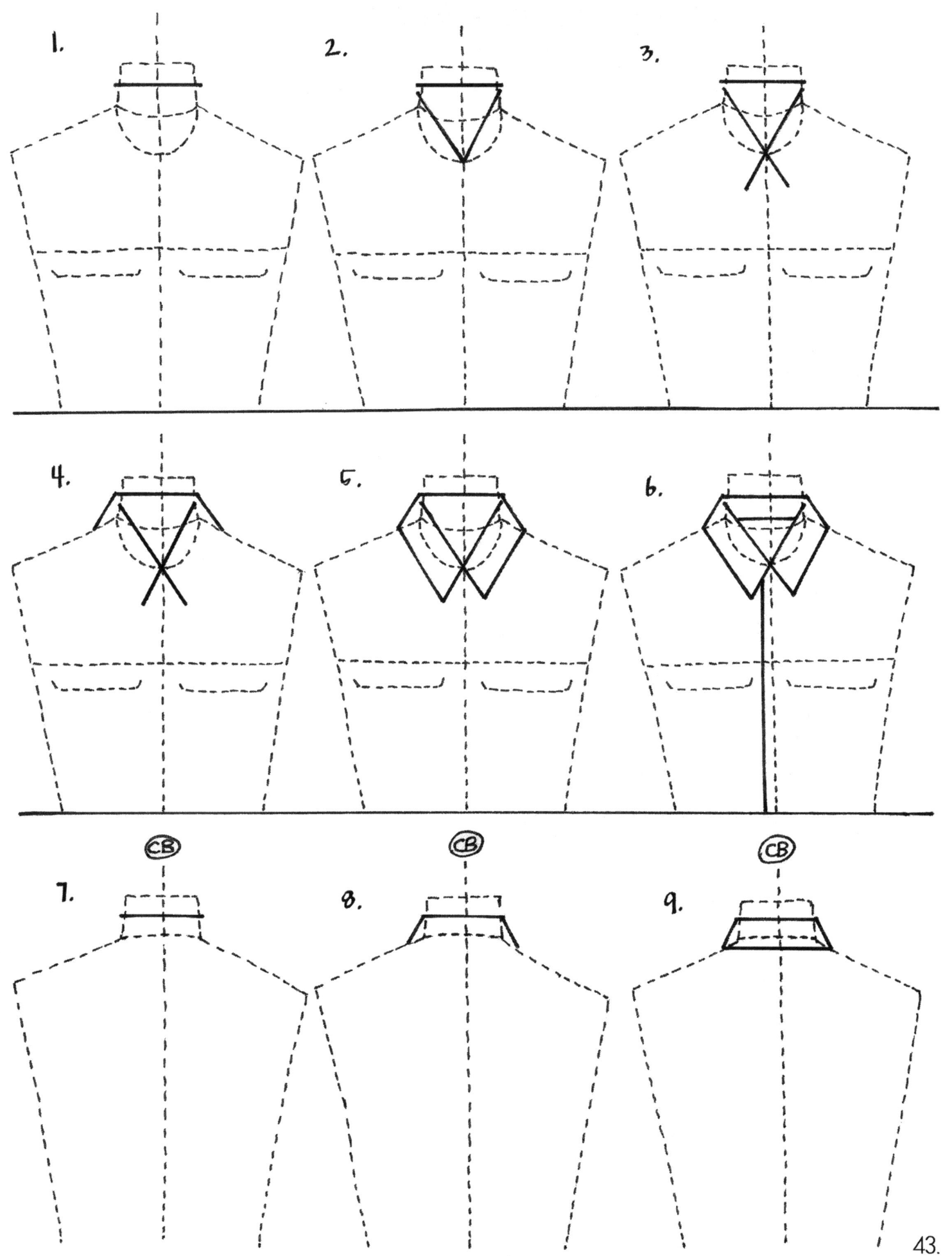

Dress Shirt: fitted

1.
- Draw the shirt collar.

2.
- Draw the shoulder line.
- Draw the armhole line, following the broken lines of the armholes in your croquis.
- From the underarm, draw the side of the shirt as an ever-so-slightly curved line. Curve in very slightly at the waist and end below the hip line.
- Draw the hem starting at the side then slightly dipping downward, eventually ending in a straight line toward the center.

3.
- Draw the outer sleeve from shoulder tip to wrist area as a straight line, curving in at the wrist.
- Draw the inner sleeve from underarm to wrist area as a straight line, curving in at the wrist.
- Draw sleeve cuff outlines on the side and hem.

4.
- Draw the other side of the shirt and sleeve.

5.
- Add all the finishing details: First draw two short lines right below the shoulders. These represent the shoulder seams of the shirt.
- Draw the front opening line, slightly to the left of the center front of the shirt.
- Draw buttons and buttonholes at the center front of the shirt. Space the buttons evenly and remember to draw the buttonholes as short up-and-down lines below the button circles.
- In each sleeve, draw a short straight line above the wrist to create a square shape that will represent the sleeve cuff.
- Finish by drawing all the necessary topstitching lines at the armholes, collar edge, front opening edge, shoulder line, cuff edges and hem.

6.
- Draw the back of the shirt collar.
- Draw the shoulder line.
- Draw the armhole and side of the shirt by sketching a line from the shoulder tip ending below hip level.
- Draw the hem starting at the side then slightly dipping downward, eventually ending in a straight line toward the center back.

7.
- Draw the other side of the shirt.
- Draw the outer sleeve from shoulder tip to wrist area as a straight line, curving in at the wrist.
- Draw the inner sleeve from underarm to wrist area as a straight line, curving in at the wrist.
- Draw sleeve cuff outlines on the side and hem.
- Draw the other sleeve repeating the above steps.

8.
- Draw a straight line about 1/2" below the back neck; this will be the back yoke.
- Draw back shirt darts by sketching vertical lines midway between side and center back that are about 1 1/4" long and slightly curve inward at the waist level.
- In the sleeves, draw two short straight lines above the wrist to create a square shape that will represent the sleeve cuff.
- Draw the sleeve button plackets at the wrist area as well as the buttons.
- Finish by drawing all the topstitching lines at the armholes, collar edge, back yoke edge, cuffs and hem.

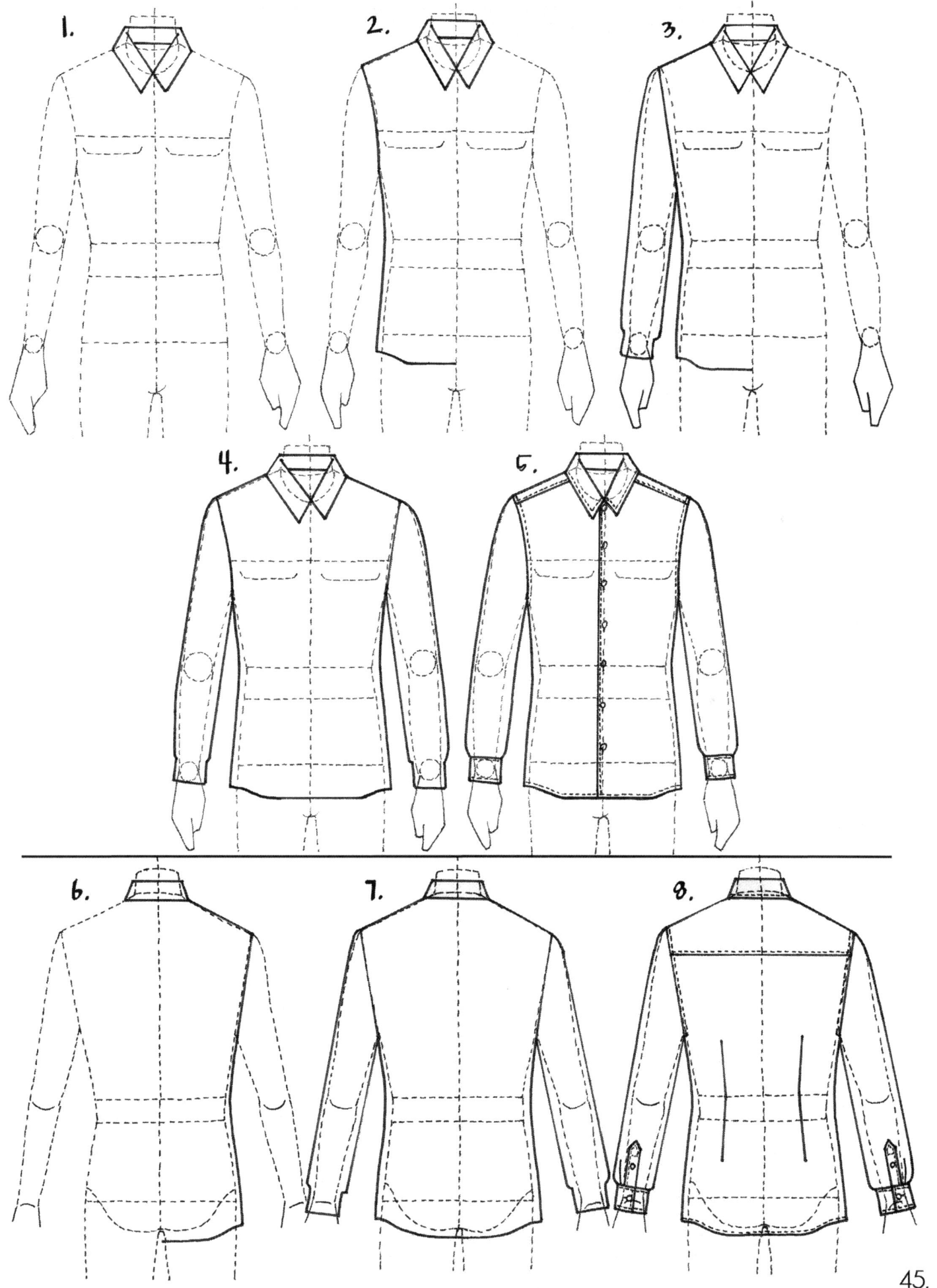

Dress Shirt: Unfitted

1.
- Draw the shirt collar. (Refer to "Shirt Collar" for detailed instructions).

2.
- Draw the shoulder line at the shoulder and slightly beyond the shoulder tip.
- Draw the armhole line, just outside the broken lines of the armholes in your croquis.
- From the underarm point, draw a straight vertical line that is outside of the croquis' torso with NO defined waist shaping.
- Draw the hem starting at the side, and then slightly dipping downward, eventually ending in a straight line toward the center front.

3.
- Draw the outline of the sleeve.
- Once you are near the wrist, make the line curve inward and then draw short vertical straight lines that end at the wrist.
- Draw a straight line connecting the two short vertical lines; this will be the bottom of the sleeve cuffs.

4.
- Draw the other side of the shirt and outline of the sleeve.

5.
- Add all the finishing details: First draw two short lines right below the shoulders, representing the shoulder seams of the shirt.
- Draw the front opening line, slightly to the left of the center front of the shirt.
- Draw buttons and buttonholes on the center front of the shirt. Space the buttons evenly and remember to draw the buttonholes as short up-and-down lines below the button circles.
- In the sleeves, draw two short straight lines above the wrist to create a square shape that will represent the sleeve cuff.
- Finish sketch by drawing all the necessary topstitching lines in the armholes, collar edge, front opening edge, shoulder line, cuff edges and hem.

6.
- Draw the back of the shirt collar.
- Draw the shoulder line extending slightly past the shoulder tip.
- Draw the armhole and side of the shirt by sketching a line from the shoulder tip ending below the hip level. This line will be straight and drawn away from the side of the croquis' torso.
- Draw the hem starting at the side then slightly dipping downward, eventually ending in a straight line toward the center back.

7.
- Draw the other side of the shirt.
- Draw outlines of the sleeves.
- Once you are near the wrists, make the line curve inward and then draw short vertical straight lines that end at the wrists.
- Draw a straight line connecting the two short vertical lines representing the bottom of the sleeve cuffs.

8.
- Draw a straight line about $\frac{1}{2}$" below the back neck; this is the back yoke.
- Add two short straight lines from the yoke line, to signify the back pleats.
- In the sleeves, draw the top lines above the wrist to create the cuff.
- Draw the sleeve button plackets at the wrist area as well as necessary buttons.
- Finish flat sketch by drawing all the necessary topstitching at the armholes, collar, back yoke, cuffs and hem.

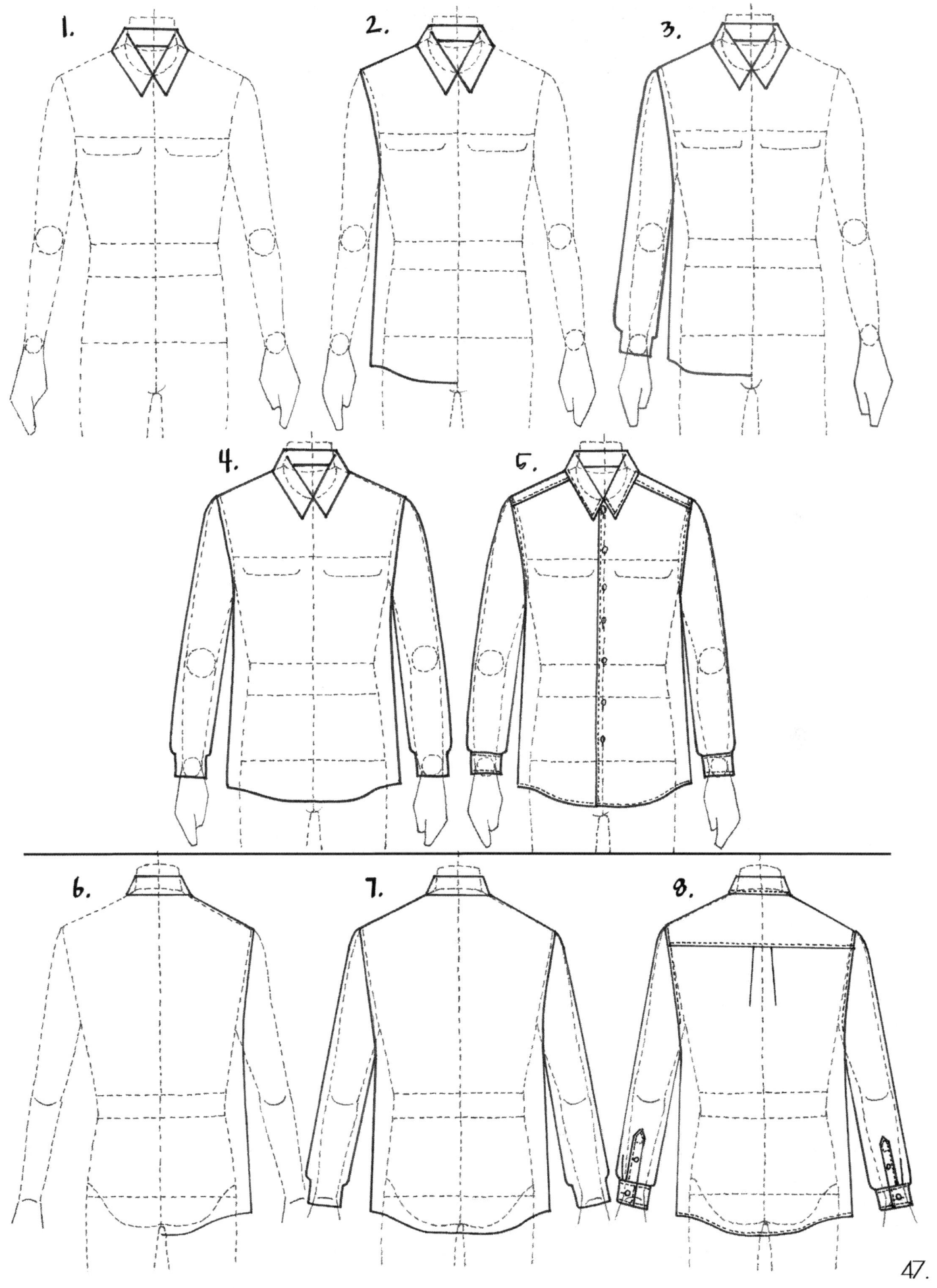

Dress Shirt: Longline

1.
   - Draw the shirt collar. (Refer to "Shirt Collar" for detailed instructions).
   - Draw the shoulder line.

2.
   - Draw the armhole and side of the shirt. Starting from shoulder tip, follow along the broken lines of the croquis' armhole and continue the line to mid-thigh level.
   - At the hem, curve inward and blend into a straight line toward the center.

3.
   - About 3/8" above the first hemline, draw another curved hemline similar to the first. This will show that the front is shorter than the back.
   - Draw a short sleeve with folded cuff. The sleeve will end midway from the shoulder to the elbow. The folded cuff is drawn like a thin rectangle that is at the bottom of the sleeve.

4.
   - Draw the other side of the shirt and sleeve.
   - Draw center front placket by drawing two straight lines—each of them slightly away from the center front.

5.
   - Finish drawing by adding buttons and buttonholes at the center front and topstitching at the collar, armholes, placket edges and hem.

6.
   - Draw the back of the collar.
   - Draw the shoulder line.
   - Draw the armhole and side of the shirt. Starting from shoulder tip and continue line to mid-thigh level.
   - At the hem, curve inward and blend into a straight line toward the center.
   - Draw half of the back yoke by sketching a straight horizontal line starting about ½" below collar, ending at the armhole.
   - Draw a short line from the back yoke to represent the back pleat.
   - Draw a short sleeve with folded cuff.
   - Draw small slash line on the side of the shirt, to represent where the side slit begins.

7.
   - Draw the other side of the shirt and sleeve.

8.
   - Add the finishing details: Draw topstitching at collar edge, armholes, back yoke and hem.

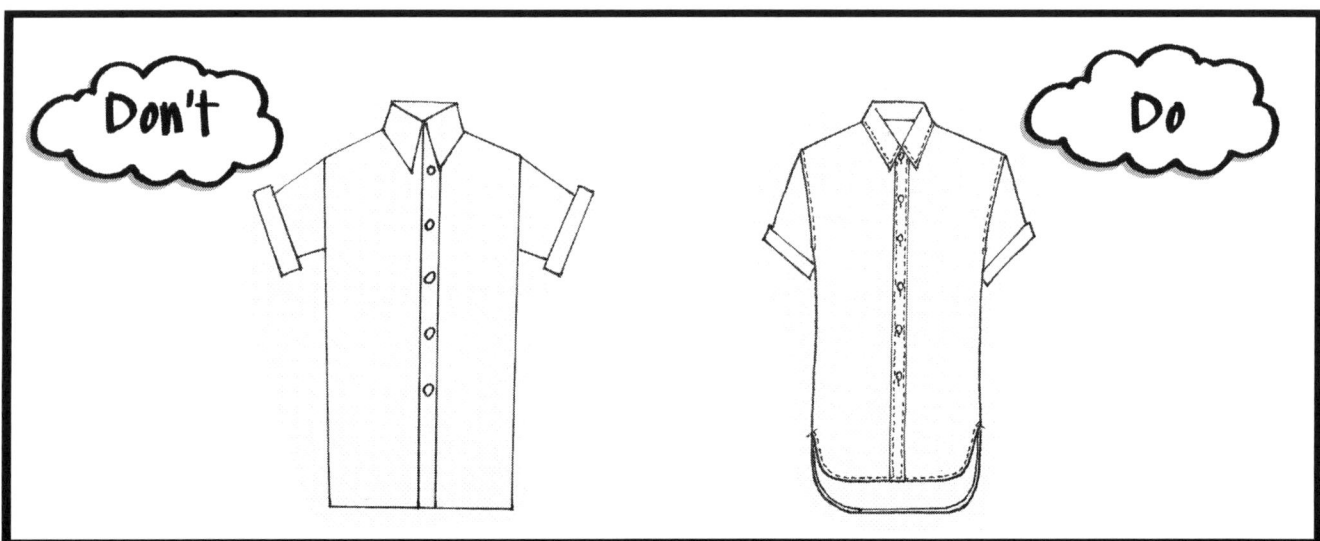

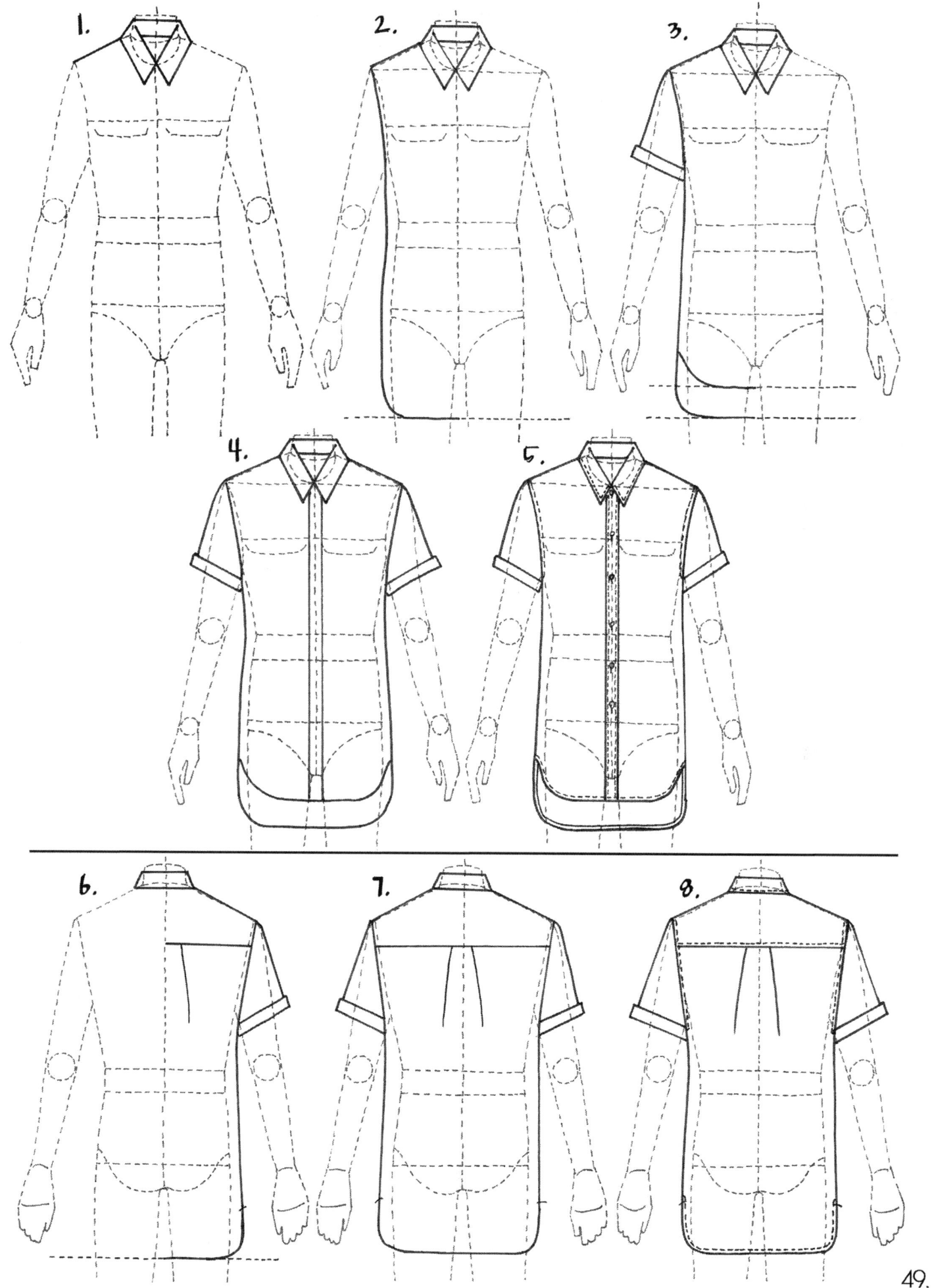

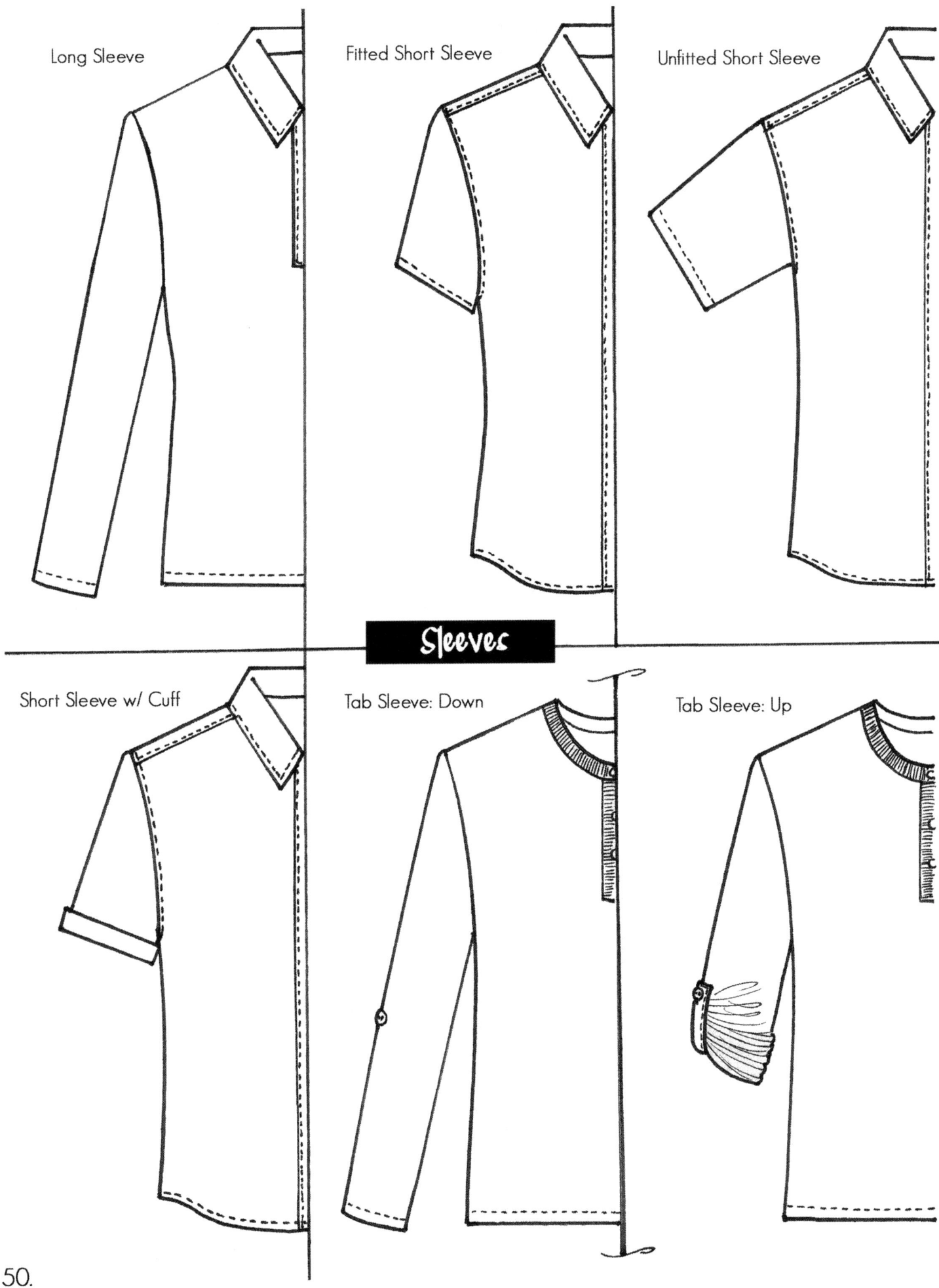

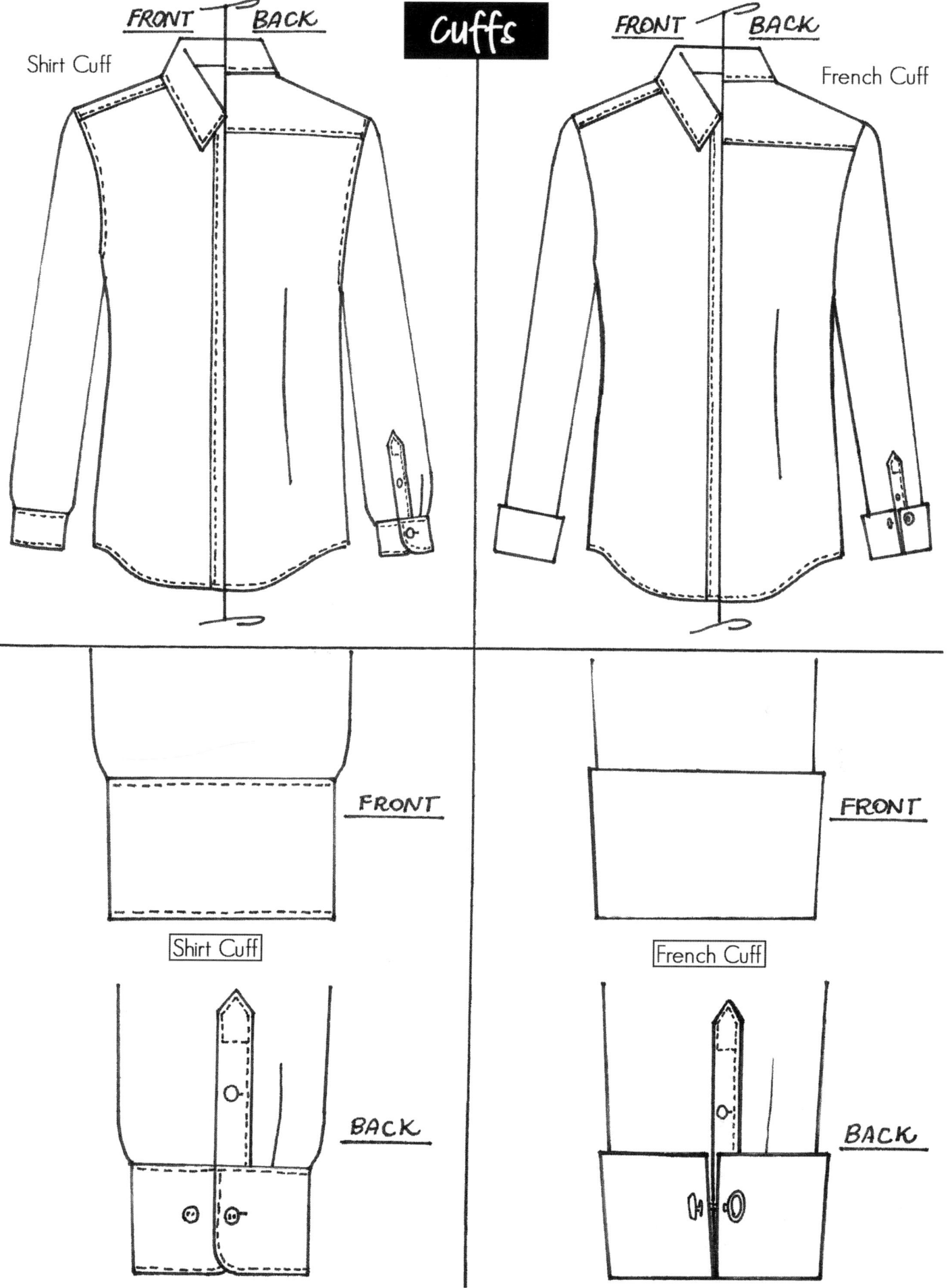

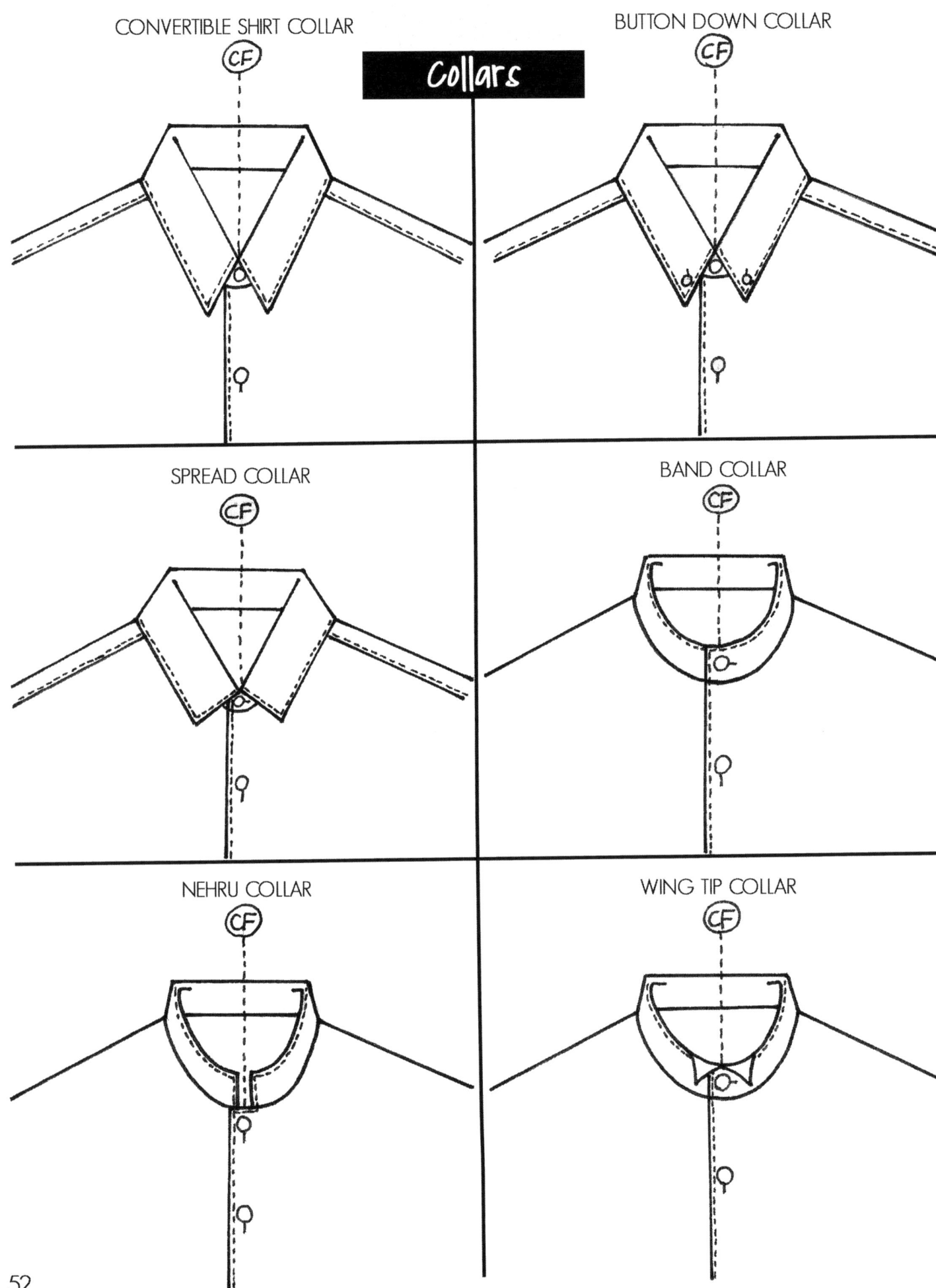

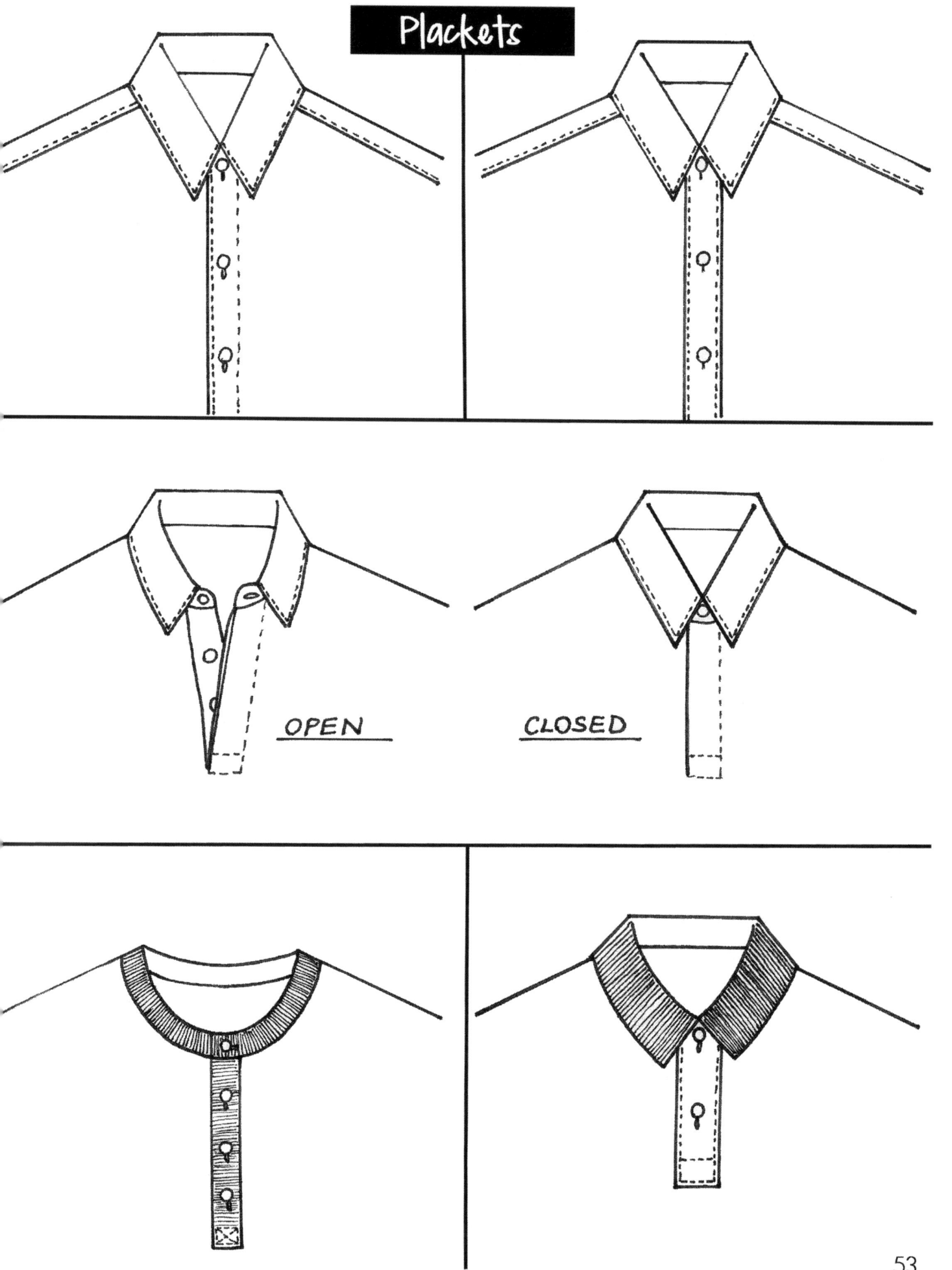

Yokes

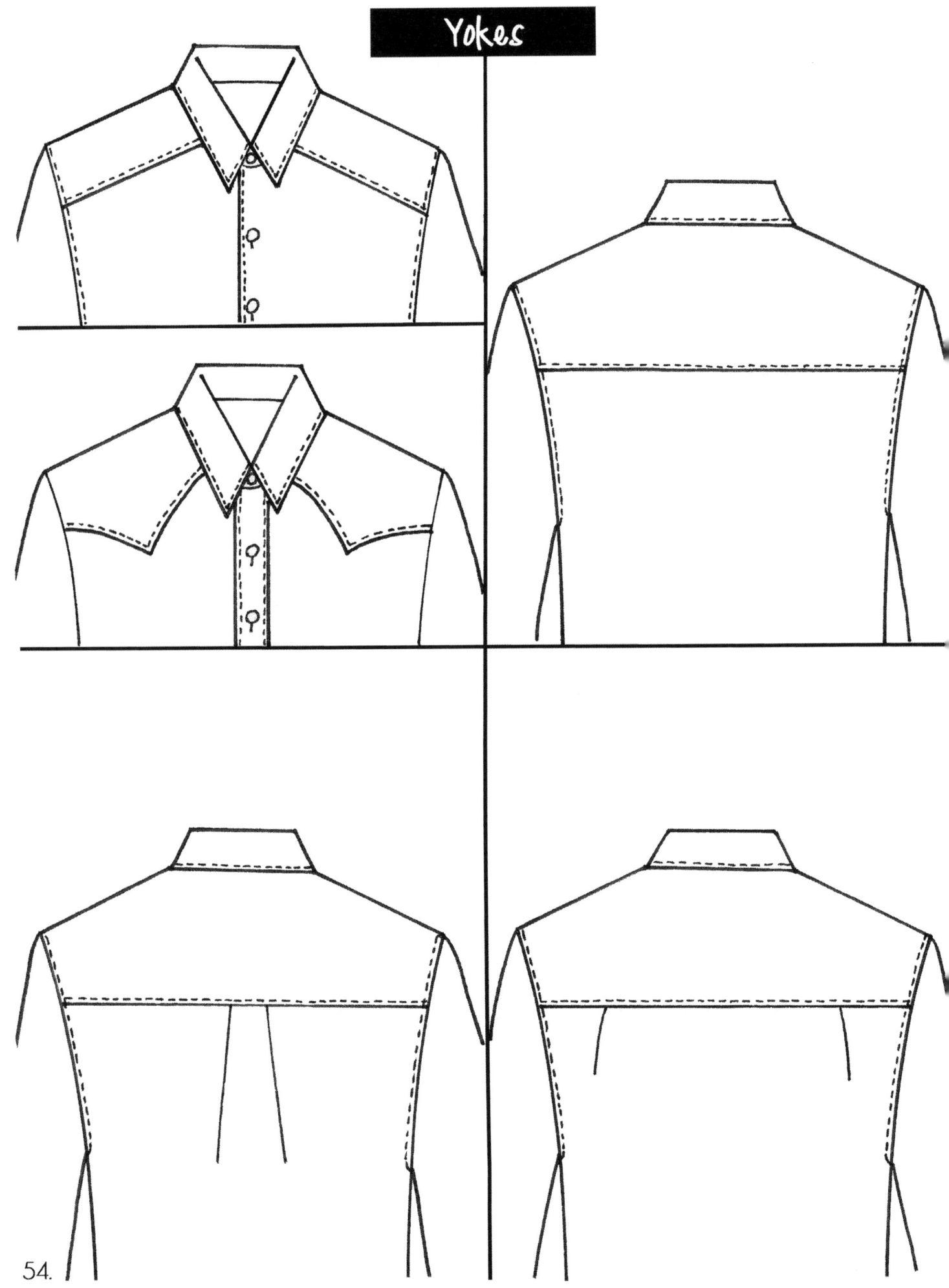

Topstitching

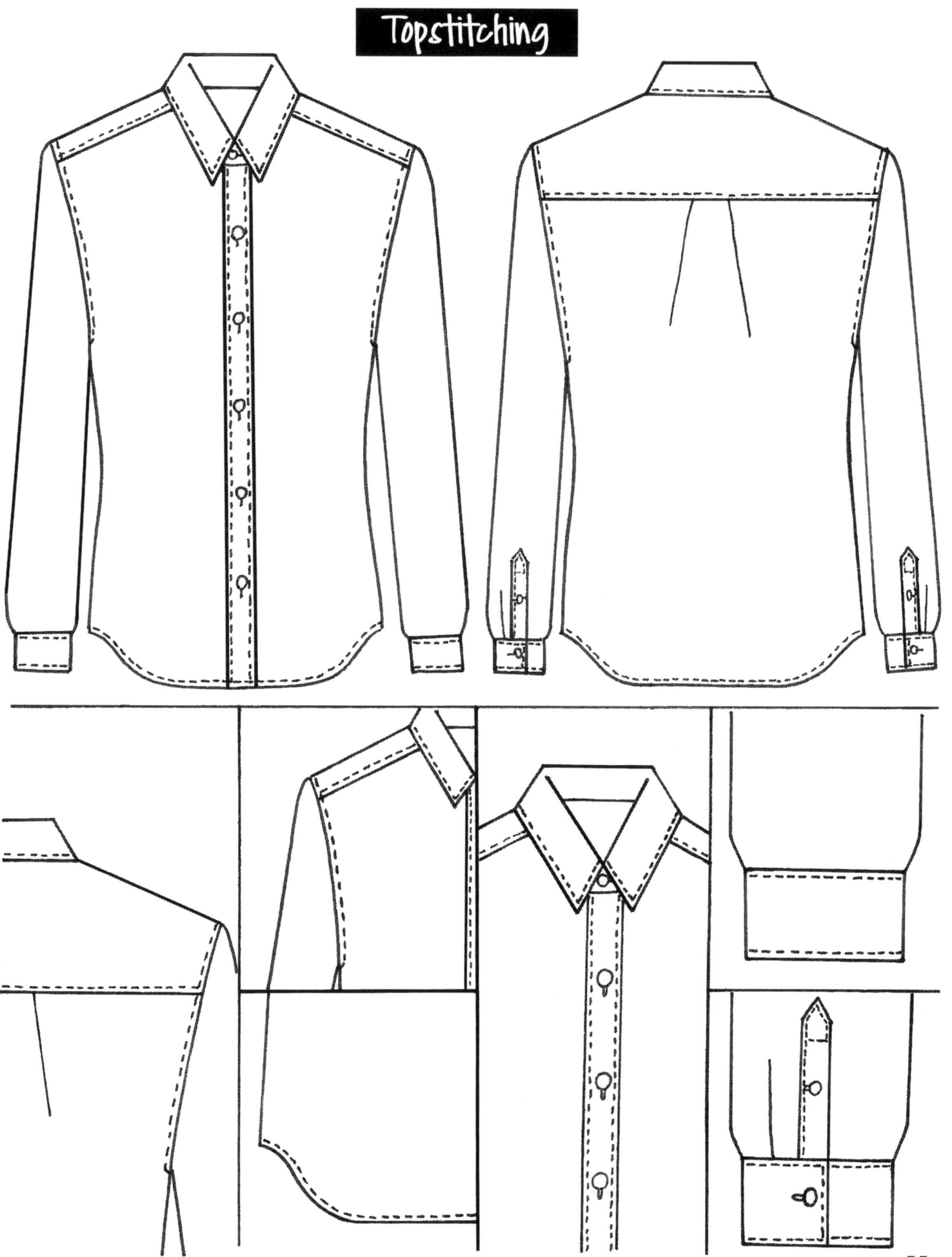

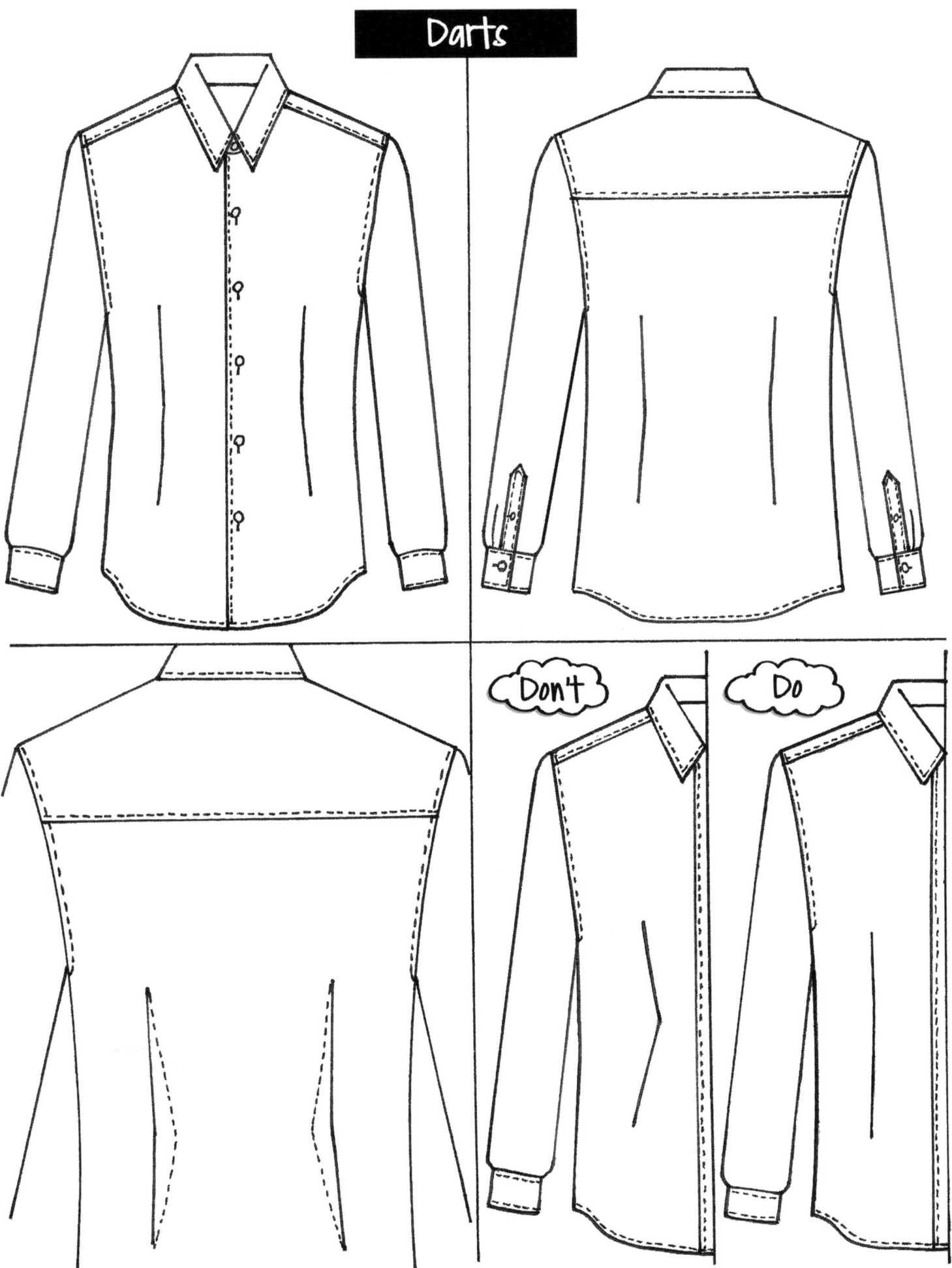

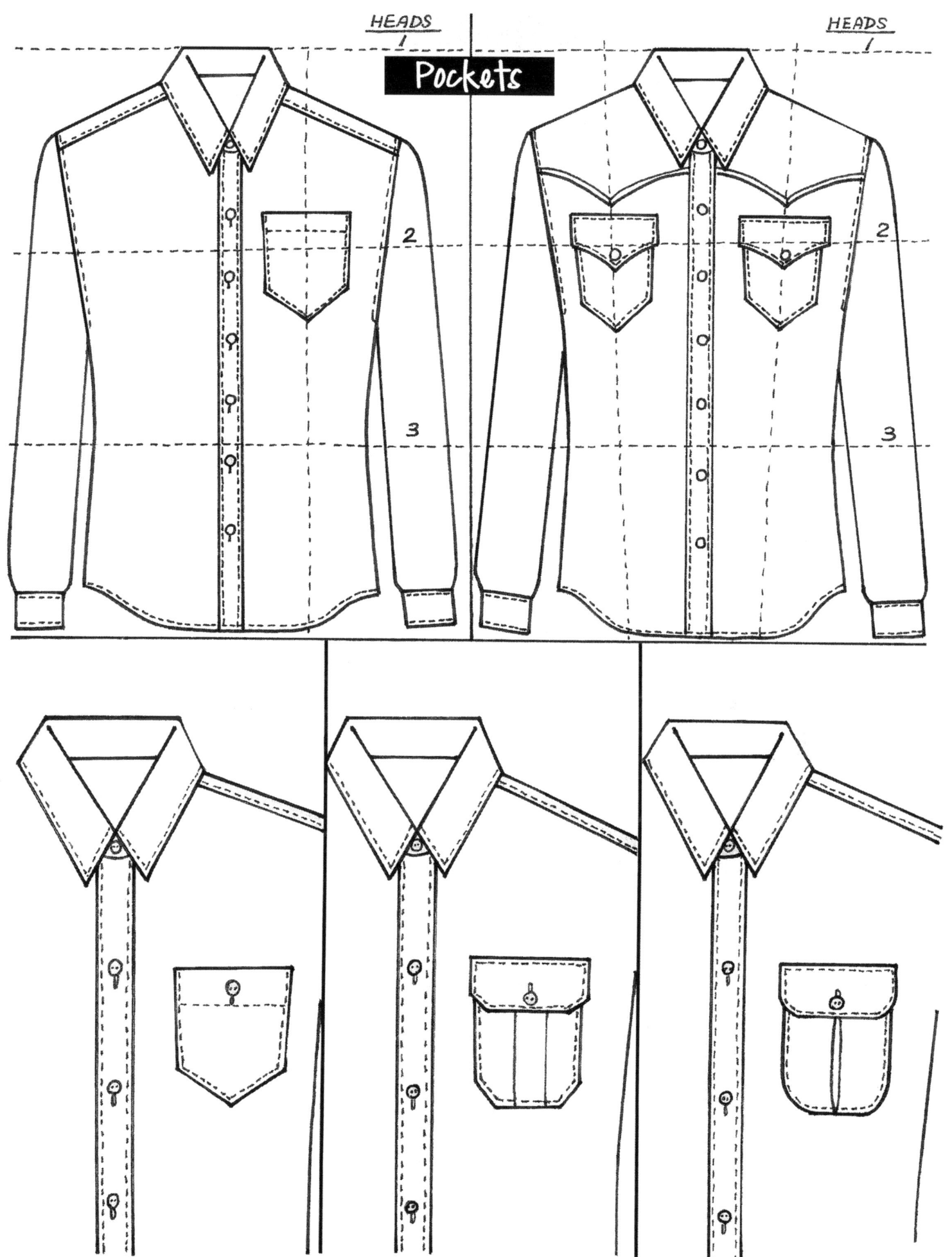

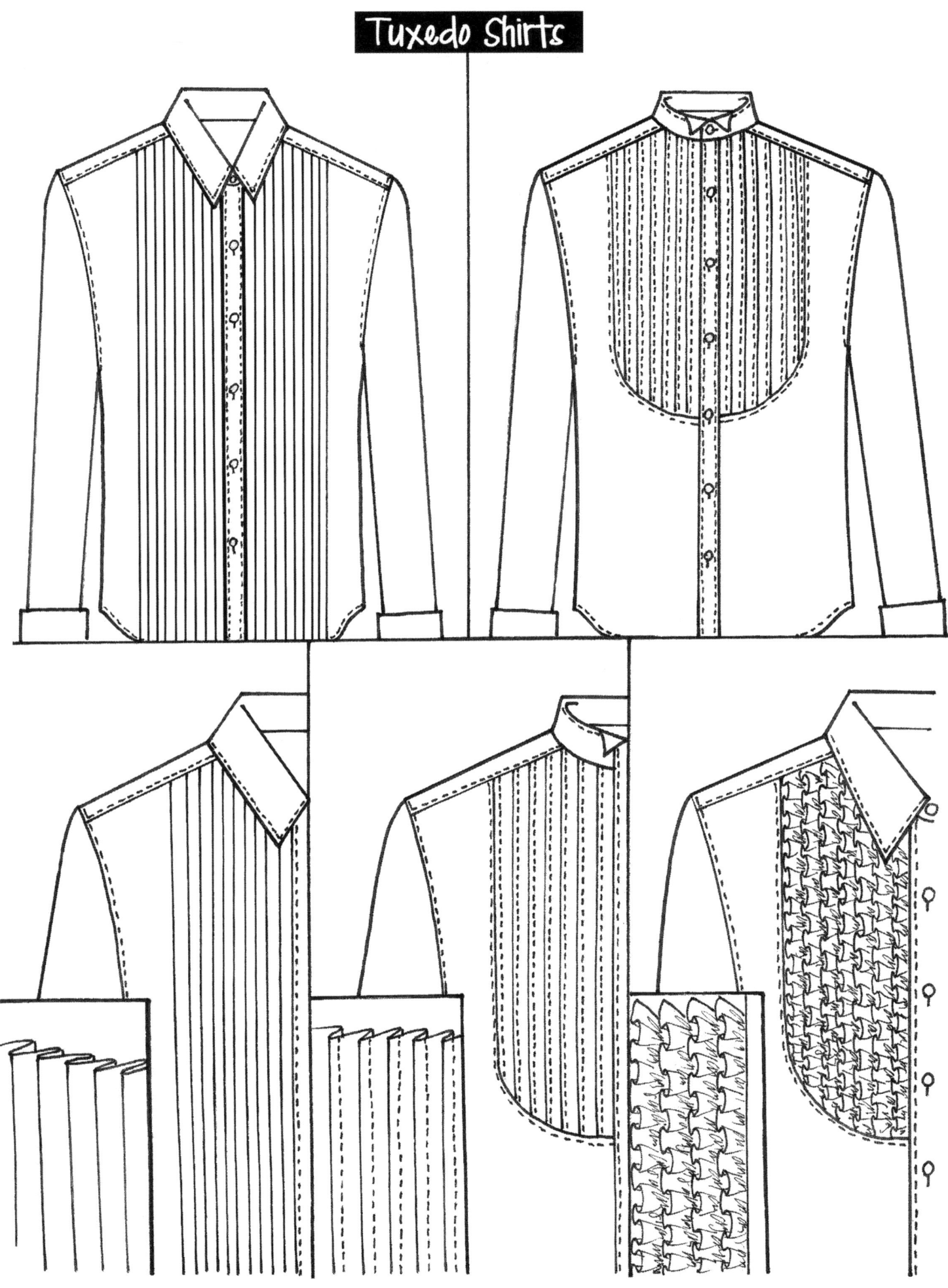

Tuxedo Shirts

Buttons

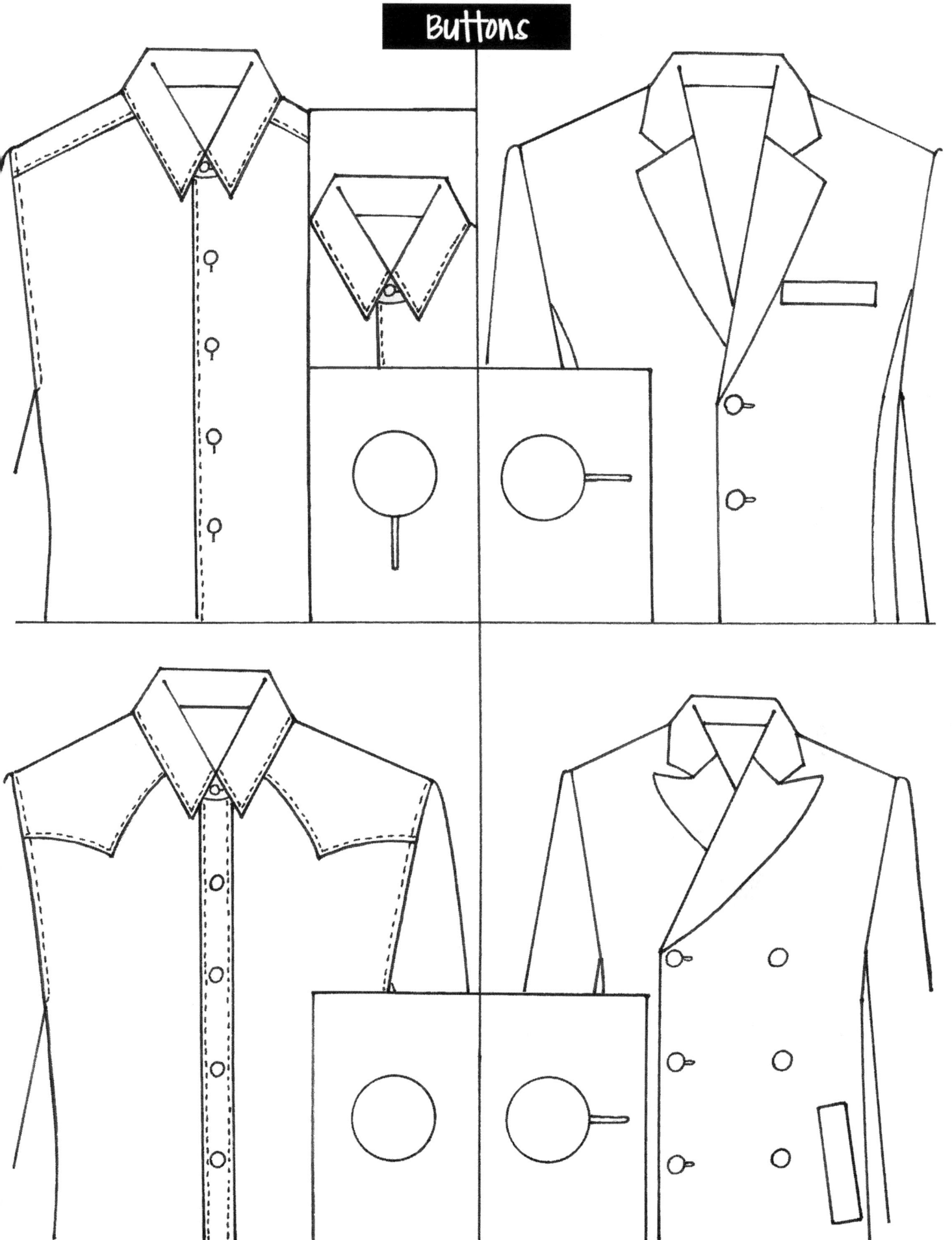

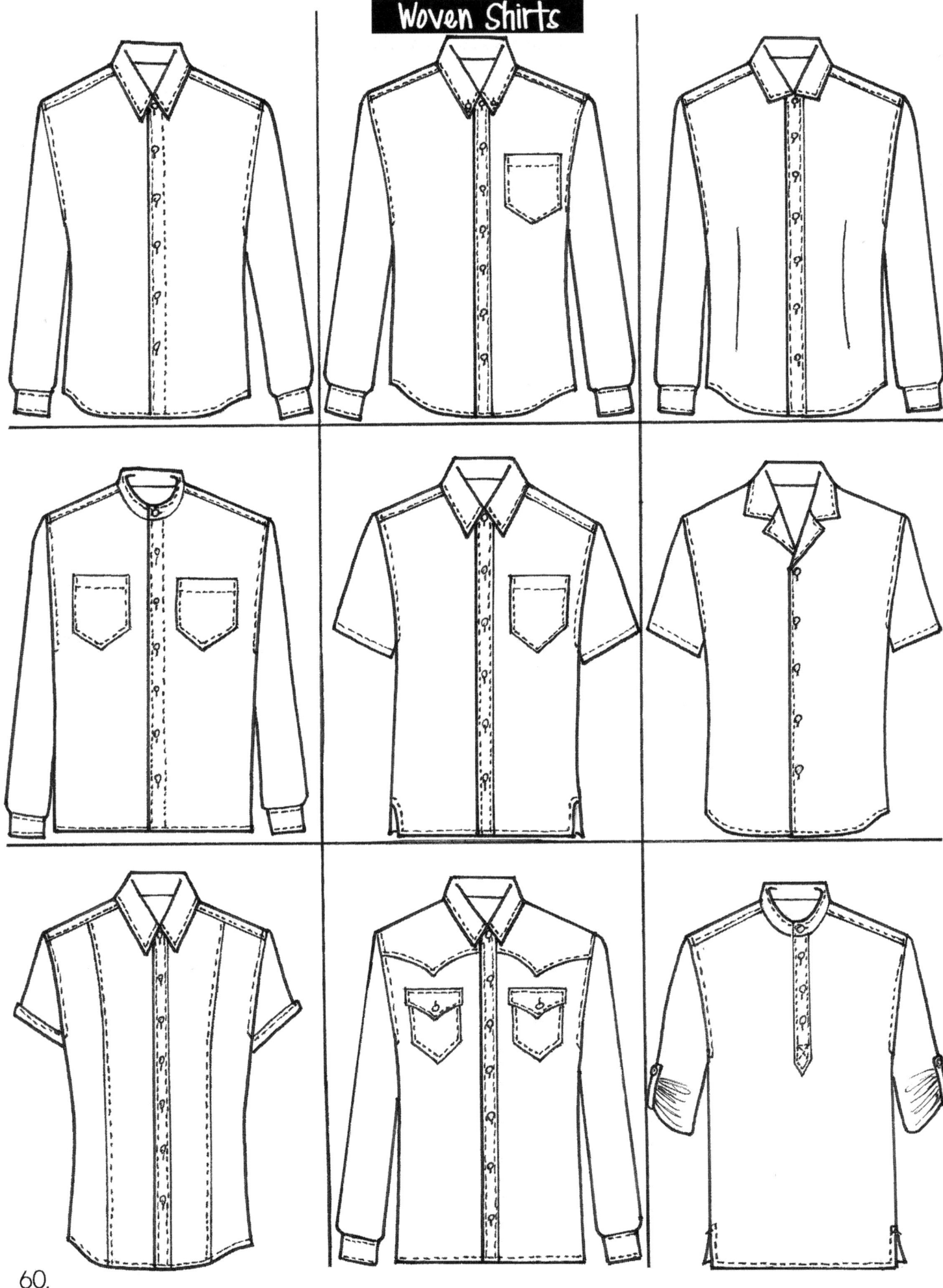

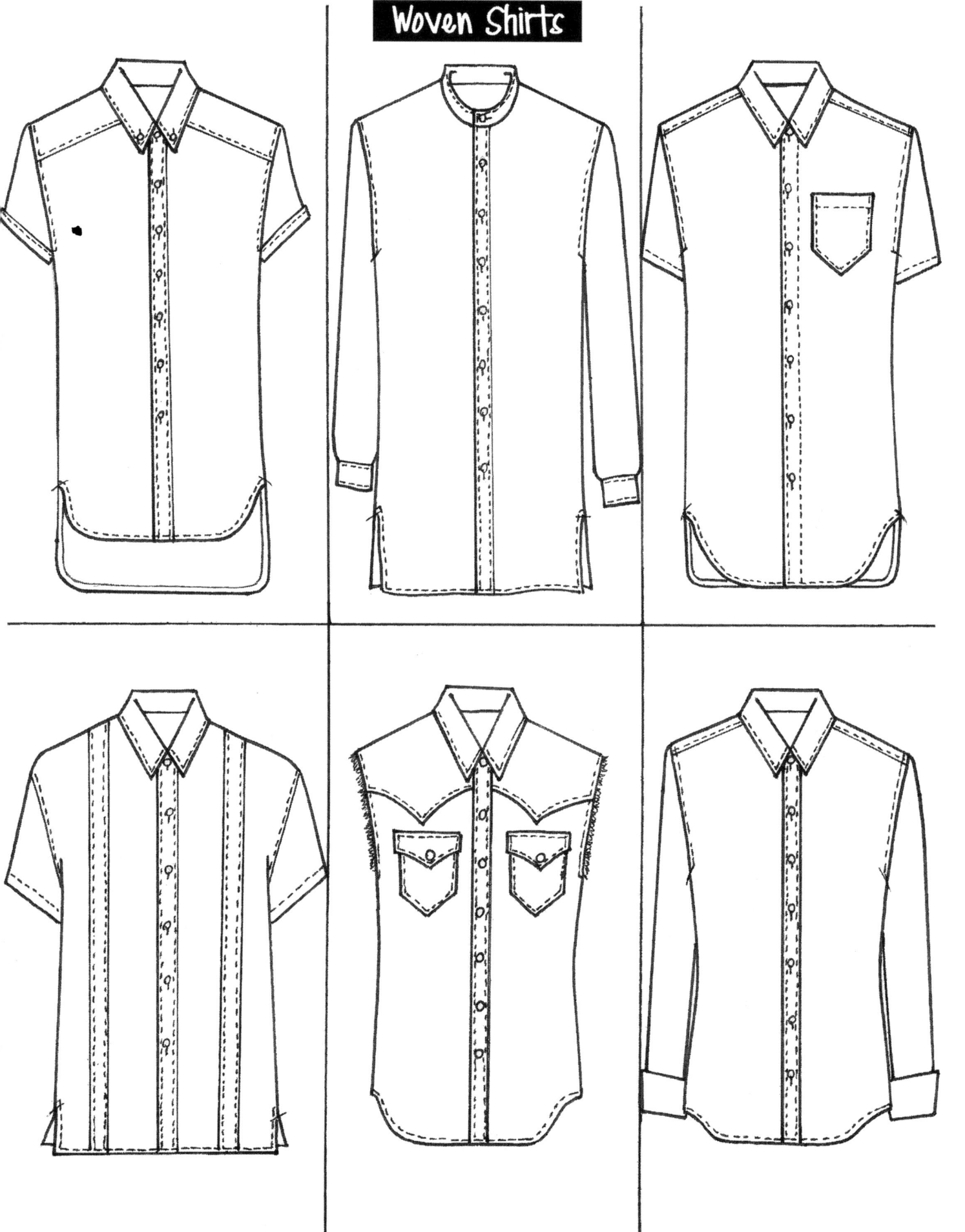

Pants

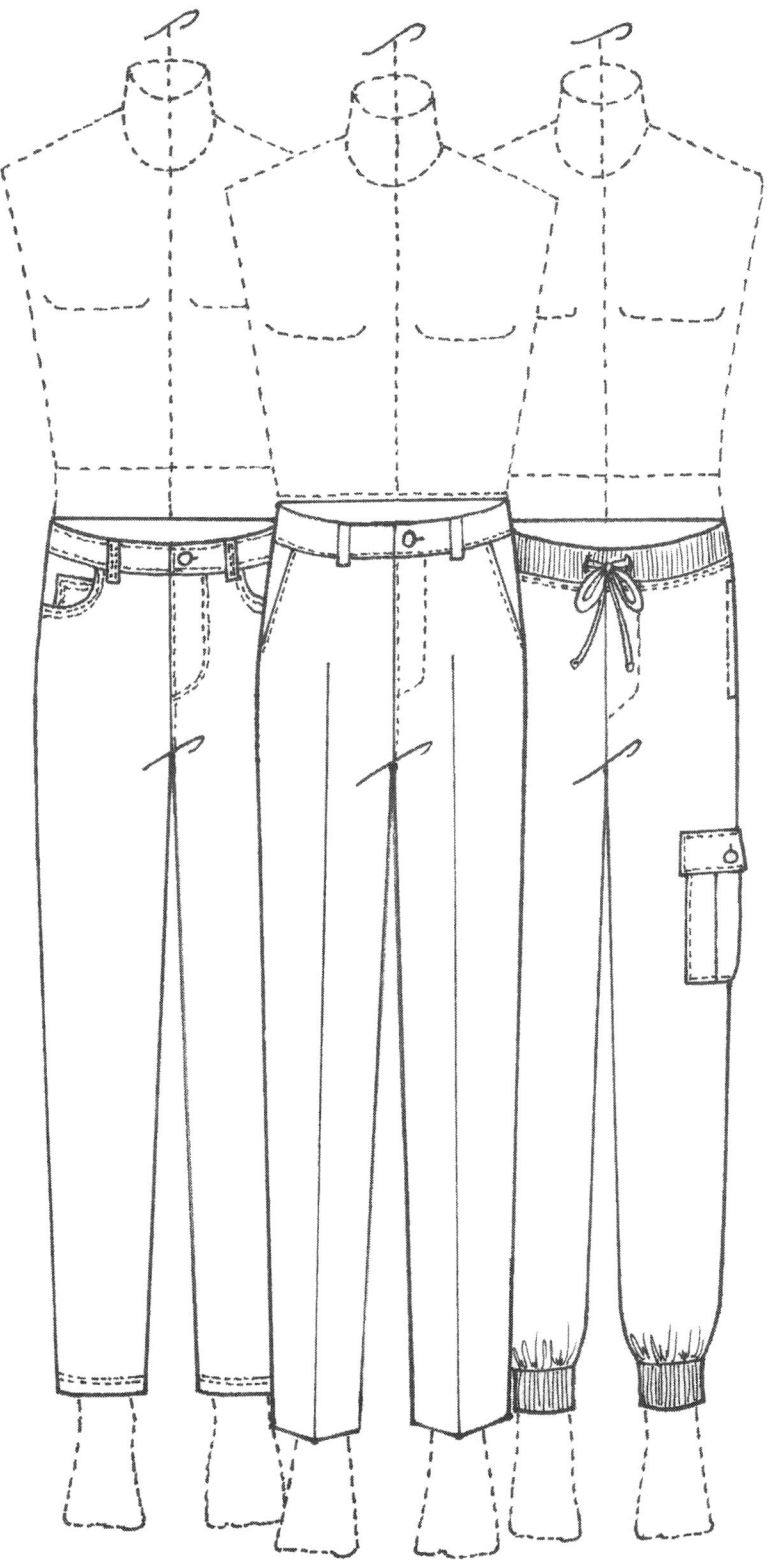

Pants: Straight Leg

1.
- Draw a straight line slightly below the waist, then draw another line below it, slightly curving downward; this second line will represent the front waist line that dips downward slightly. Draw a straight line at center front and a "slash" line at the crotch to signify the front crotch.

2.
- When drawing the flat sketch of the pants, draw one leg of the pants first.
- Beginning at the low waist line, draw a straight line, from top to ankle area, right next to the outer leg.

3.
- For the inner leg line, draw a straight line from the crotch point to the ankle area.
- To draw the hem, connect the outer leg and inner leg lines with a straight horizontal line.
- Draw the waistband line parallel to the top waist line, slightly below it (about 1/4"-3/8").
- Draw the belt loop on the waistband midway between the side and center front.

4.
- Draw the other leg of the pants, waistband and belt loop following the same directions as the first leg.

5.
- Finish by adding details such as the front fly stitching, front button, side pockets and hem stitching.

6.
- Draw the back waistband line right below the waist.
- Draw a straight line from top to ankle area right next to the outer leg.
- For the inner leg line, draw a straight line from crotch point to ankle.
- For the hem, connect the outer leg and inner leg lines with a straight horizontal line.
- Draw the waistband line parallel to the top waist line, slightly below it about 1/4"-3/8".
- Draw belt loops on the waistband-one on the center back and the other midway between the center back and the side.

7.
- Draw the other leg of the pants, waistband and belt loop following the same directions as the first leg. Add a long slanted slash line at the back buttocks level to signify the back.

8.
- Finish by adding details such as the back welt pockets, waist darts, and necessary topstitching at the waistband, center back seam as well as the hem.

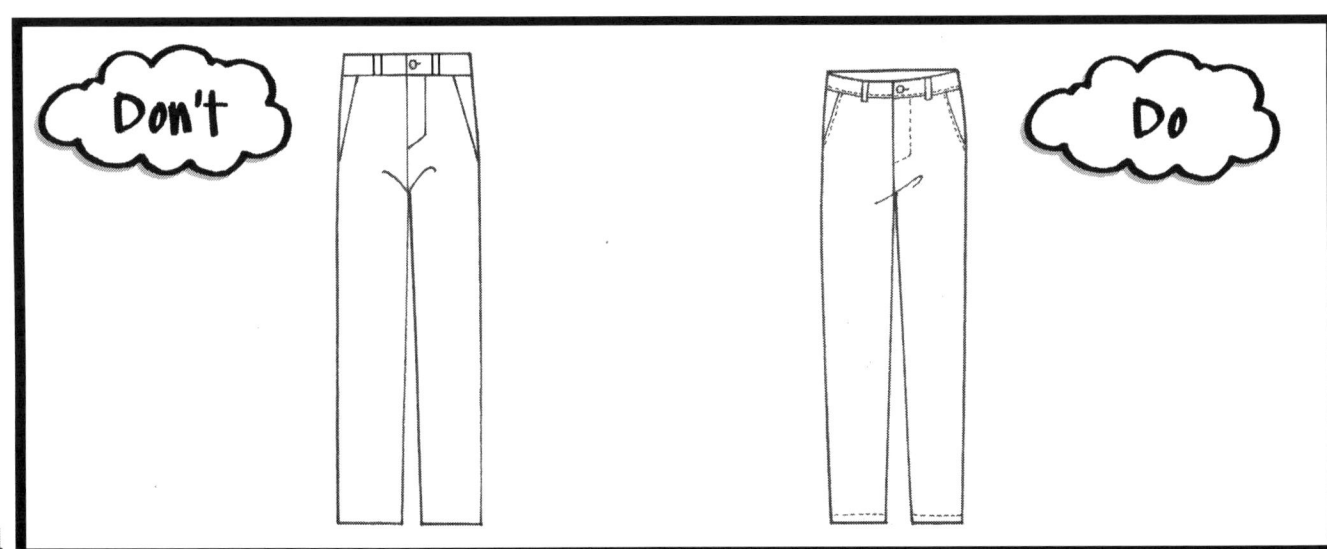

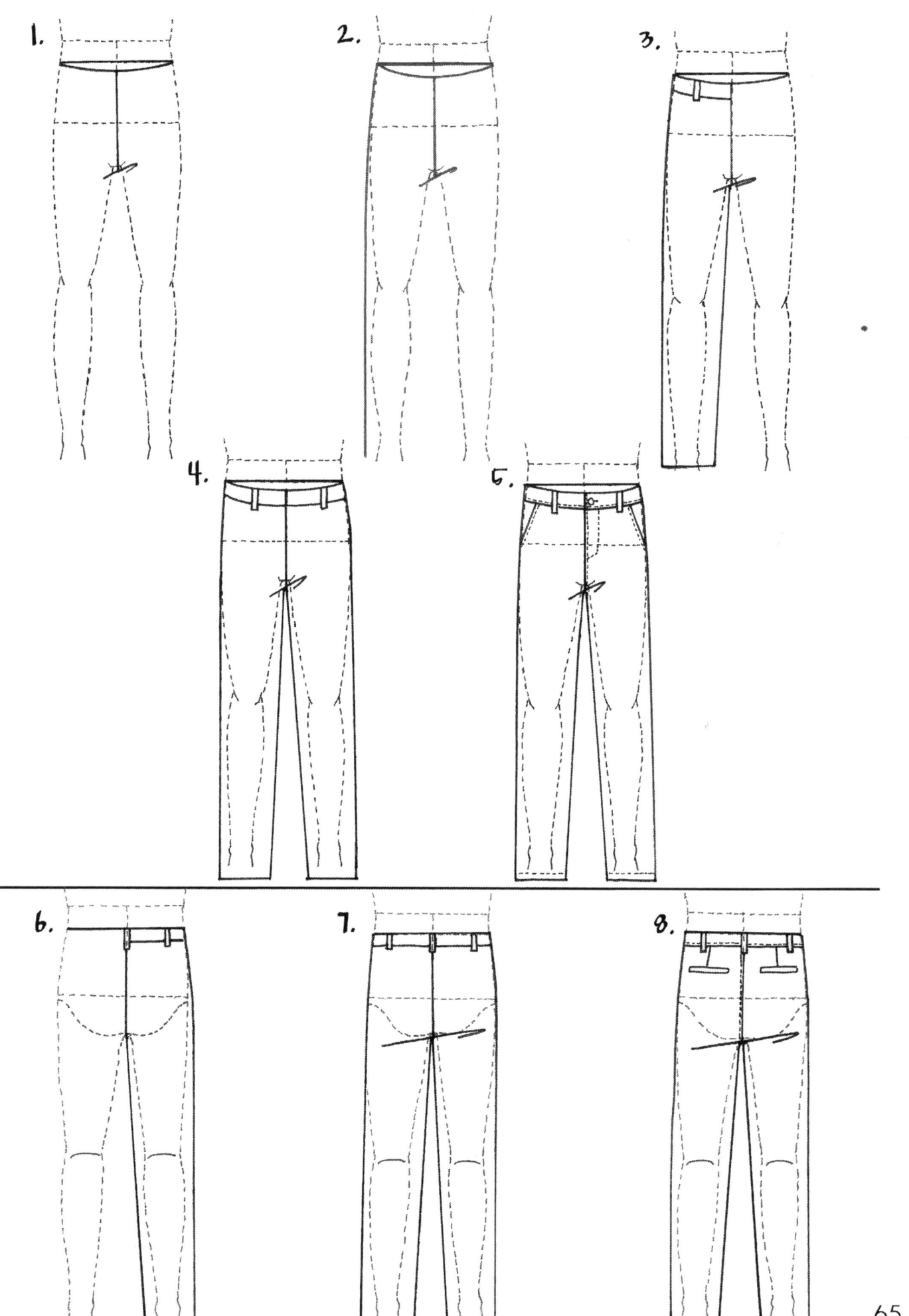

Pants: Joggers

Front:

1.
- Draw a straight line slightly below the waist, then draw another line below it, slightly curving downward; this second line will represent the front waist line that dips downward slightly.
- Draw a straight line at center front and a "slash" line to signify the front crotch.

2.
- Draw the waistband by sketching a curved line parallel to the first curved line, about 1/4" below it.

3.
- Draw the outer leg by sketching a line from the waist to around ankle level, following closely to the leg of the Croquis.
- When reaching the ankle level, curve in slightly and then draw a short vertical line, showing the side of the ribbed ankle band.
- For the inner pant line, draw a straight line from the crotch level to around the ankle.
- When reaching the ankle level, curve in slightly and then draw a short vertical line, as you did with outer leg.
- Connect the vertical straight lines at the ankle with a short horizontal line to show the hem of the pants.

4.
- Draw the other side of the pants following the same directions as the first pant leg.

5.
- Finish the Joggers by adding all the necessary details:
- First, draw the waist tie at the center front area of the waistband.
- Draw the gather-lines inside the waistband to illustrate the "elasticized" waist.
- Draw short straight lines at the ankle bands to show the ribbing.
- Draw gather lines above the ankle band to illustrate the gathering effect that occurs in this area.
- Lastly, draw the side pockets and any necessary stitching.

Back:

6.
- To draw the waist, begin by sketching a straight line right below the waist, representing the back waist of the pants.
- Draw the waistband by sketching a straight line parallel to the first waist line, about 1/4" below it.
- Draw the center back seam line.
- Draw the Back Jogger Pant leg following the same directions as the front.

7.
- Draw the other side of the pants following the same directions as the first pant leg. Add a slightly angled "slash" line at the buttocks level, showing that this is the BACK of the pants. This slash line is longer than the front one.

8.
- Finish the Joggers by adding all the necessary details.
- First, draw the gather-like lines inside the waistband to illustrate the "elasticized" waist.
- Draw short straight lines at the ankle bands to show ribbing.
- Draw gather lines above the ankle band to illustrate the gathering effect that occurs in this area.
- Lastly, draw the back pockets (here, they often include zippers as well) and any necessary stitching.

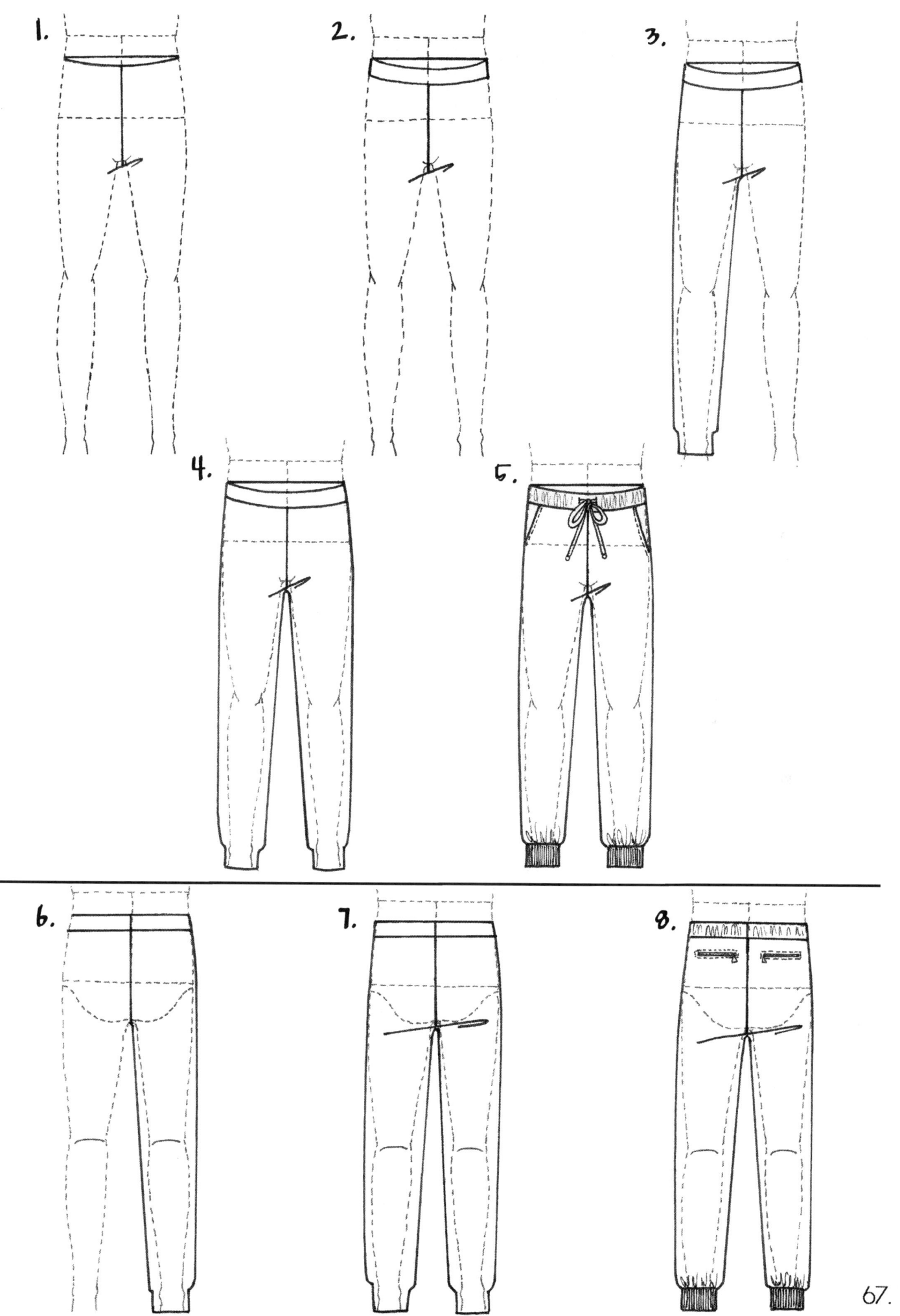

Pants: Drop Crotch

Use Men's Croquis with spread legs when drawing Drop Crotch Pants

1.
- Draw the waist by sketching a straight line right below the waist, representing the back of the waist. Draw a line slightly curving downward at the center front. This curved line represents the front waist that dips slightly lower than the back.
- Draw a straight vertical line at the center front, making this line extend past the crotch level to show the drop crotch effect (about 3/8" beyond the crotch).
- Draw a small angled "slash" line at the end of the center front line to illustrate that this is the FRONT of the pants.

2.
- For the outer leg line, draw a straight line from the waist to ankle level. Keep this line close to the leg of the Croquis.

3.
- For the inner leg line, start at the crotch with a slightly curved line that blends into a straight line down to the ankle.
- Connect the outer and inner leg lines with a short horizontal line to show the hem.

4.
- Draw the other leg of the pants in the same manner you sketched the first one.
- Draw the waistband by adding a second curved line parallel to the front waist line and about 1/4" below it.
- Add belt loops to the waistband.
- Draw a "half-moon" curved line around the front crotch; this shows the extra gusset panel usually seen in Drop Crotch Pants that creates extra ease and movement.

5.
- Finish by adding necessary details: Front fly stitching, front opening button, side pockets, coin pocket and topstitching at the waistband, around pockets, front gusset, center front seam, and hem.

6.
- For the back of the pant, draw half of the waistband by sketching a straight line below the waist and another one 1/4" below the first waist line. Draw the belt loops.
- Draw a straight vertical line at the center back, making this line extend past the buttocks level to show the "drop crotch" effect (about 3/8" beyond crotch).
- Draw a long angled "slash" line at the end of the center back to illustrate that this is the BACK of the pants.
- For the outer leg line, draw a straight line from the waist to ankle level. Keep this line close to the leg of the Croquis.
- For the inner leg line, start at the crotch with a slightly curved line that blends into a straight line down to the ankle.
- Connect the outer and inner leg lines with a short horizontal line to show the hem.

7.
- Draw the other leg of the pant in the same manner you sketched the first one, as well as draw the other half of the waistband and belt loop.
- Draw a "half-moon" curved line around the back crotch in the same manner you did for the front, showing the extra gusset panel.

8.
- Finish by adding necessary details such as the back yoke, back pockets, topstitching at the waistband, around pockets, yoke, back gusset, center back seam, and hem.

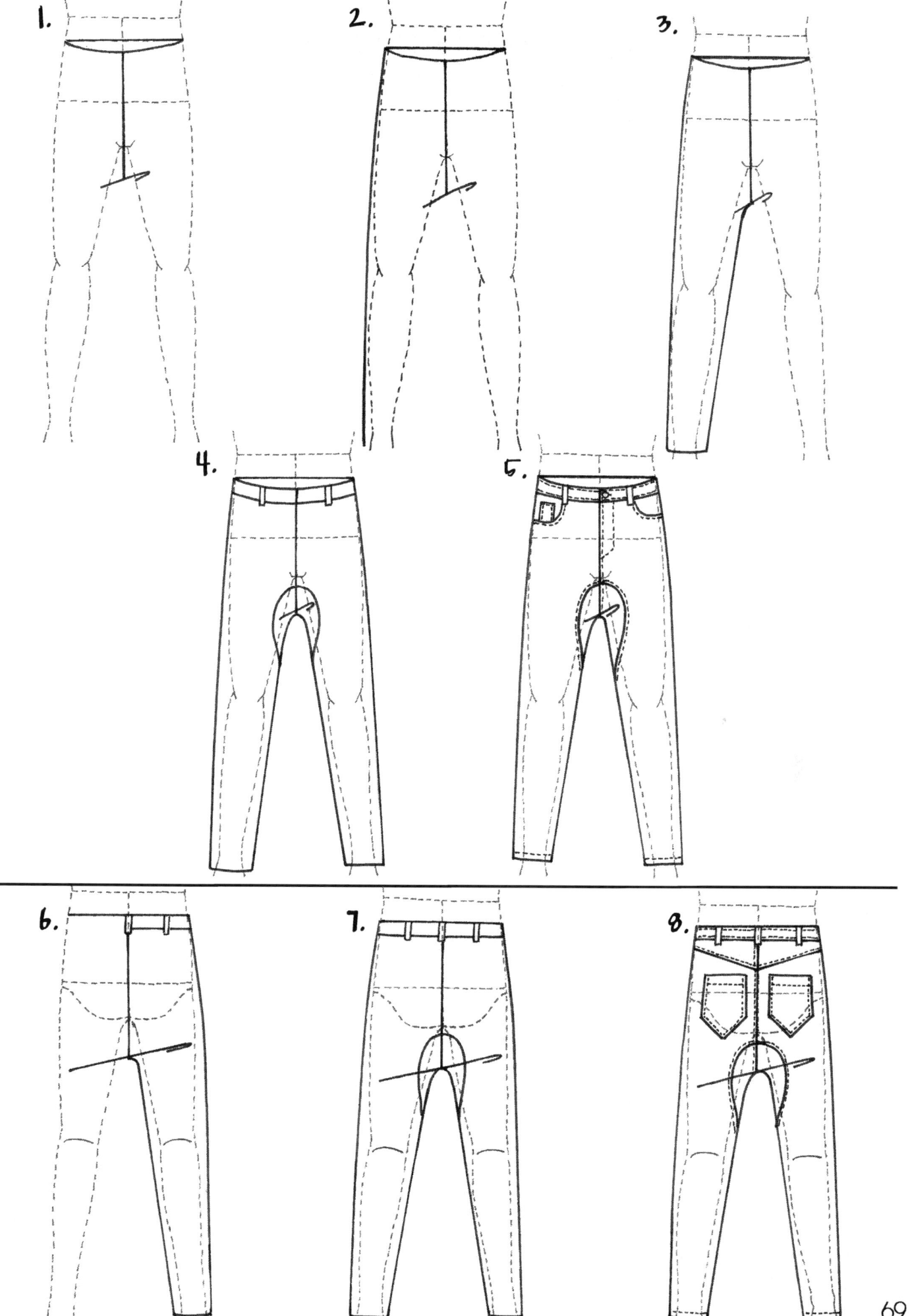

Pants: Jeans

Front:

1.
- For the waistline, draw a straight line right below the waist, representing the back waist.
- Draw a curved line dipping slightly downward at center front representing the front waist.
- Draw a straight line at center front crotch.
- Draw a short slightly angled "slash" line at the center front crotch point to represent the front of the jeans.

2.
- Draw half of the waistband and belt loop.

3.
- For the leg, start by drawing a line at the outer leg from waist to ankle level, keeping this line very close to the leg of your Croquis.
- Draw the inner leg by sketching a straight line from the crotch point to the ankle level. Keep this line close to the leg of your Croquis.
- Connect these lines with a short straight line which will be the hem. This line should be about 1/2" long.

4.
- Draw the other leg of the Jeans as well as the waistband and belt loop.

5.
- Finish the drawing by adding the details associated with jeans, such as side pockets, coin pocket, fly front stitching and all the necessary topstitching at waistband, around pockets, center front seam, inner leg and hem.

Back:

6.
- Draw one leg of the jeans in the same manner as you did for the front, including the waistband, belt loops and waistband patch.
- Draw a straight line at the center back, stopping at back buttocks level.

7.
- Draw the other leg of the Jeans as well as the waistband and belt loop.
- Draw the back yoke.
- Draw a slightly angled long "slash" line at the back buttocks area to represent the back of the jeans.

8.
- Finish the drawing by adding the details associated with jeans such as back pockets as well as all the necessary topstitching at the waistband, pockets, yoke, belt loops, center back seam, side seam and hem.

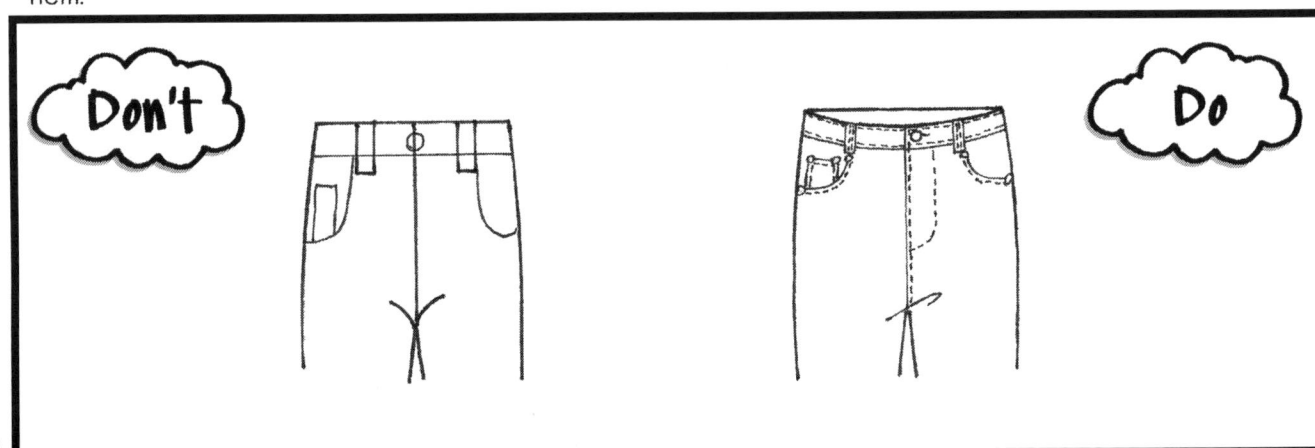

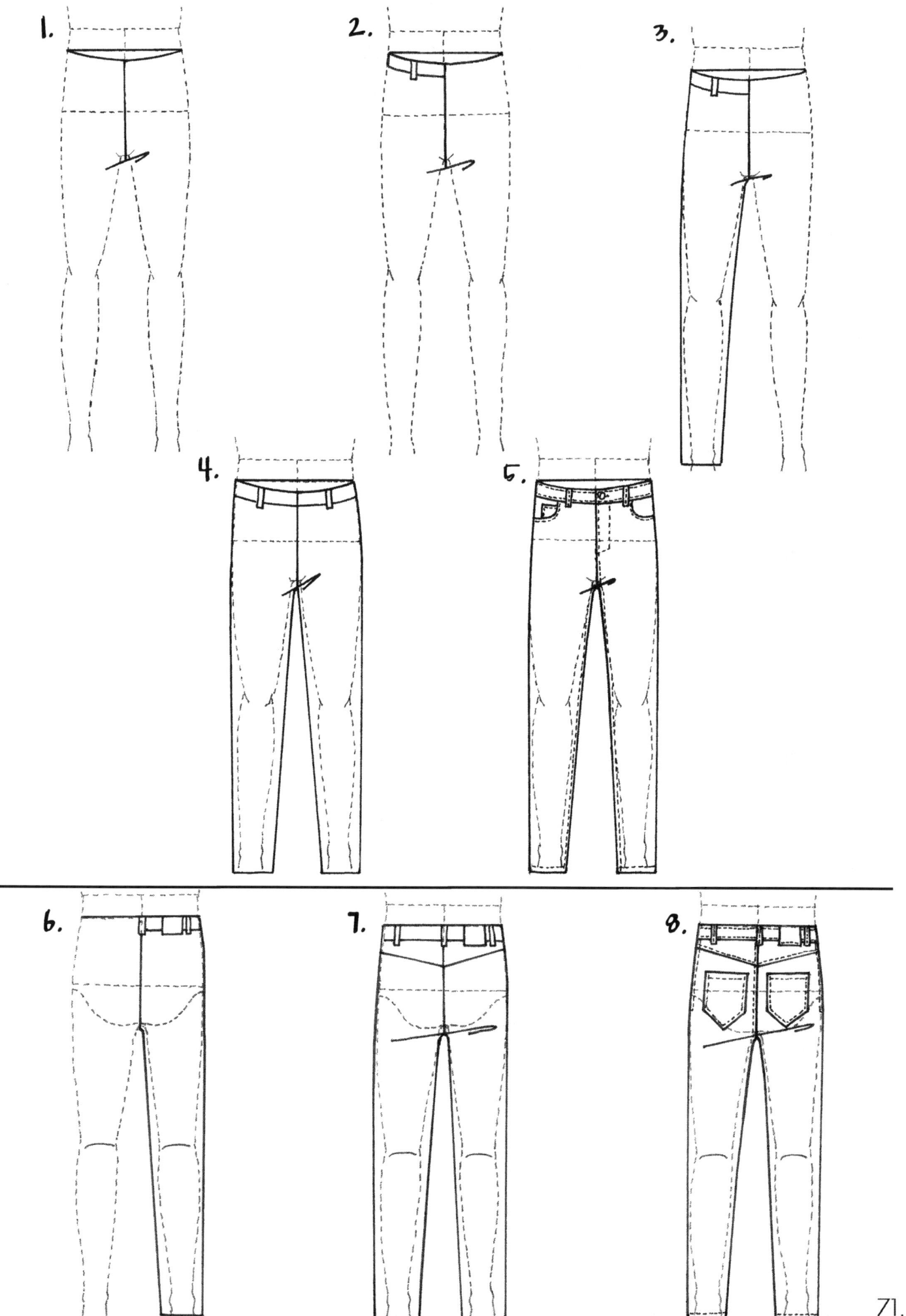

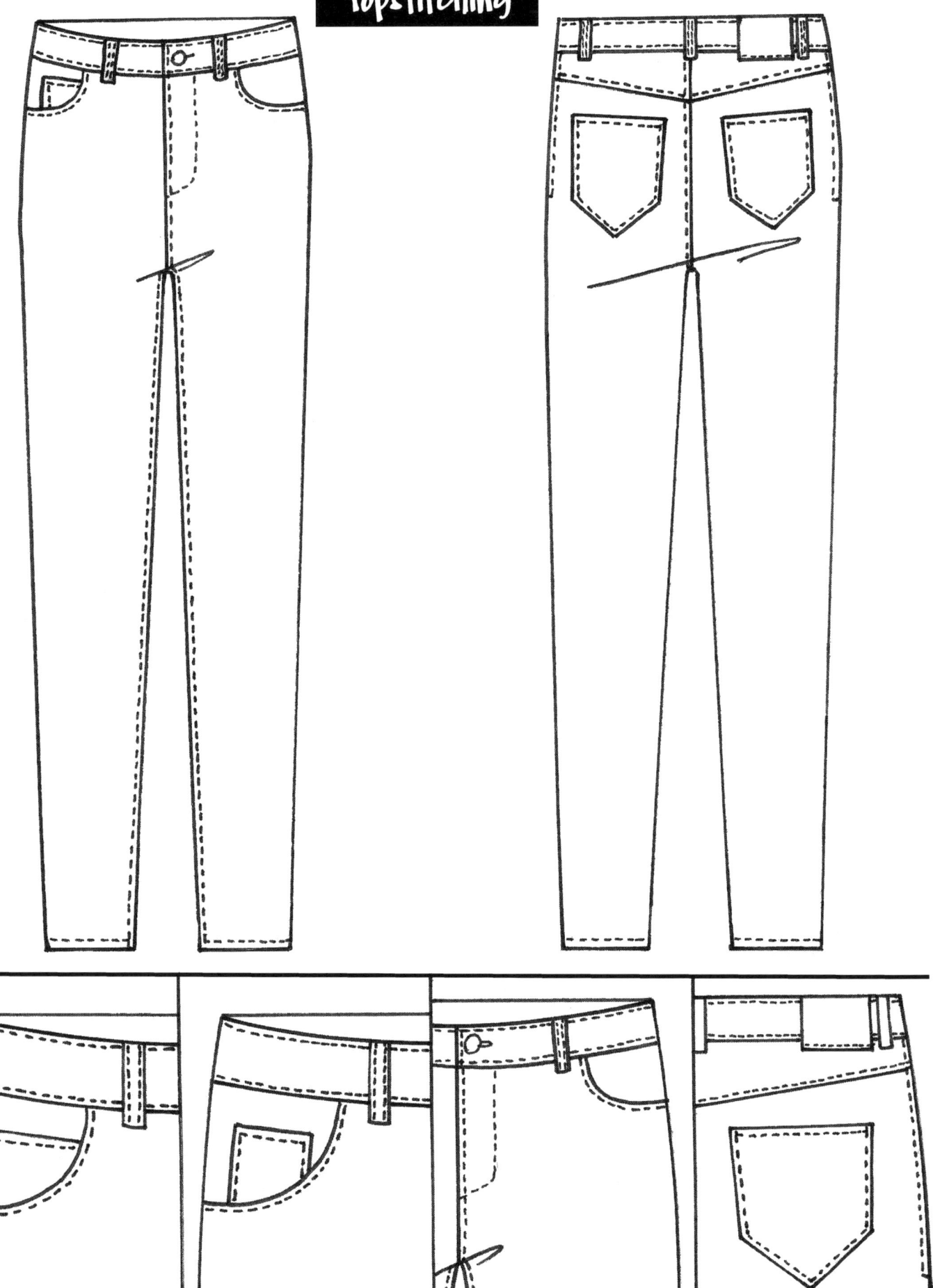

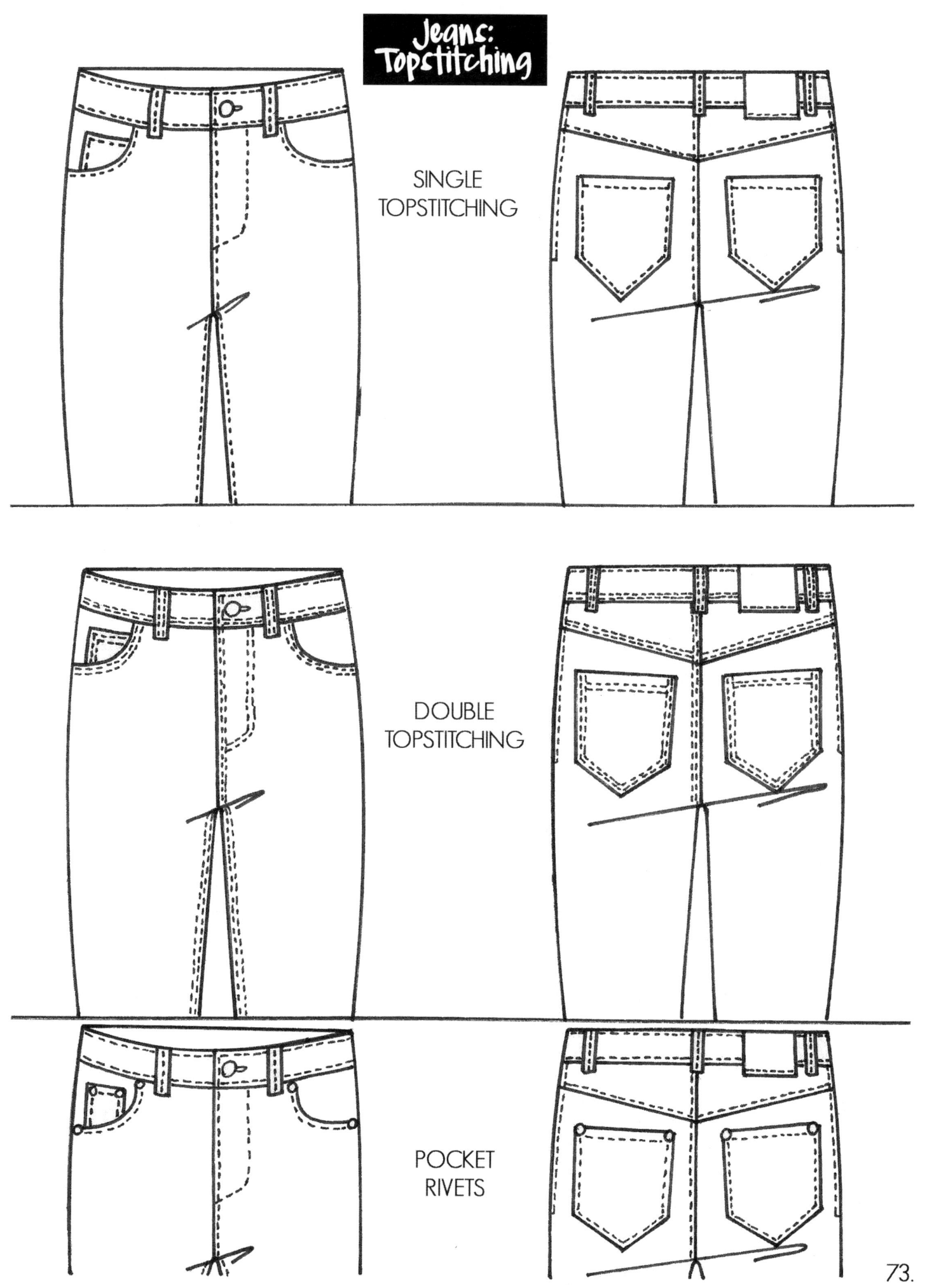

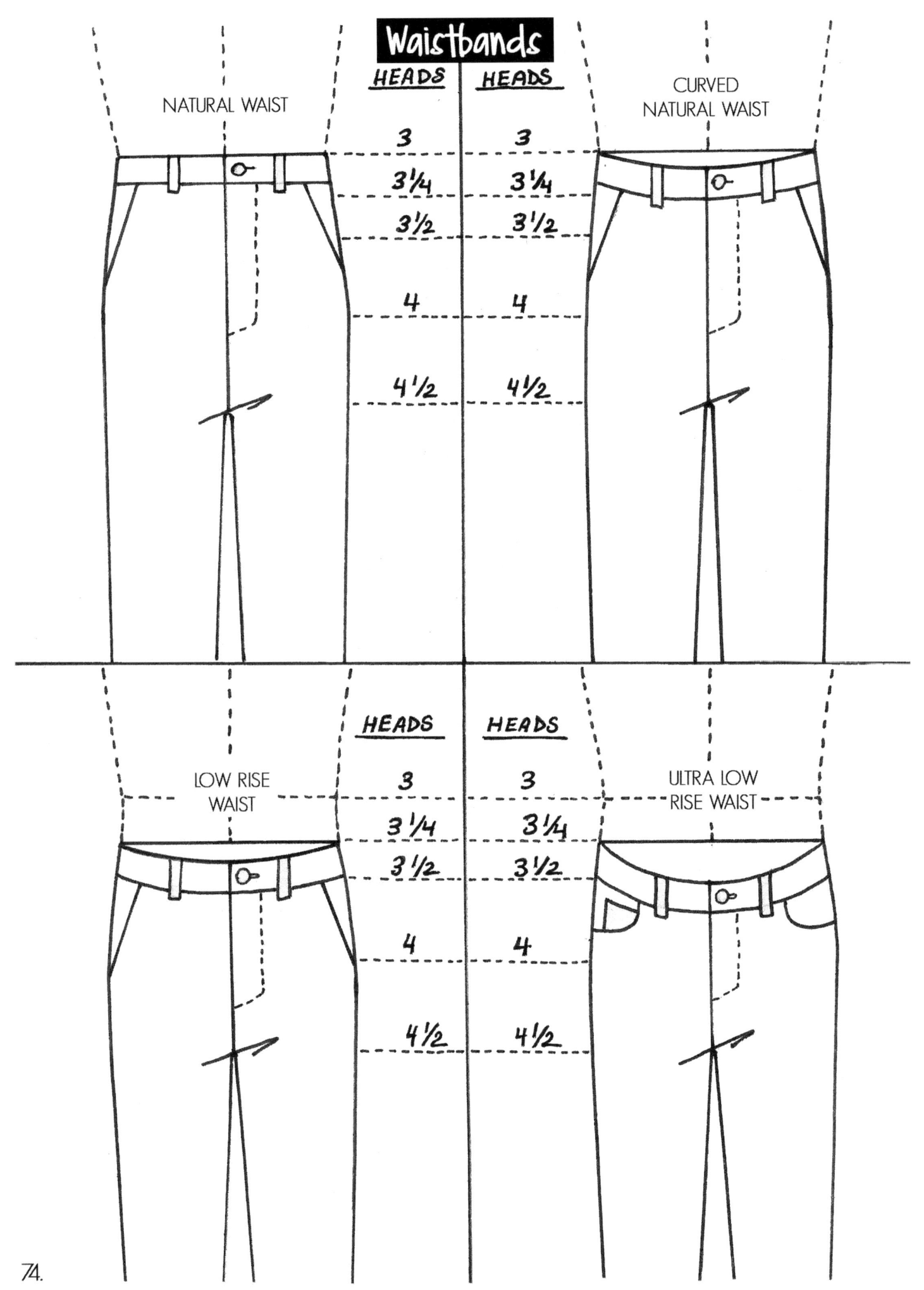

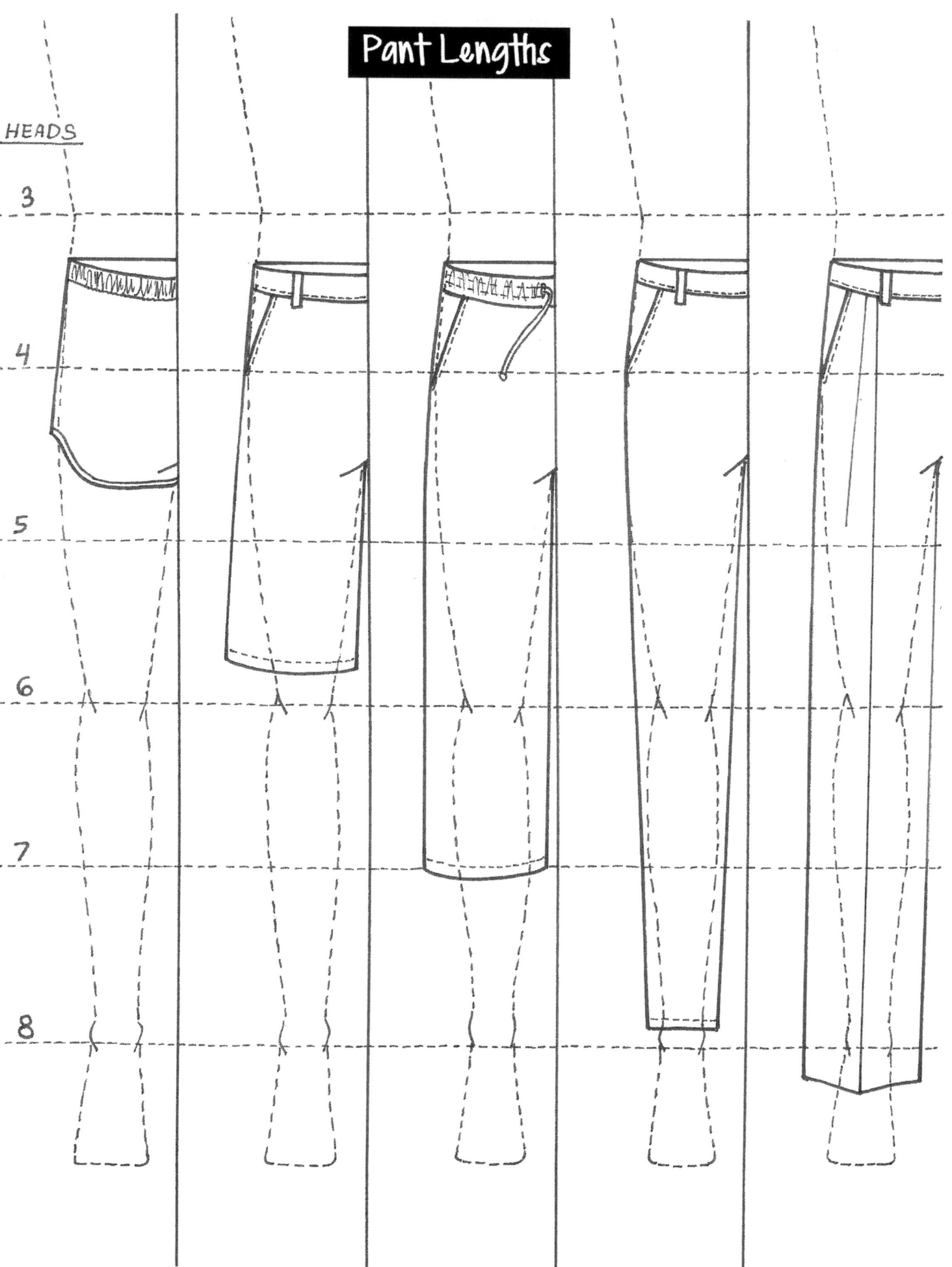

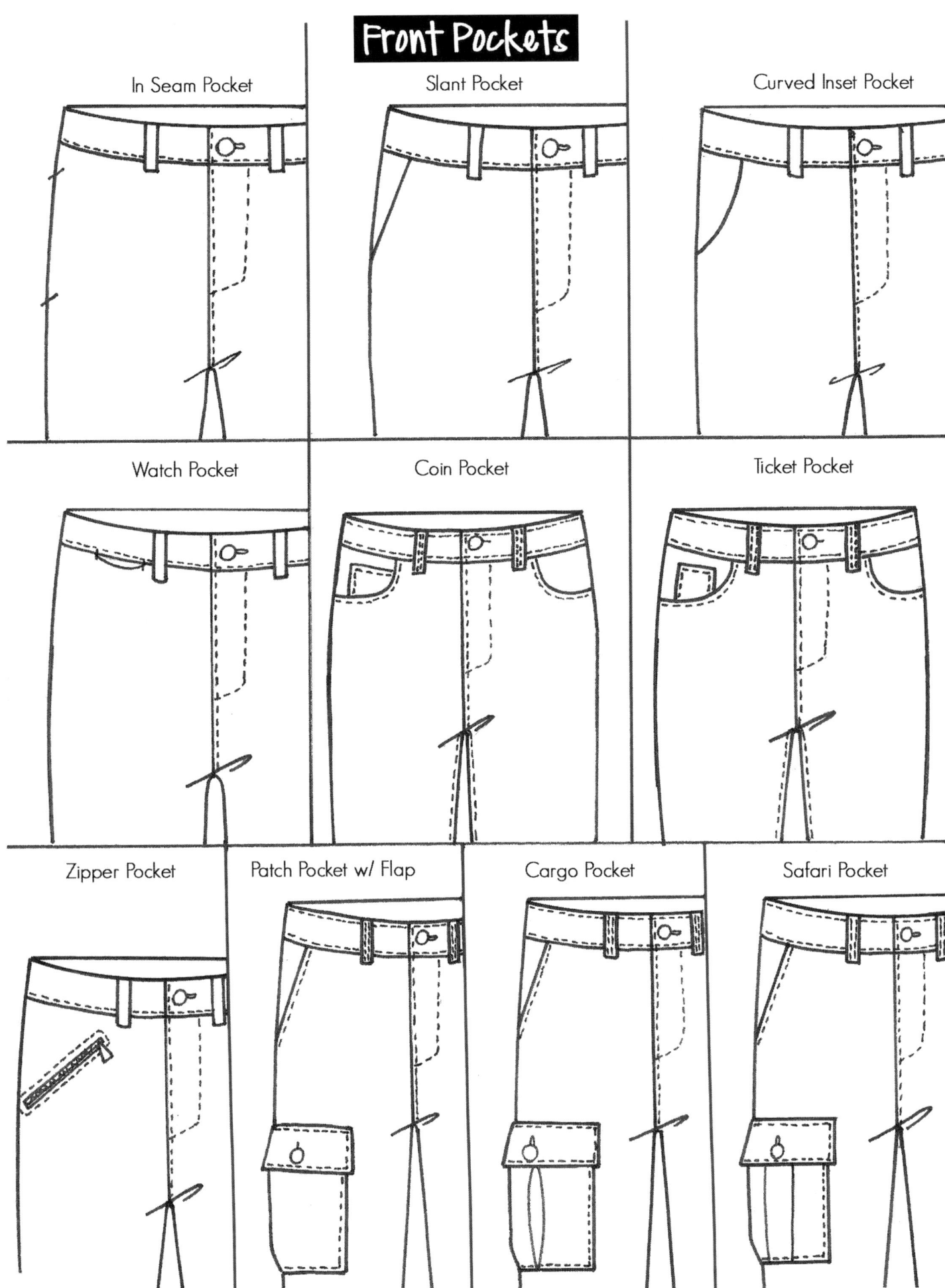

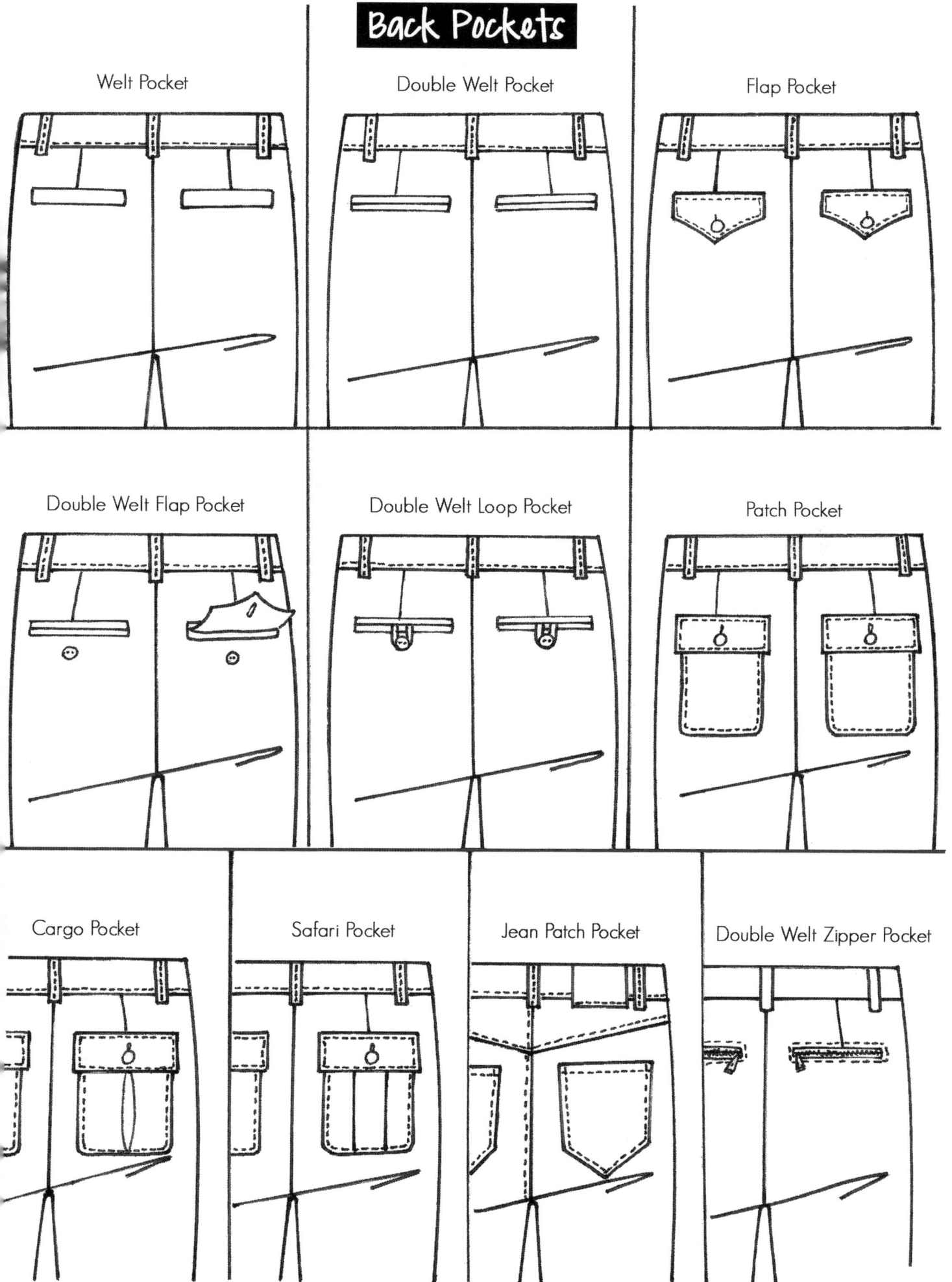

Hems

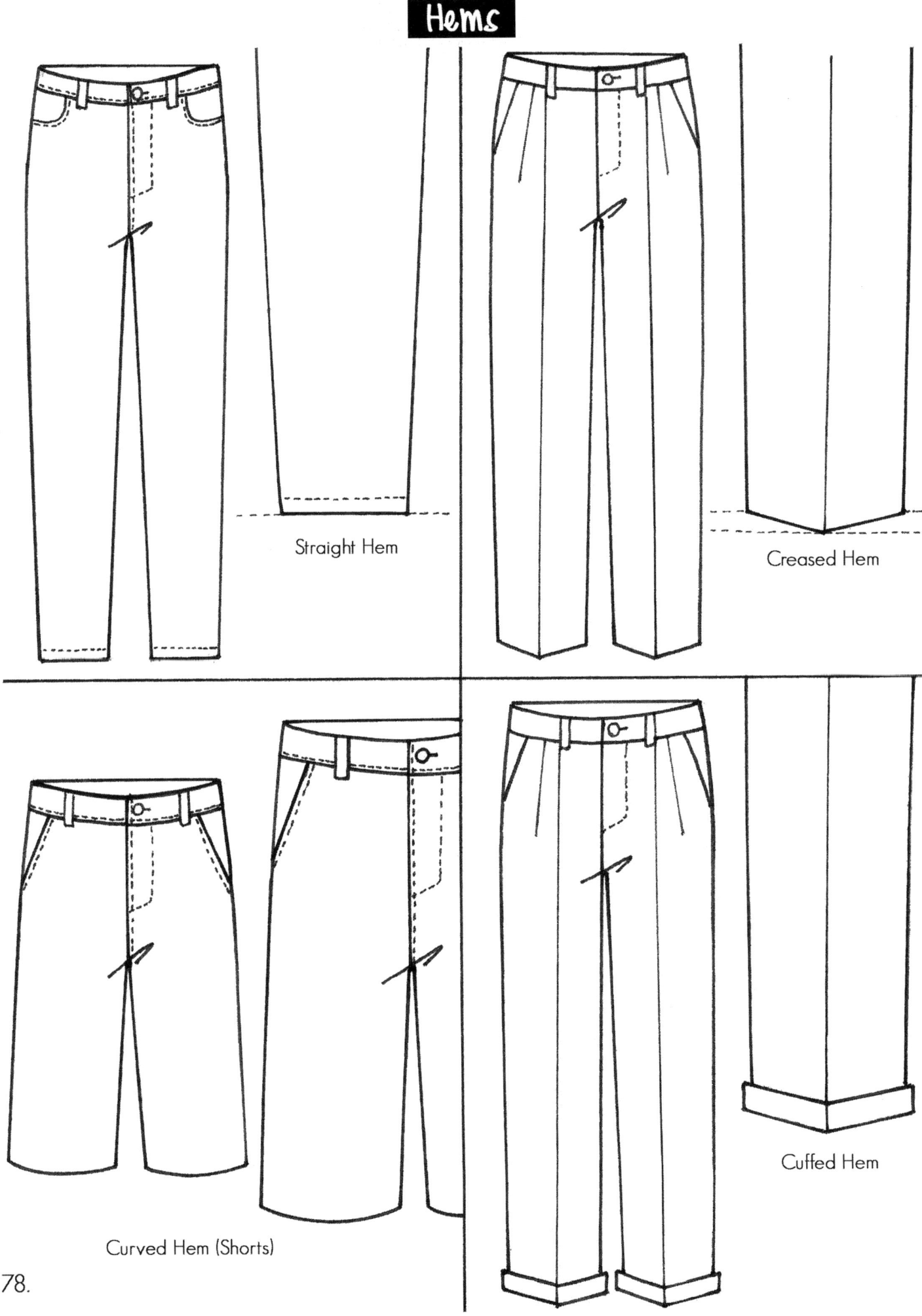

Straight Hem

Creased Hem

Curved Hem (Shorts)

Cuffed Hem

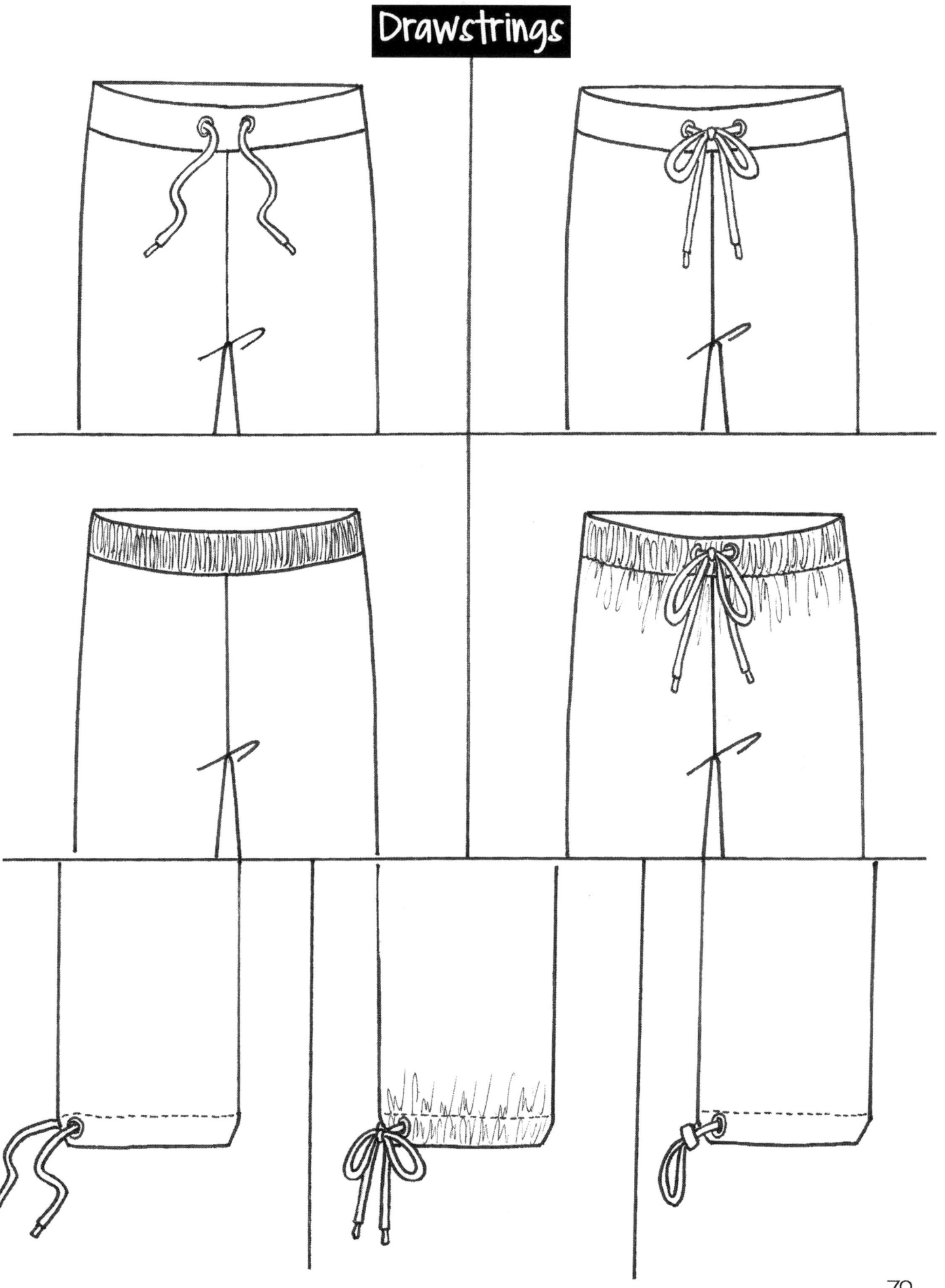

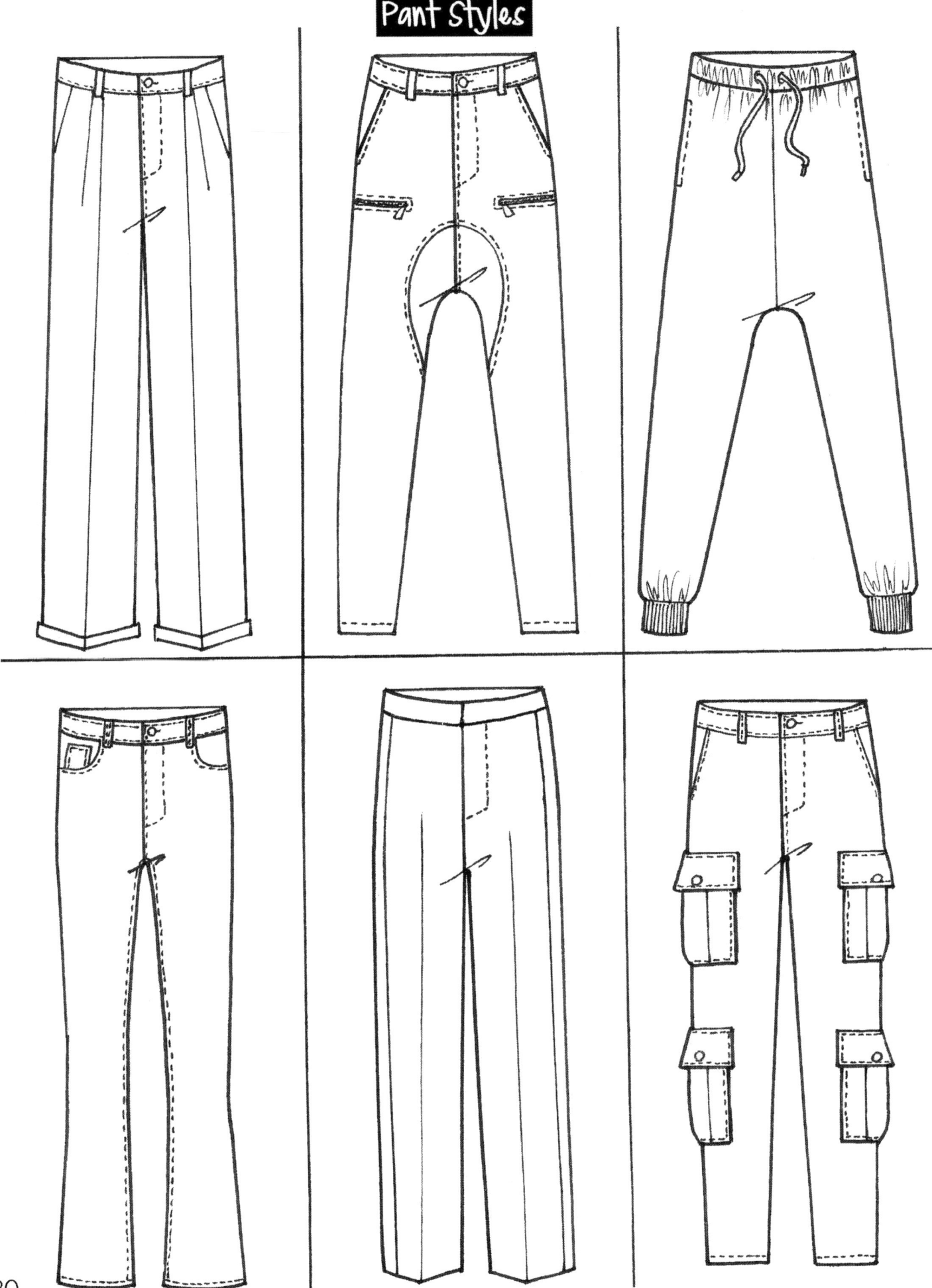

Pant Styles

81.

Pant Styles

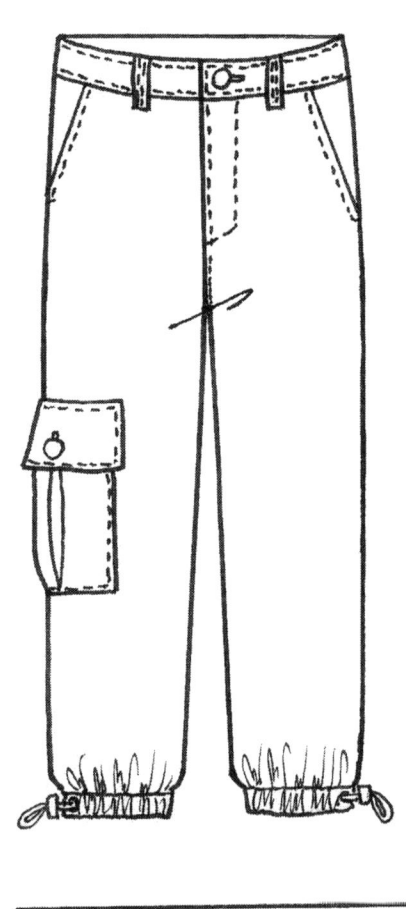
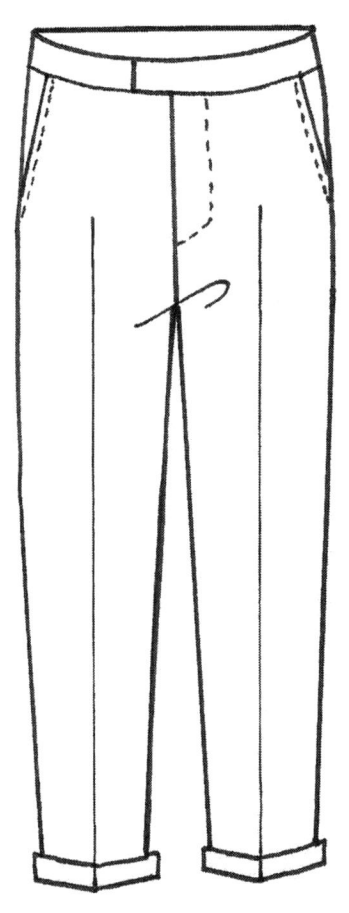
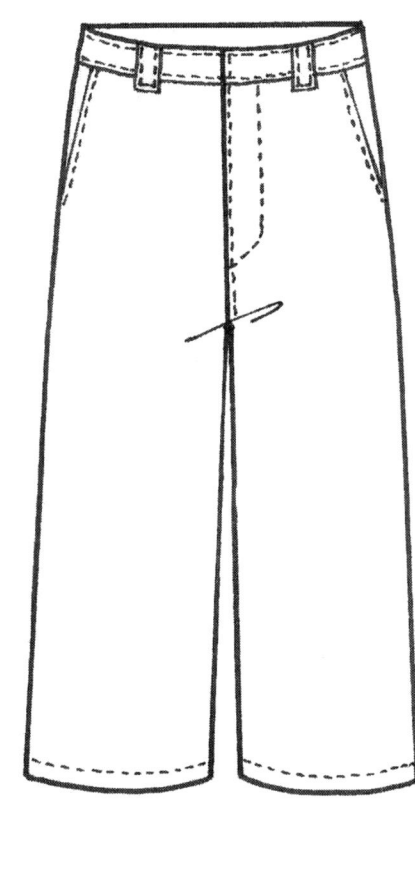
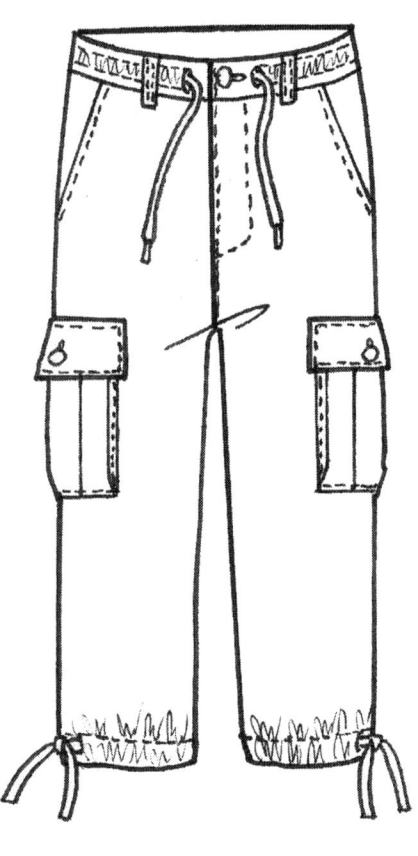
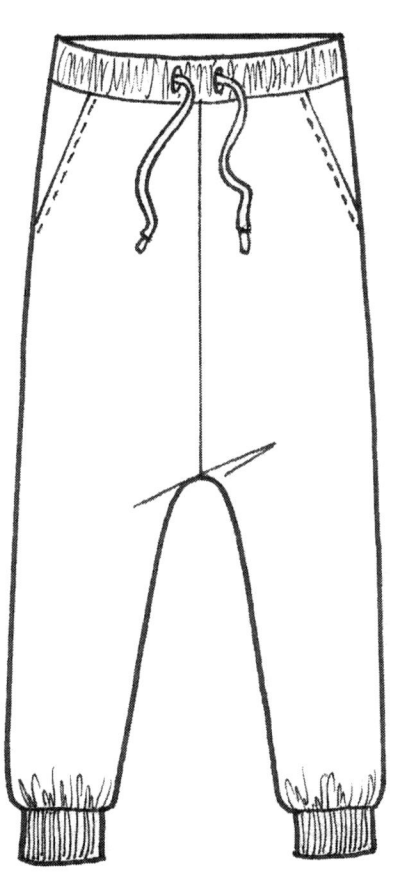
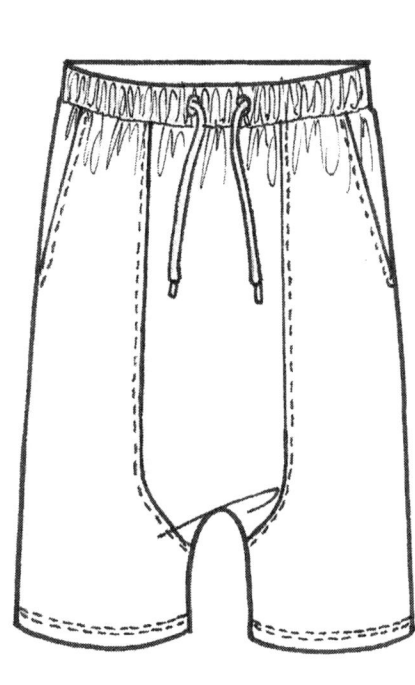

Jackets

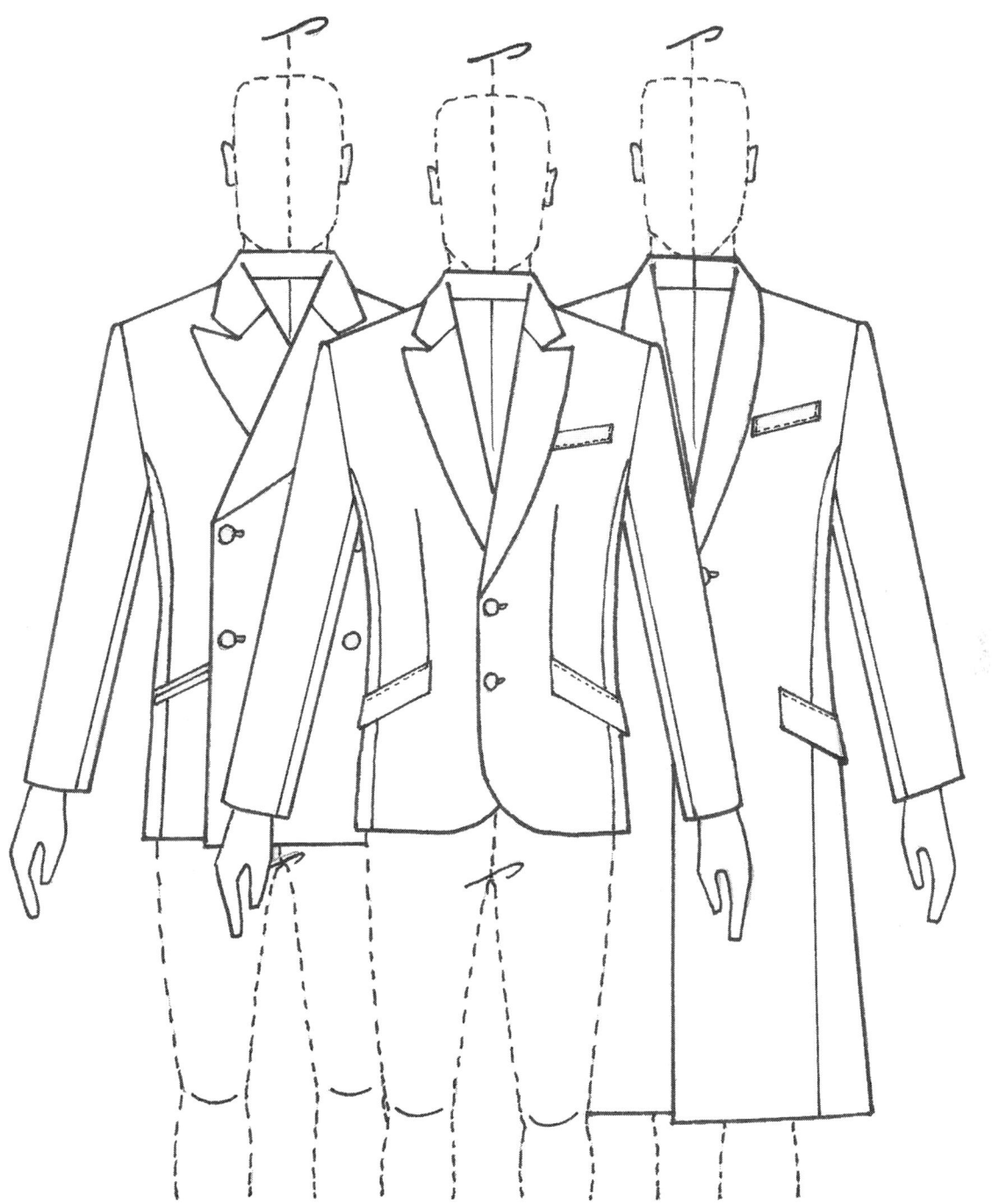

Jackets: Notched Collar

1.
- Draw a "halo"; a short vertical straight line mid-neck level on the Croquis. This represents the collar neckline top edge.

2.
- Draw two long straight lines, slightly angled, that cross over below the chest.
- The beginning of these lines should come from the "halo" line but DO NOT touch it. Notice the right line gives the impression that it is over the left line (broken lines). This shows that the lapel cross-over is from left to right for menswear.
- The end of these two cross-lines finish slightly away from center front.

3.
- At the end of the lines, continue drawing a straight line next to the center front representing the front opening of the Jacket.

4.
- Draw two short slightly angled lines, from the "halo" (collar neck edge line) to the shoulder. These lines represent the side shape of the jacket's collar.

5.
- At the front neckline level, draw two short slightly angled lines, almost in the same angle as the previous two short lines you drew up top.
- Mark the middle of these lines with a small mark. These lines represent the edge of the Notched Lapel and the small mark is where the Collar will meet the Lapel.

6.
- From the end of these two short lines, draw two curved, knife-like shapes all the way to the center front edges. You have now drawn the actual Jacket Lapels.

7.
- Go back to the top area. At that small mark you previously drew, draw two short lines in an upward angle.

8.
- Now connect these two short lines with the lines you drew previously that touched the shoulders. You have now drawn the rest of the collar that is sewn to the Jacket Lapel.

9.
- Finish your Notched Collar/Lapel by erasing the lines from underneath (the previous broken lines that represented the jacket that is crossing under) and add the buttons and buttonholes.

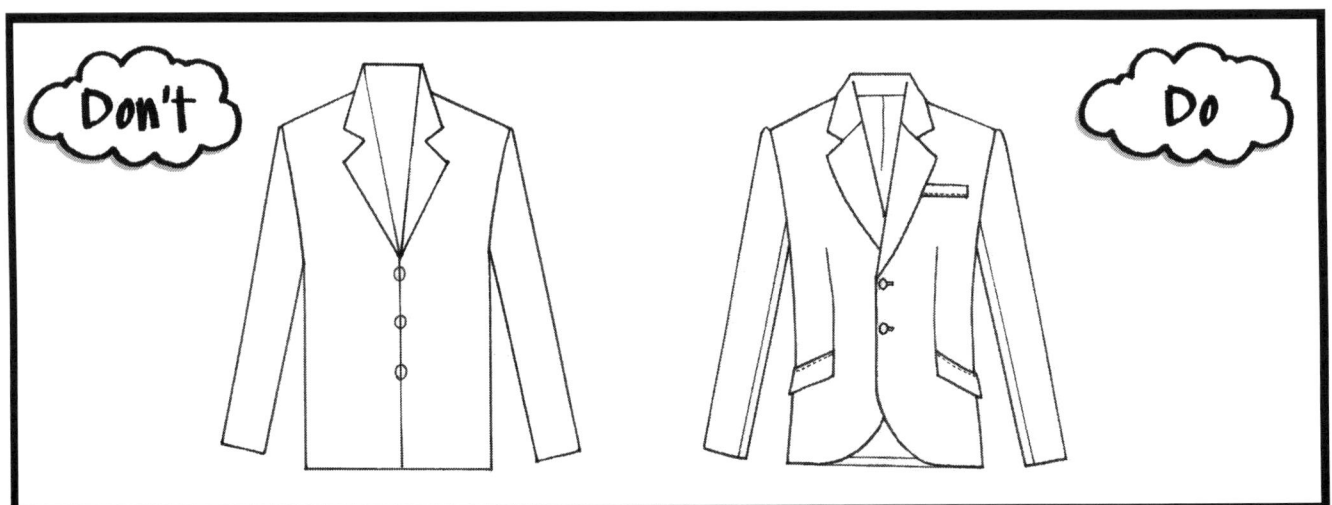

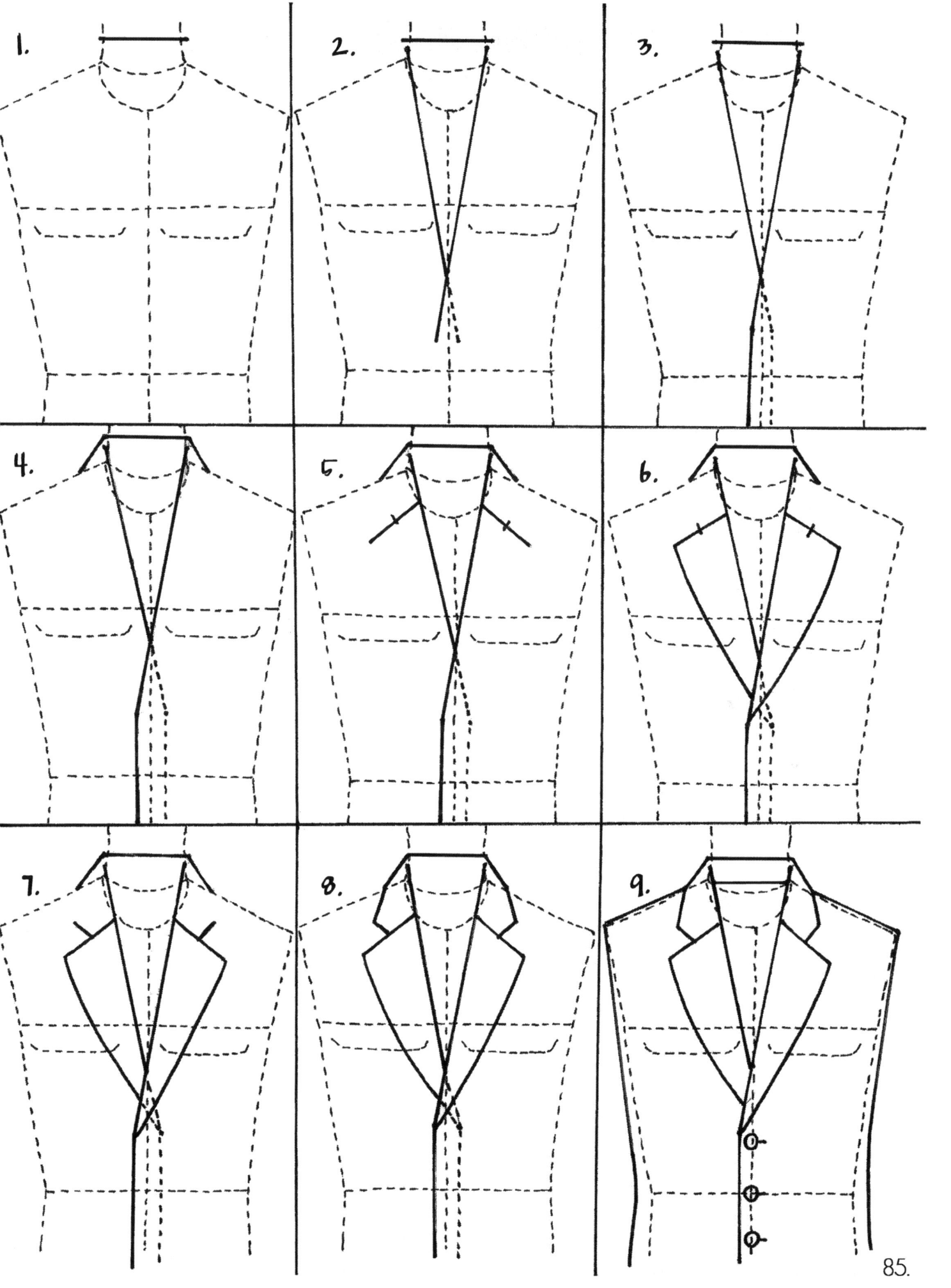

Notched Collar Jacket: Fitted

1.
- Draw the Notched Collar/Lapel according to the instructions on the previous page.
- Draw the center front edge of the Jacket line slightly away from the actual center front of the Croquis.
- Jackets DO NOT CLOSE right at the center front, but slightly away from it.
- The buttons and buttonholes are drawn at the center front.
- You can curve the hem of this center front line depending on the style of the Jacket.

2.
- Continue by drawing the shape of the jacket using the steps below:
- Draw the shoulder line.
- Draw a line that begins from shoulder tip, straight through the armhole area, curved in slightly at the waist.
- End the line below the hip level.
- Notice that this line is drawn slightly away from the Croquis' body and not directly following the lines of the Croquis, although still fairly fitted.
- Draw the hem of the Jacket as a straight line from the side to the center front.
- You can curve the hem right at the center front line depending on the style of the Jacket.
- Draw the Jacket sleeve as shown. Starting at the shoulder tip; begin with a slight curve "bump" to represent the cap of a tailored jacket sleeve.
- Draw straight lines on either side of the arm, down to the wrist area. These lines represent the outer and inner lines of the sleeve.
- Finish off with a short straight line connecting these two sleeve lines. This short line represents the bottom of the sleeve.

3.
- Draw the other side of the Fitted Jacket.

4.
- Finish the flat sketch with the following details:
- Draw a straight line inside the sleeve right next to the inner sleeve line. This is the undersleeve seam.
- Draw the waist area darts as slightly curved lines at the Princess Line area.
- Draw the chest welt pocket and welt pockets right below the waist and directly below the waist darts.

5.
- Draw the back of the collar at the neckline; this will look like a thin "trapezoid".

6.
- Draw the shoulder line.
- Draw the side of the Jacket, starting from shoulder tip, down the back side and end below the hip level.
- Notice the slightly fitted shape around the waist area.
- Draw a straight horizontal line from the side of the Jacket to the center back. This is half of the hem.
- Draw the sleeve.

7.
- Draw the other side of the Jacket and the other sleeve.
- In addition, draw a straight line at center back. This line represents the center back seam of the Jacket.
- Draw a small "slash" mark below the waist at center back and a small "rabbit ear" triangular shape at the center back hem to show the back vent opening of the Jacket.

8.
- Finish off with the Details:
- Draw a straight line inside each sleeve representing the undersleeve seam.
- Draw small circles near the wrist at the positions shown on the sleeve to show sleeve buttons.
- Draw straight-to-slightly curved lines by the sides of the Jacket representing the side panel seams.

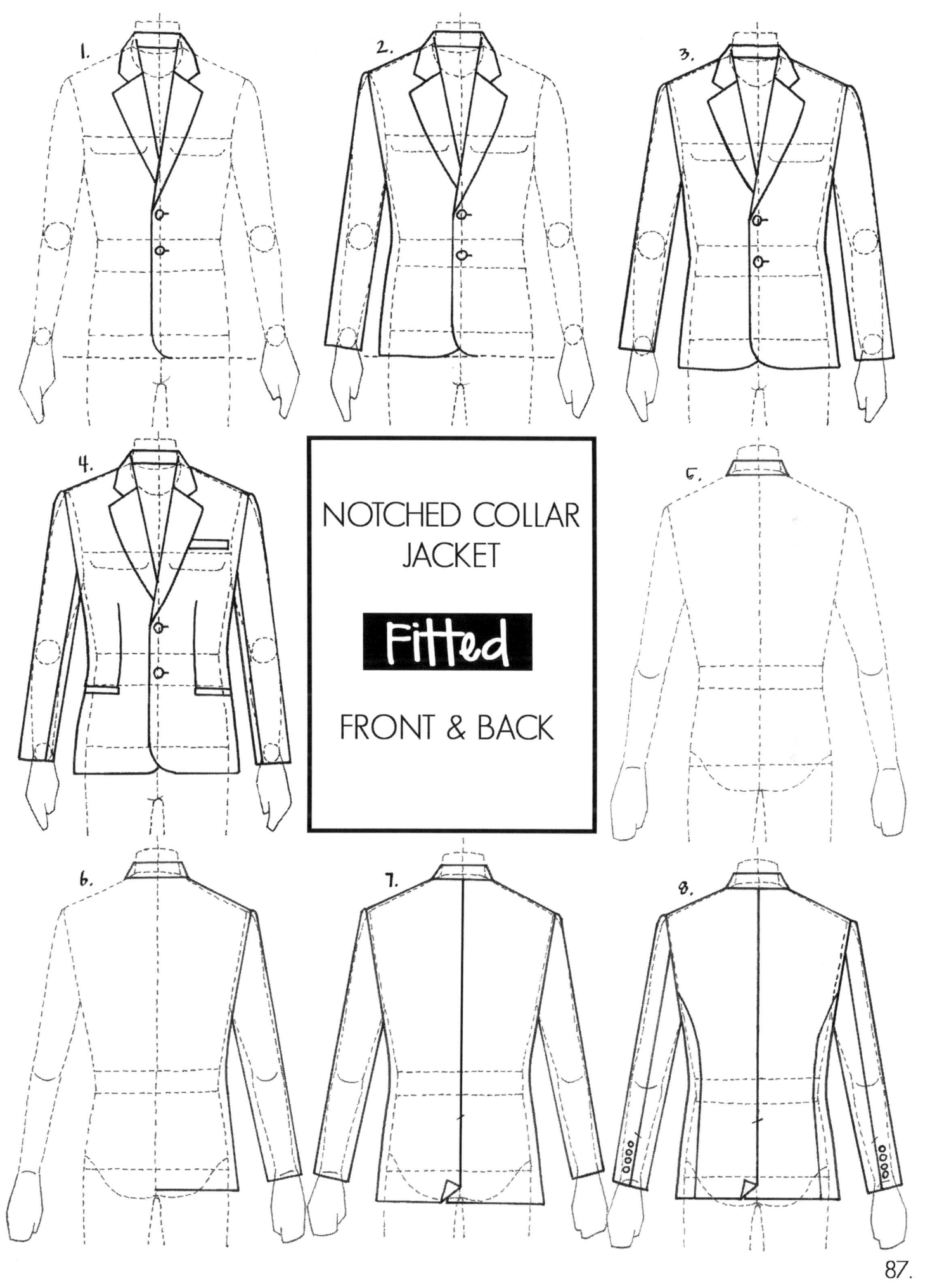

Notched Collar Jacket: Unfitted

1.
- Draw the Notched Collar/Lapel according to the instructions on the previous page.
- Draw the center front edge of the Jacket line slightly away from the actual center front of the Croquis.
- Jackets DO NOT CLOSE right at the center front, but slightly away from it.
- The buttons and buttonholes are drawn at the center front.
- You can curve the hem of this center front line depending on the style of the Jacket.

2.
- Continue by drawing the shape of the jacket using the steps below:
- Draw the shoulder line.
- Draw a line that begins from shoulder tip and continues straight through the armhole area. Continue drawing a straight, un-fitted line that ends below the hip level.
- Notice that this line is drawn slightly AWAY from the Croquis' body to show that it is not a fitted Jacket.
- Draw the hem of the Jacket as a straight line from the side to the center front.
- You can curve the hem right at the center front line depending on the style of the Jacket.
- Draw the Jacket sleeve as shown. Starting at the shoulder tip; begin with a slight curve "bump" to represent the cap of a tailored jacket sleeve.
- Draw straight lines on either side of the arm, down to the wrist area. These lines represent the outer and inner lines of the sleeve.
- Finish off with a short straight line connecting these two sleeve lines. This short line represents the bottom of the sleeve.

3.
- Draw the other side of the Unfitted Jacket.

4.
- Finish the flat sketch with the following details:
- Draw a straight line inside the sleeve right next to the inner sleeve line. This is the undersleeve seam.
- Draw the chest pocket, and pocket flaps right below the waist. These "flaps" are slightly angled and not perfectly horizontal.

5.
- Draw the back of the collar at the neckline; this will look like a thin "trapezoid".

6.
- Draw the shoulder line.
- Draw the side of the Jacket, starting from shoulder tip, down the back side and end below the hip level.
- Notice this line is straight and away from the Croquis' body.
- Draw a straight horizontal line from the side of the Jacket to the center back. This is half of the hem.
- Draw the sleeve.

7.
- Draw the other side of the Jacket and the other sleeve.
- In addition, draw a straight line at center back. This line represents the center back seam of the Jacket.
- Draw a small "slash" mark below the waist at center back and a small "rabbit ear" triangular shape at the center back hem to show the back vent opening of the Jacket.

8.
- Finish off with the Details:
- Draw a straight line inside each sleeve representing the undersleeve seam.
- Draw small circles near the wrist at the positions shown on the sleeve to show sleeve buttons.

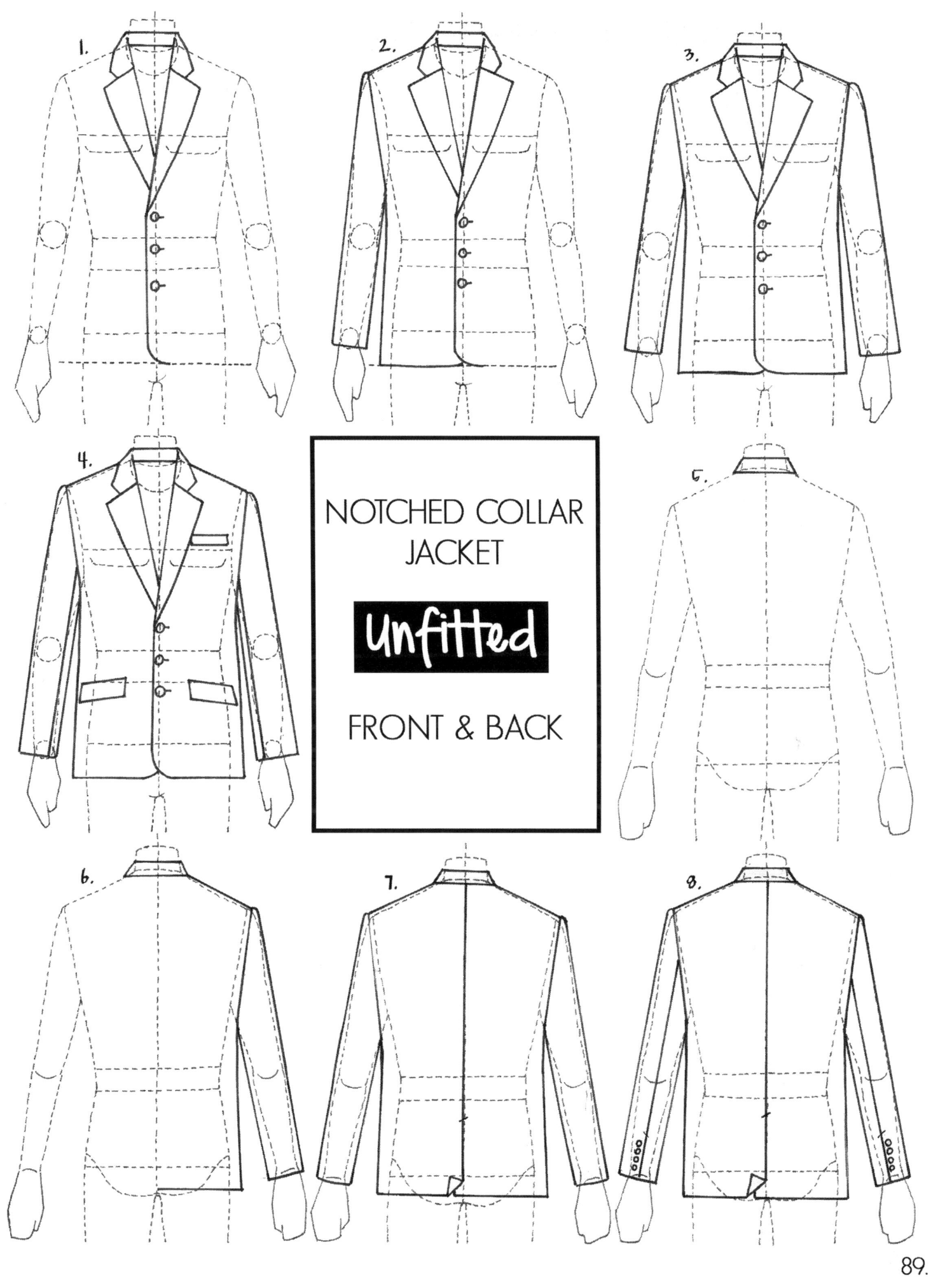

Jackets: Shawl Collar

1.
- Draw a "halo"; a short vertical straight line mid-neck level on the Croquis. This represents the collar neckline top edge.

2.
- Draw two long straight lines, slightly angled, that cross over below the chest.
- The beginning of these lines should come from the "halo" line but DO NOT touch it. Notice the right line gives the impression that it is over the left line (broken lines). This shows that the lapel cross-over is from left to right for menswear.
- The end of these two cross-lines finish slightly away from center front.

3.
- At the end of the lines, continue drawing a straight line next to the center front representing the front opening of the Jacket.

4.
- Draw two short slightly angled lines, from the "halo" (collar neck edge line) to the shoulder. These lines represent the side shape of the jacket's collar.

5.
- From the end of one of the short collar lines, draw a straight-to-curved line that will end where the jacket crosses over. This line will represent the Shawl Collar.

6.
- Repeat Step #5 on the other side.

7.
- Erase the center front area of the right Shawl Collar, representing that this portion of the collar is UNDER the other side of the jacket.

8.
- Draw back neckline collar line and center back neckline collar line.

9.
- Finish your Shawl Collar by drawing the rest of the jacket shape and adding the buttons and buttonholes.

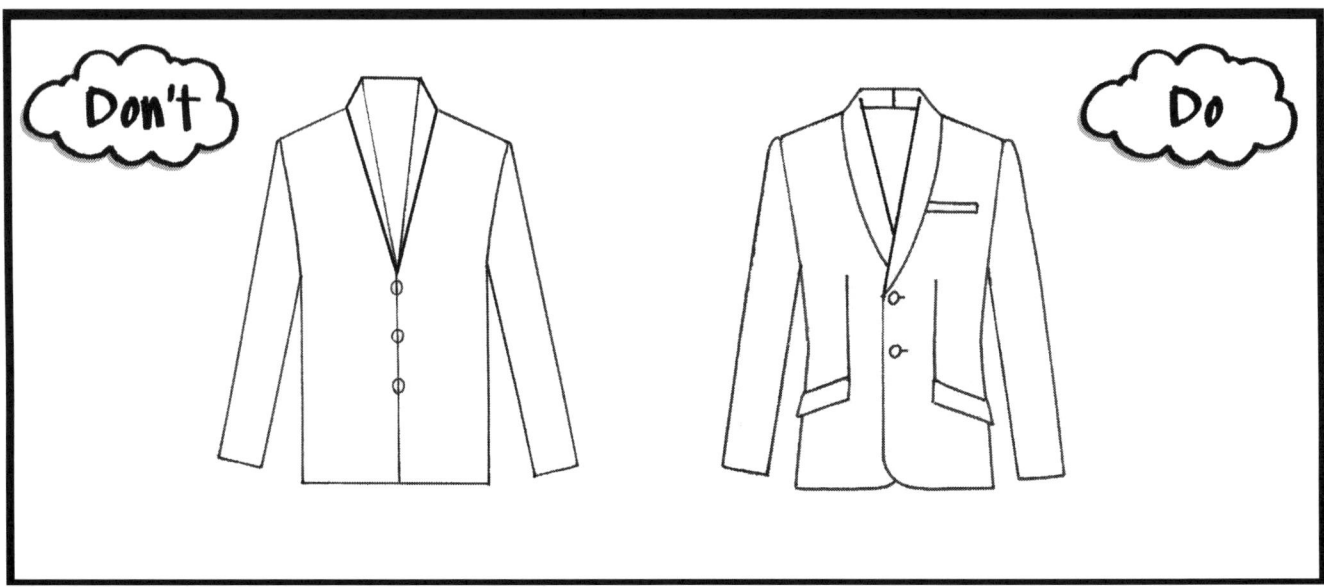

90.

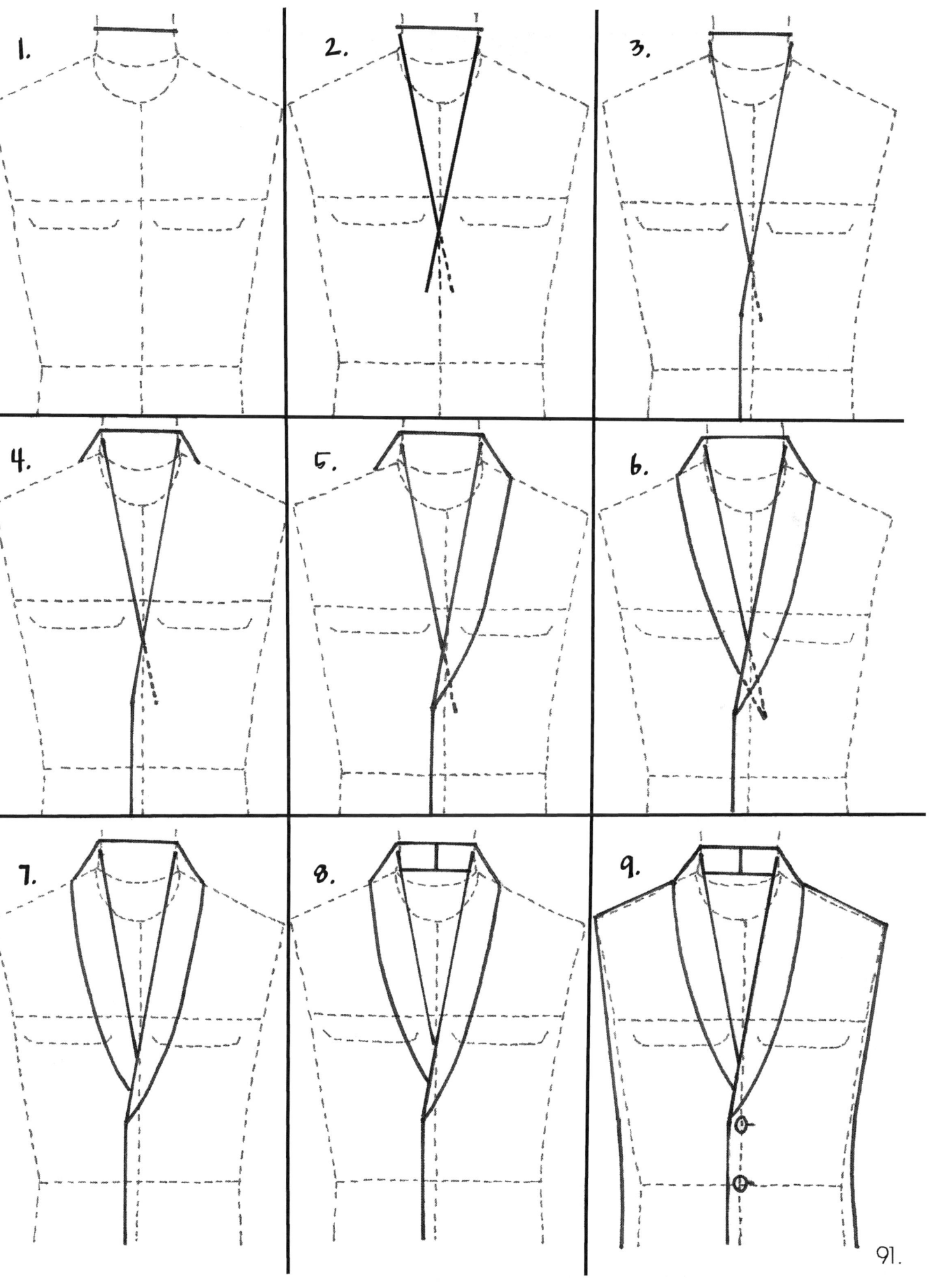

Shawl Collar Jacket

1.
- Draw the Notched Collar/Lapel according to the instructions on the previous page.
- Draw the center front edge of the Jacket line slightly away from the actual center front of the Croquis.
- Jackets DO NOT CLOSE right at the center front, but slightly away from it.
- The buttons and buttonholes are drawn at the center front.
- You can curve the hem of this center front line depending on the style of the Jacket.

2.
- Continue by drawing the shape of the jacket using the steps below:
- Draw the shoulder line.
- Draw a line that begins from shoulder tip, straight through the armhole area, curved in slightly at the waist.
- End the line below the hip level.
- Notice that this line is drawn slightly away from the Croquis' body and not directly following the lines of the Croquis, although still fairly fitted.
- Draw the hem of the Jacket as a straight line from the side to the center front.
- You can curve the hem right at the center front line depending on the style of the Jacket.
- Draw the Jacket sleeve as shown. Starting at the shoulder tip; begin with a slight curve "bump" to represent the cap of a tailored jacket sleeve.
- Draw straight lines on either side of the arm, down to the wrist area. These lines represent the outer and inner lines of the sleeve.
- Finish off with a short straight line connecting these two sleeve lines. This short line represents the bottom of the sleeve.

3.
- Draw the other side of the Shawl Collar Jacket.

4.
- Finish the flat sketch with the following details:
- Draw the waist area darts as slightly curved lines at Princess Line area.
- Draw the chest welt pocket and flap pockets right below the waist and directly below the waist darts.

5.
- Draw the back of the collar at the neckline; this will look like a thin "trapezoid".

6.
- Draw the shoulder line.
- Draw the side of the Jacket, starting from shoulder tip, down the back side and end below the hip level.
- Notice the slightly fitted shape around the waist area.
- Draw a straight horizontal line from the side of the Jacket to the center back. This is half of the hem.
- Draw the sleeve.

7.
- Draw the other side of the Jacket and the other sleeve.
- In addition, draw a straight line at center back. This line represents the center back seam of the Jacket.
- Draw a small "slash" mark below the waist at center back and a small "rabbit ear" triangular shape at the center back hem to show the back vent opening of the Jacket.

8.
- Finish off with the Details:
- Draw a straight line inside each sleeve representing the undersleeve seam.
- Draw small circles near the wrist at the positions shown on the sleeve to show sleeve buttons.
- Draw straight-to-slightly curved lines by the sides of the Jacket representing the side panel seams.

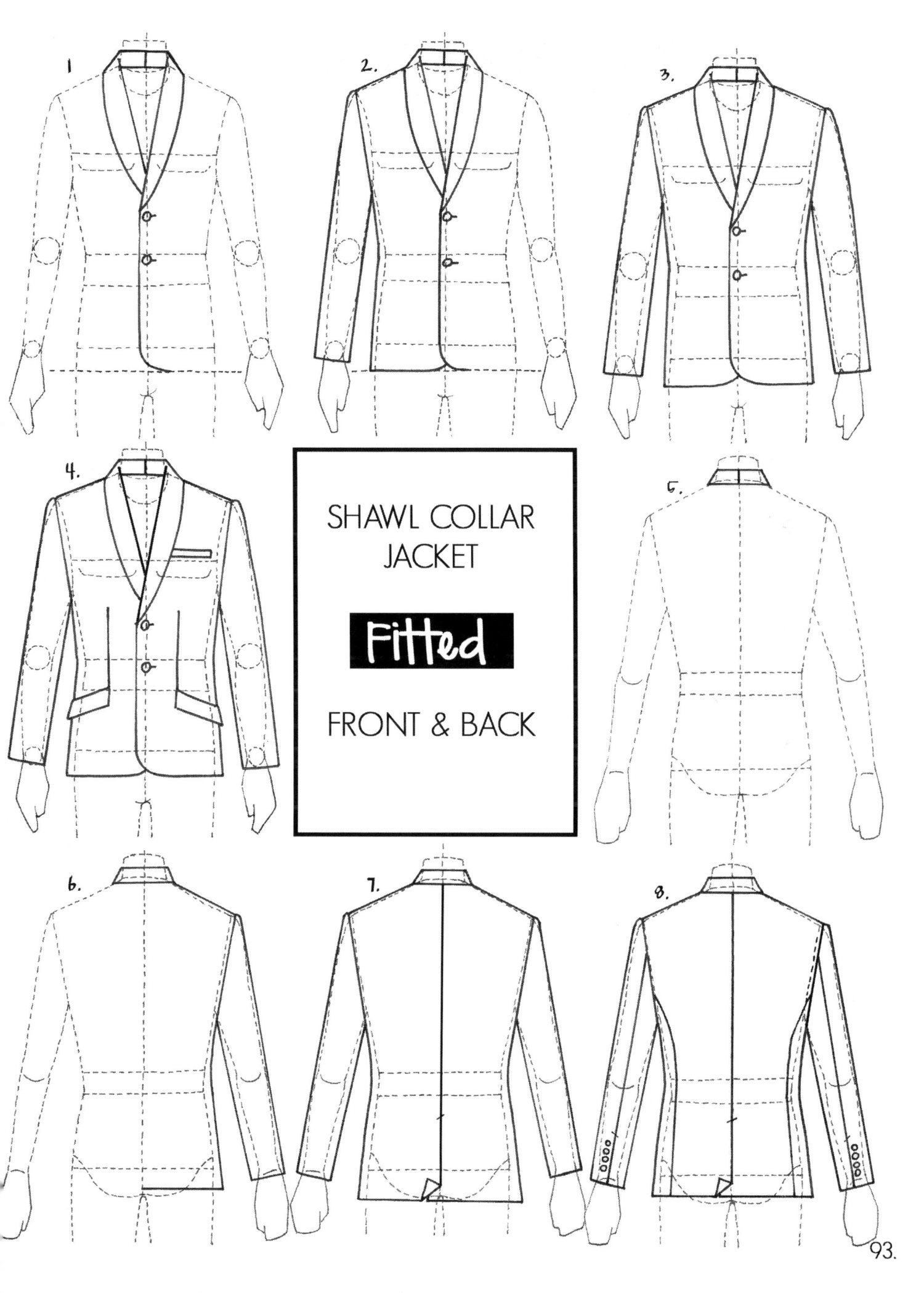

Jackets: Double Breasted Collar

1.
- Draw a "halo"; a short vertical straight line mid-neck level on the Croquis. This represents the collar neckline top edge.

2.
- Draw an "X" as shown, beginning from the "halo" line but making sure NOT to have these lines touch that "halo" line.
- Notice the right line gives the impression that it is over the left line (broken lines). This shows that the lapel cross-over is from left to right for menswear.
- Make sure the intersection of these two lines finish slightly away from center front.
- Each line should end mid-torso at the Princess line area of the body.
- Part of the "X" should be drawn lightly since you will erase it later. It is seen here as a broken line; this represents the under part of the Double Breasted Lapel that is hidden underneath.

3.
- Draw vertical straight lines from the end of the "X" lines. These represent the front opening of the Double Breasted Jacket.
- Note that one of those lines will be drawn lightly (seen here as a broken line) to be erased later.

4.
- Go back to the neck area and draw two short angled straight lines from the "halo" to the shoulder. These represent the sides of the collar.

5.
- At the front neckline area, at the "X" lines, draw a very open "V" shape with a short mark in the middle. This represents the notched area of the lapel.

6.
- From the edge of the previous open "V" lines, draw a curved knife-like shape, down to the front opening. This is the Lapel of the Jacket.
- Note that one of them is drawn lightly (broken lines) to be erased later since it will be hidden underneath.

7.
- Draw two small lines that extend out of the middle of the open "V".

8.
- Draw a line from these two short lines, back to the shoulder collar lines. This completes the collar portion of the Double Breasted Lapel.

9.
- Erase all of the broken lines so part of the lapel remains hidden underneath.
- Add buttons: Only one row of the buttons (the ones closest to the opening of the jacket) will have button holes.

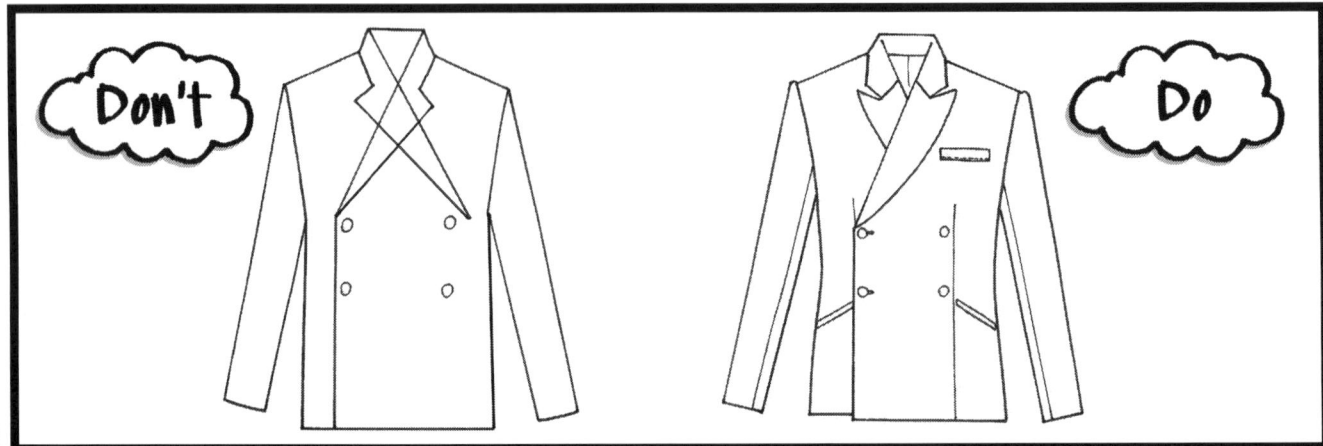

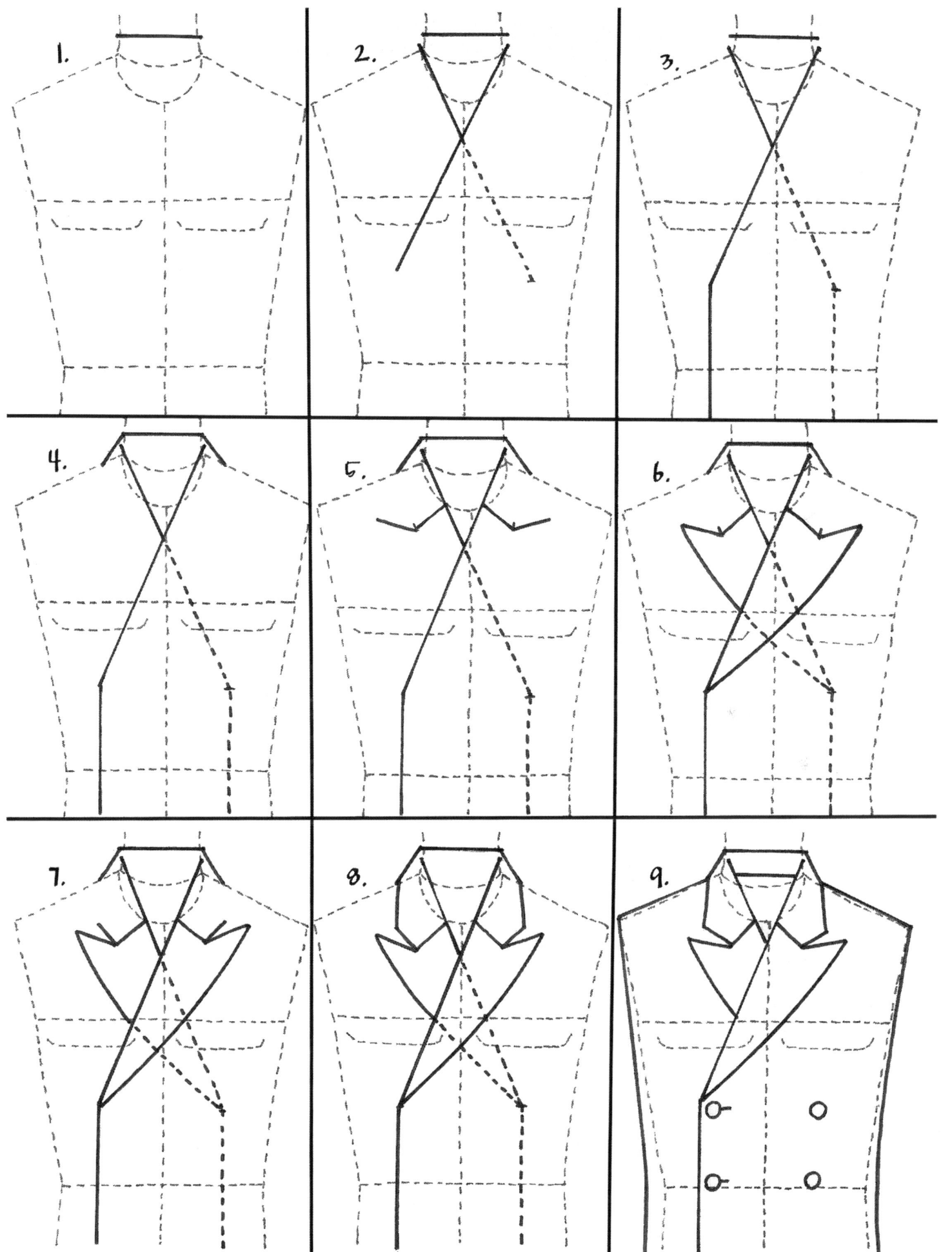

Double Breasted Jacket

1.
- Draw the Notched Collar/Lapel according to the instructions on the previous page.
- Draw the center front edge of the Jacket line slightly away from the actual center front of the Croquis.
- Jackets DO NOT CLOSE right at the center front, but slightly away from it.
- The buttons and buttonholes are drawn at the center front.
- You can curve the hem of this center front line depending on the style of the Jacket.

2.
- Continue by drawing the shape of the jacket using the steps below:
- Draw the shoulder line.
- Draw a line that begins from shoulder tip, straight through the armhole area, curved in slightly at the waist.
- End the line below the hip level.
- Notice that this line is drawn slightly away from the Croquis' body and not directly following the lines of the Croquis, although still fairly fitted.
- Draw the hem of the Jacket as a straight line from the side to the center front.
- You can curve the hem right at the center front line depending on the style of the Jacket.
- Draw the Jacket sleeve as shown. Starting at the shoulder tip; begin with a slight curve "bump" to represent the cap of a tailored jacket sleeve.
- Draw straight lines on either side of the arm, down to the wrist area. These lines represent the outer and inner lines of the sleeve.
- Finish off with a short straight line connecting these two sleeve lines. This short line represents the bottom of the sleeve.

3.
- Draw the other side of the Shawl Collar Jacket.

4.
- Finish the flat sketch with the following details:
- Draw the waist area darts as slightly curved lines at Princess Line area.
- Draw the chest welt pocket and flap pockets right below the waist and directly below the waist darts.

5.
- Draw the back of the collar at the neckline; this will look like a thin "trapezoid".

6.
- Draw the shoulder line.
- Draw the side of the Jacket, starting from shoulder tip, down the back side and end below the hip level.
- Notice the slightly fitted shape around the waist area.
- Draw a straight horizontal line from the side of the Jacket to the center back. This is half of the hem.
- Draw the sleeve.

7.
- Draw the other side of the Jacket and the other sleeve.
- In addition, draw a straight line at center back. This line represents the center back seam of the Jacket.
- Draw a small "slash" mark below the waist at center back and a small "rabbit ear" triangular shape at the center back hem to show the back vent opening of the Jacket.

8.
- Finish off with the Details:
- Draw a straight line inside each sleeve representing the undersleeve seam.
- Draw small circles near the wrist at the positions shown on the sleeve to show sleeve buttons.
- Draw straight-to-slightly curved lines by the sides of the Jacket representing the side panel seams.

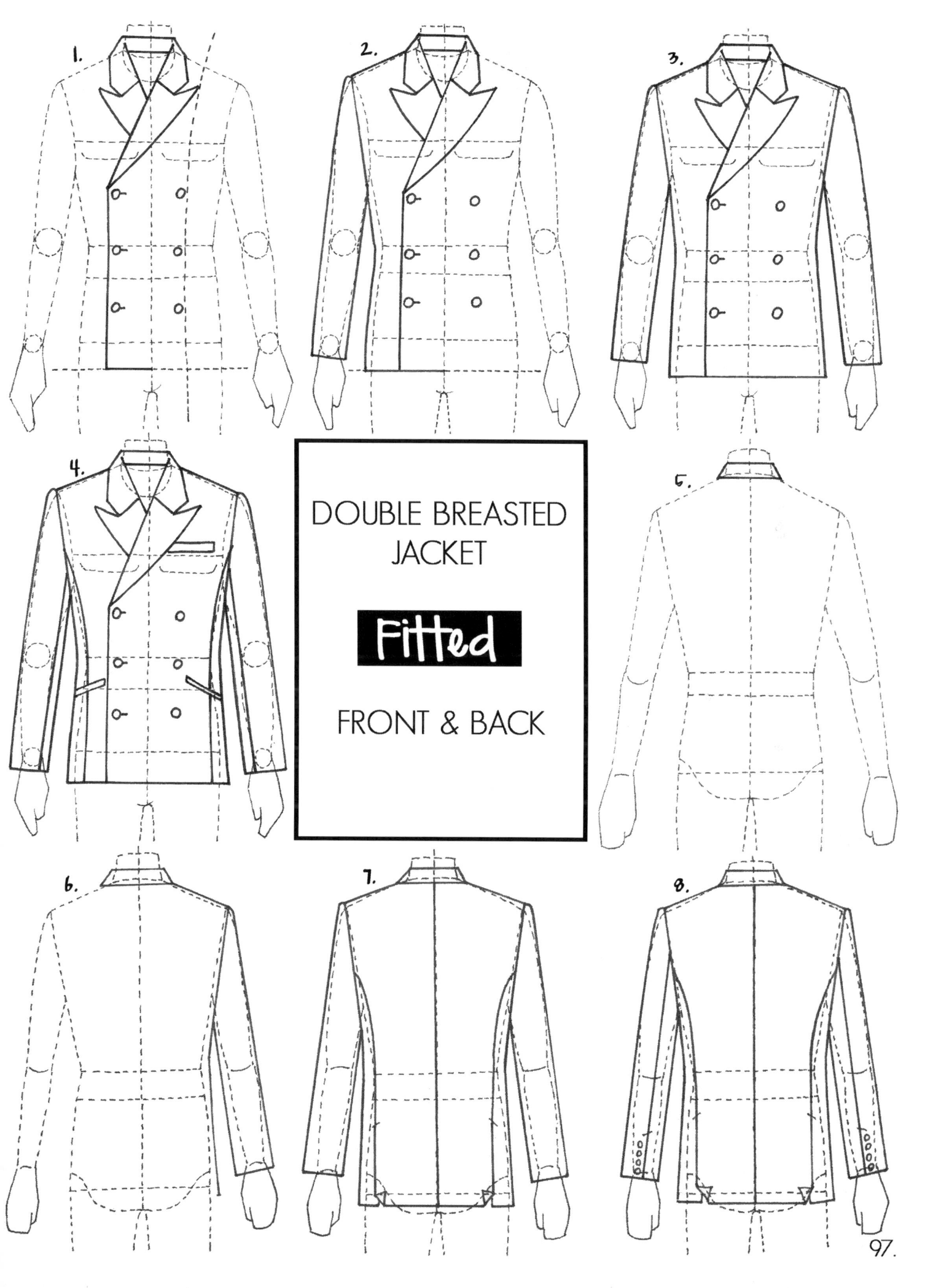

Single Breasted Coat

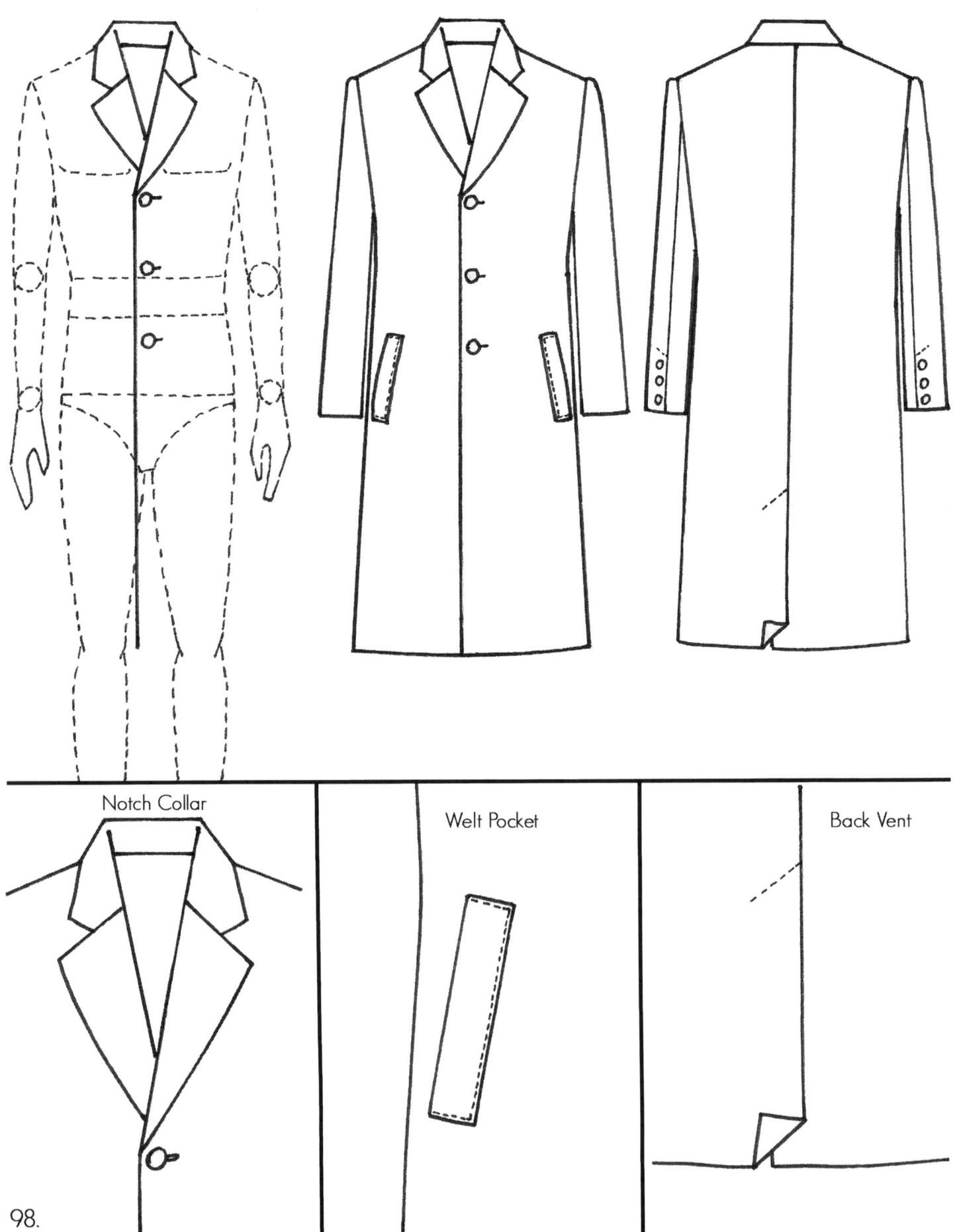

Notch Collar

Welt Pocket

Back Vent

Double Breasted Trench Coat

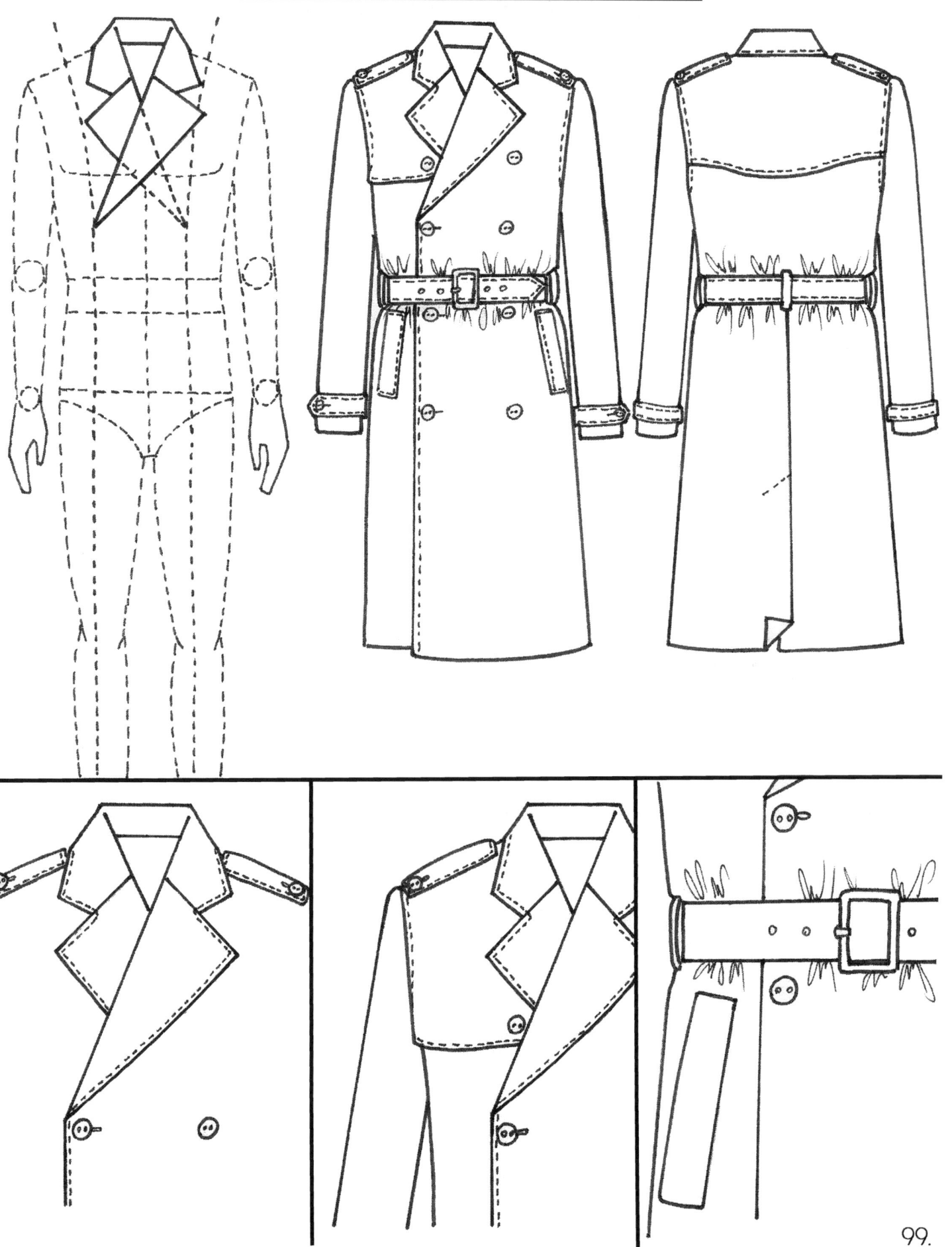

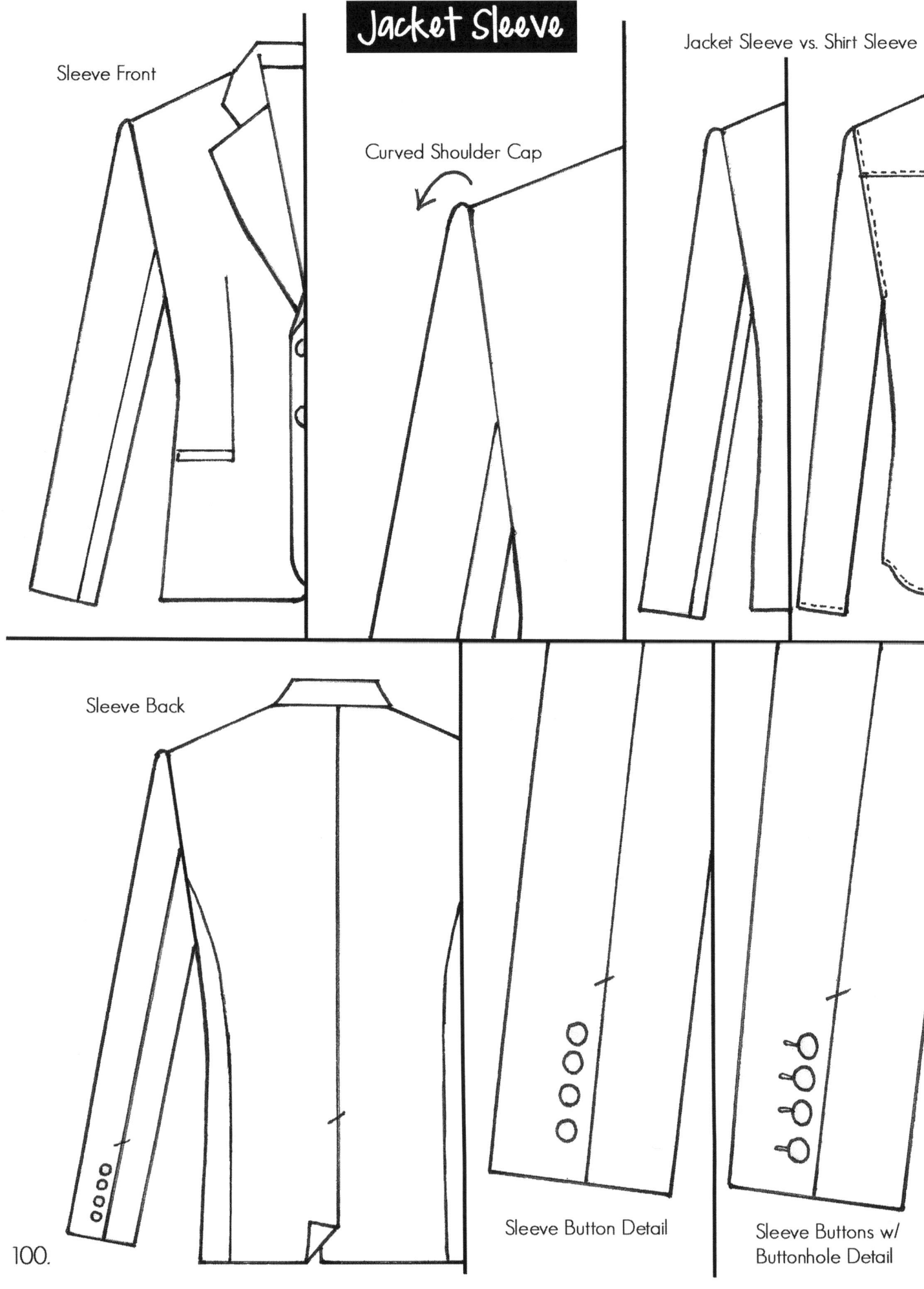

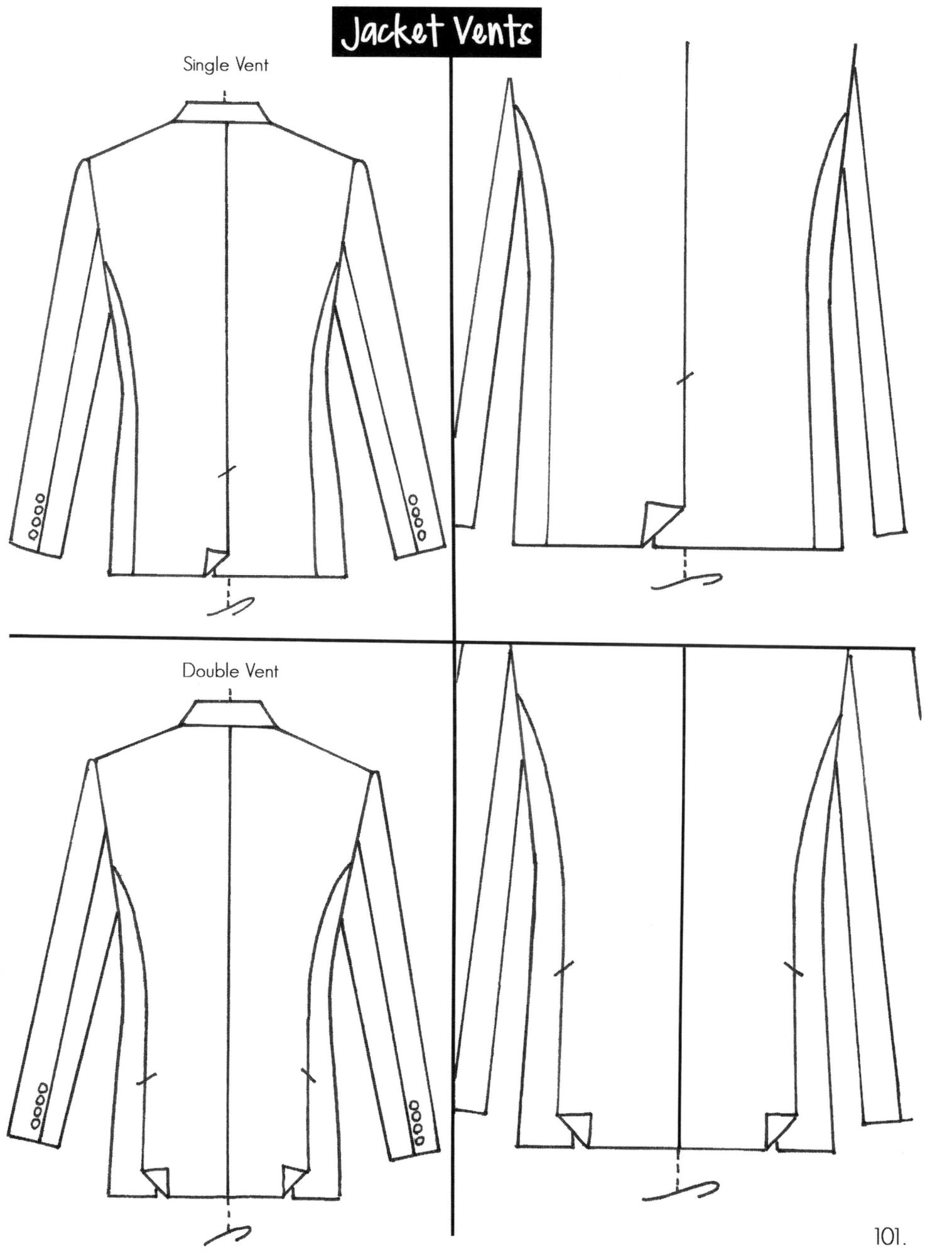

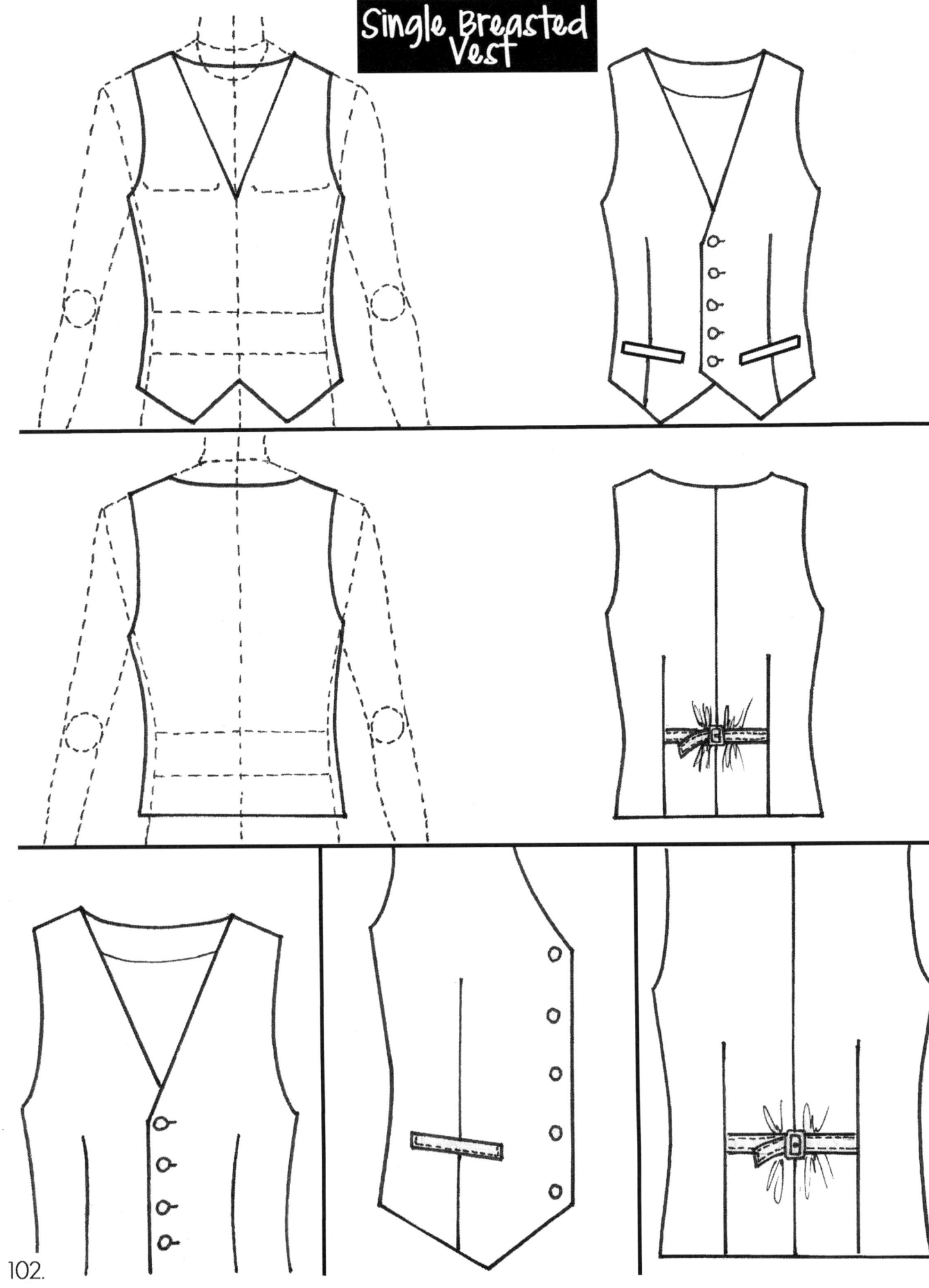

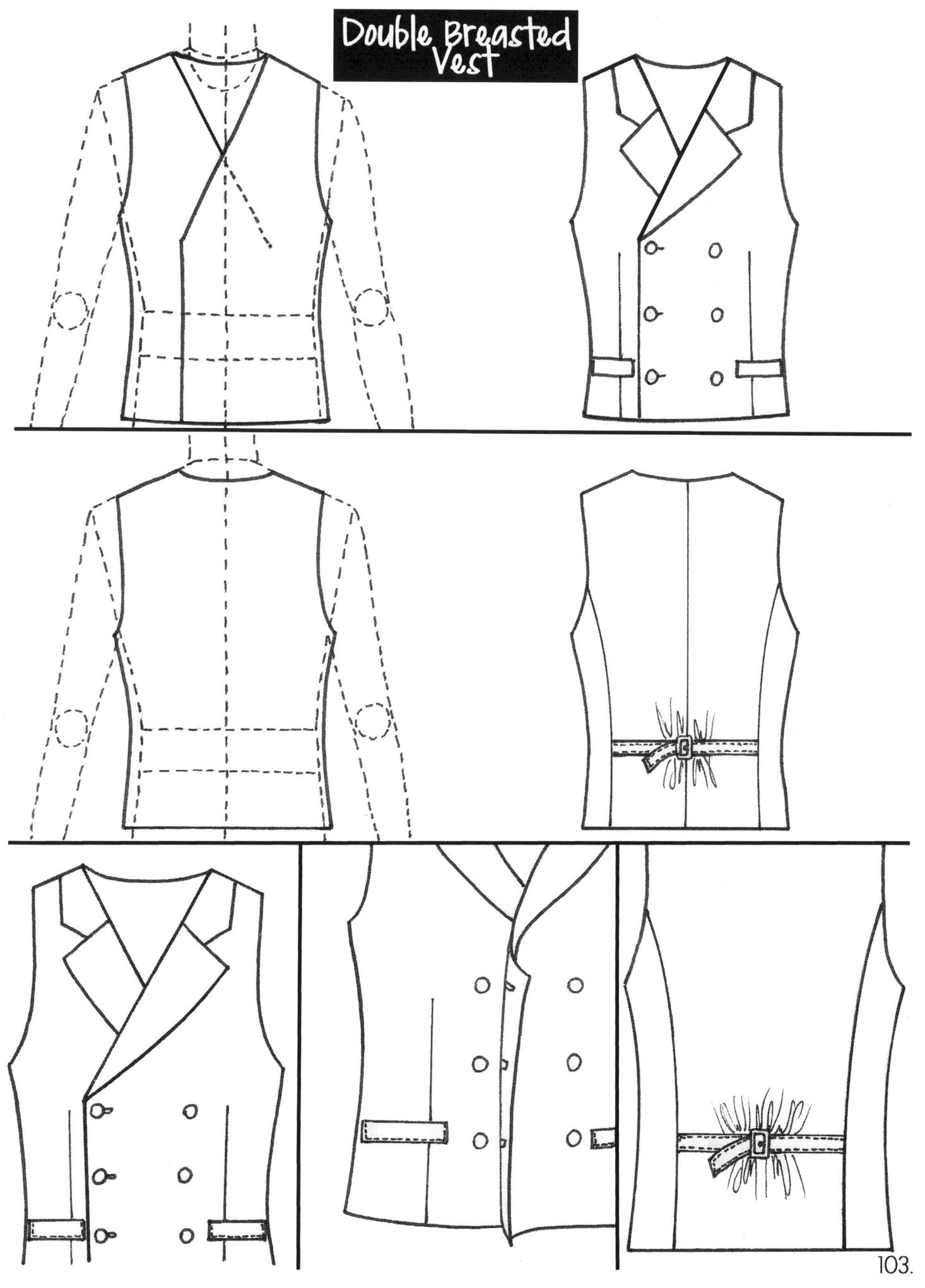

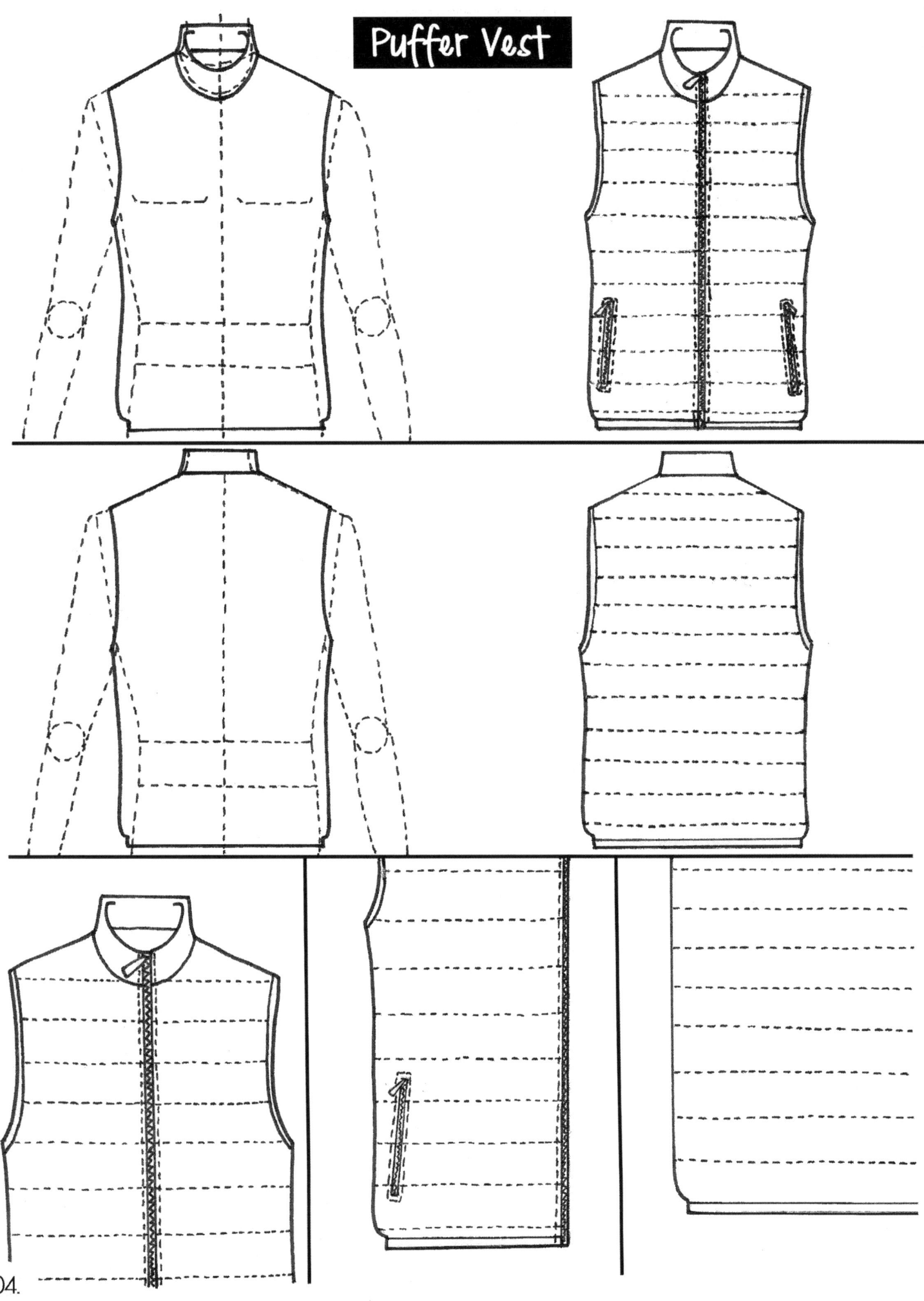

Single Breasted Jackets

105.

Double Breasted Jackets

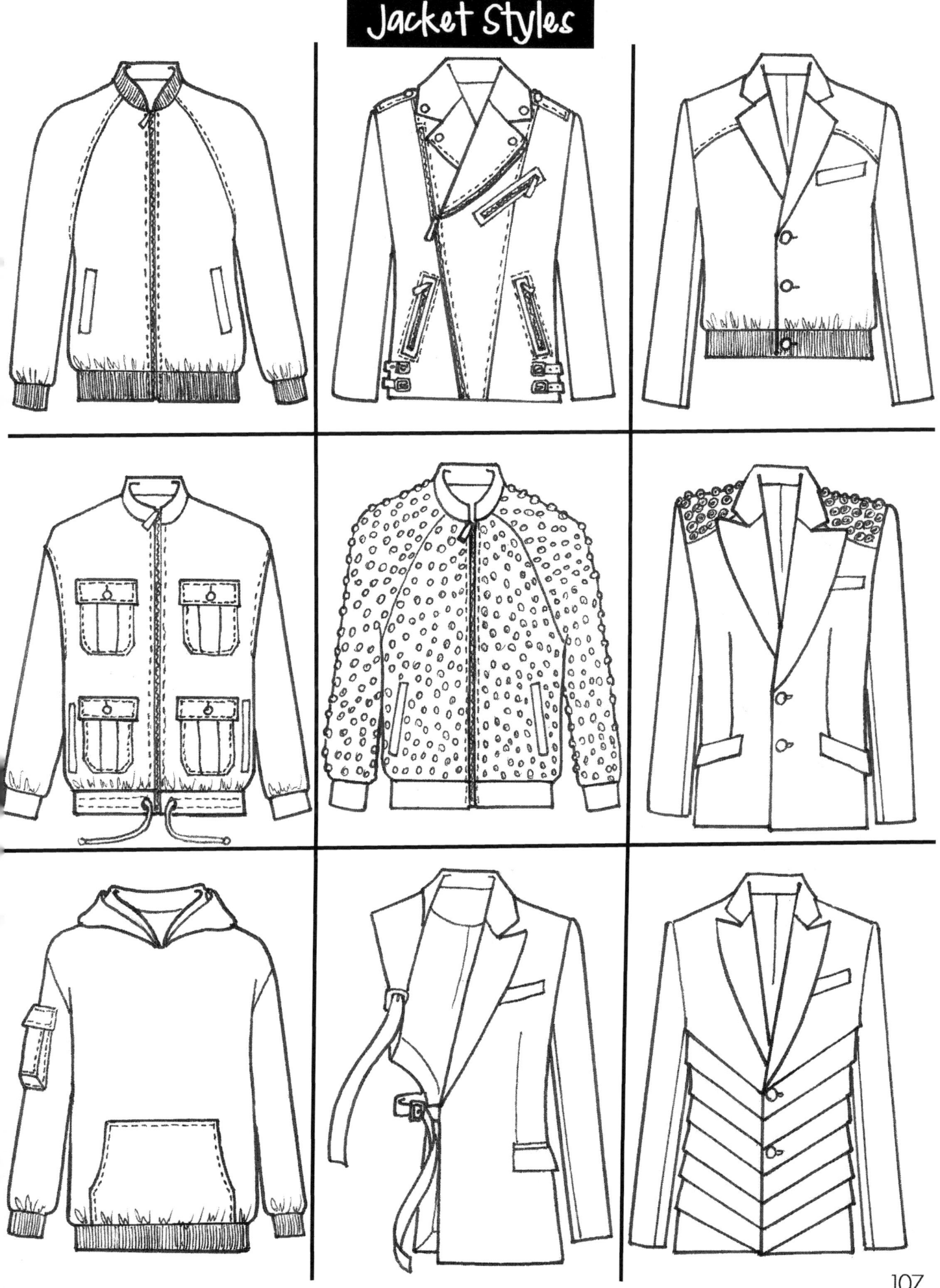

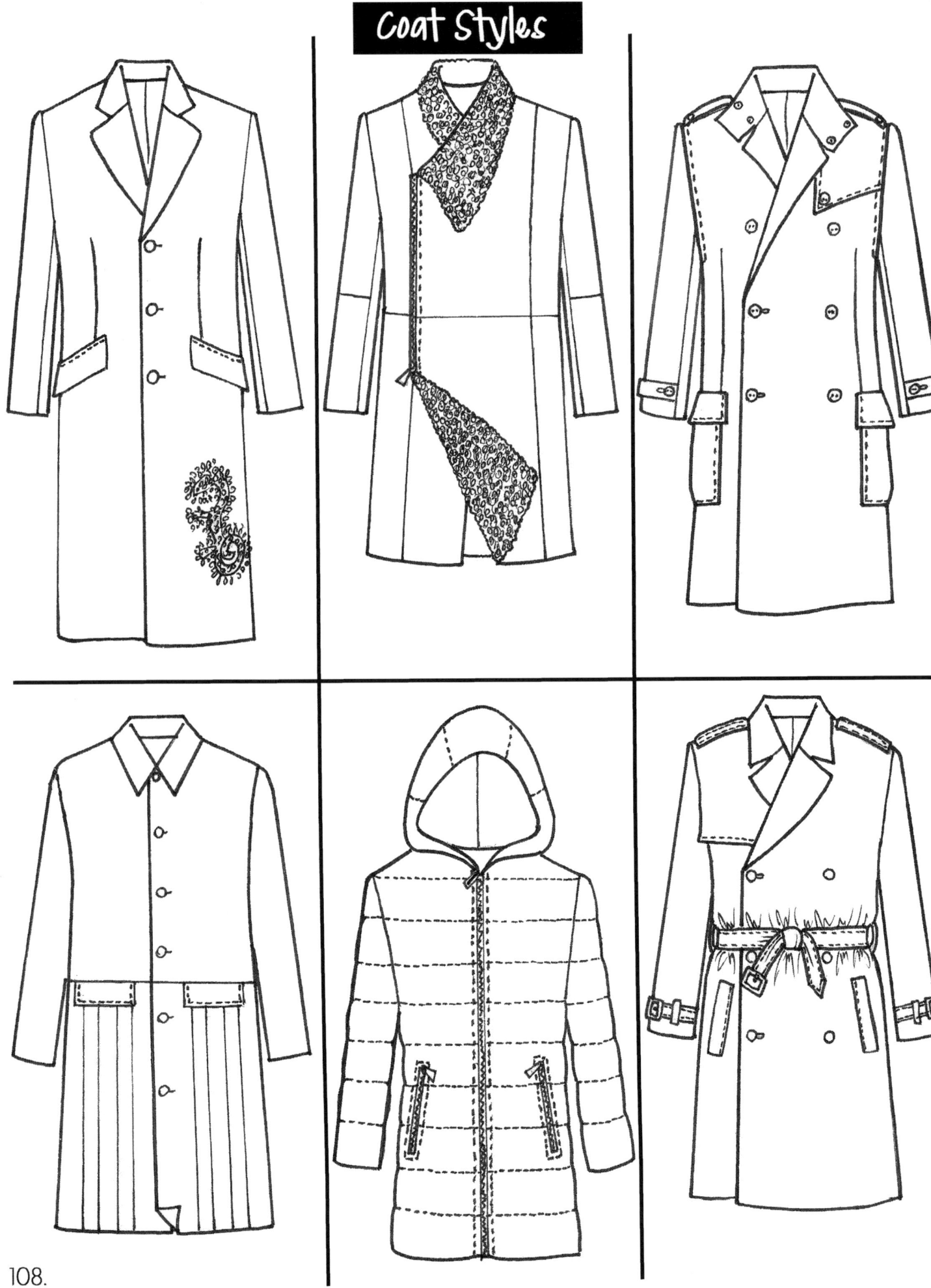

Made in the
USA
Middletown, DE